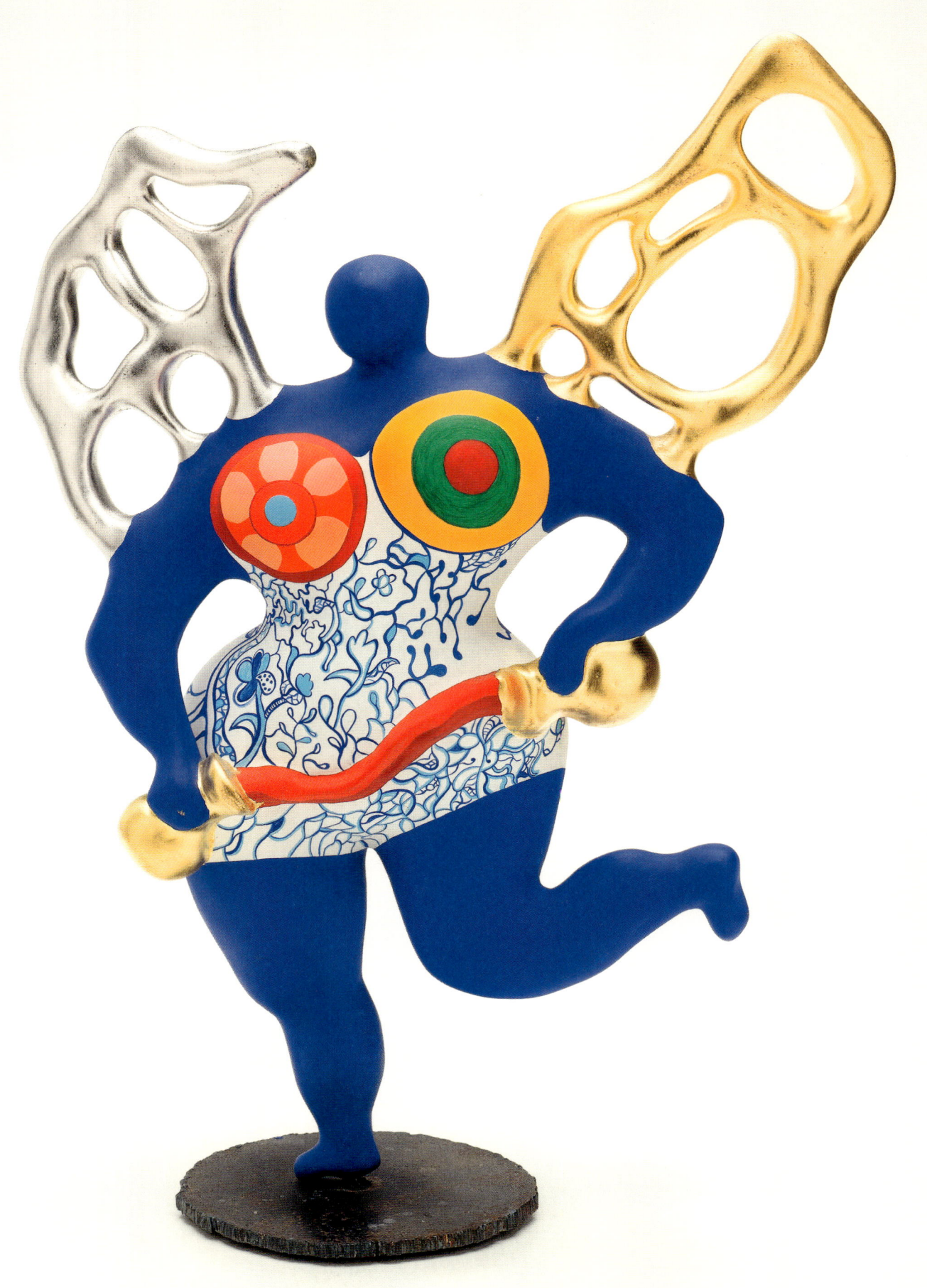

Janis Mink

Niki de Saint Phalle

1930–2002

A Wild, Wild Weed

TASCHEN

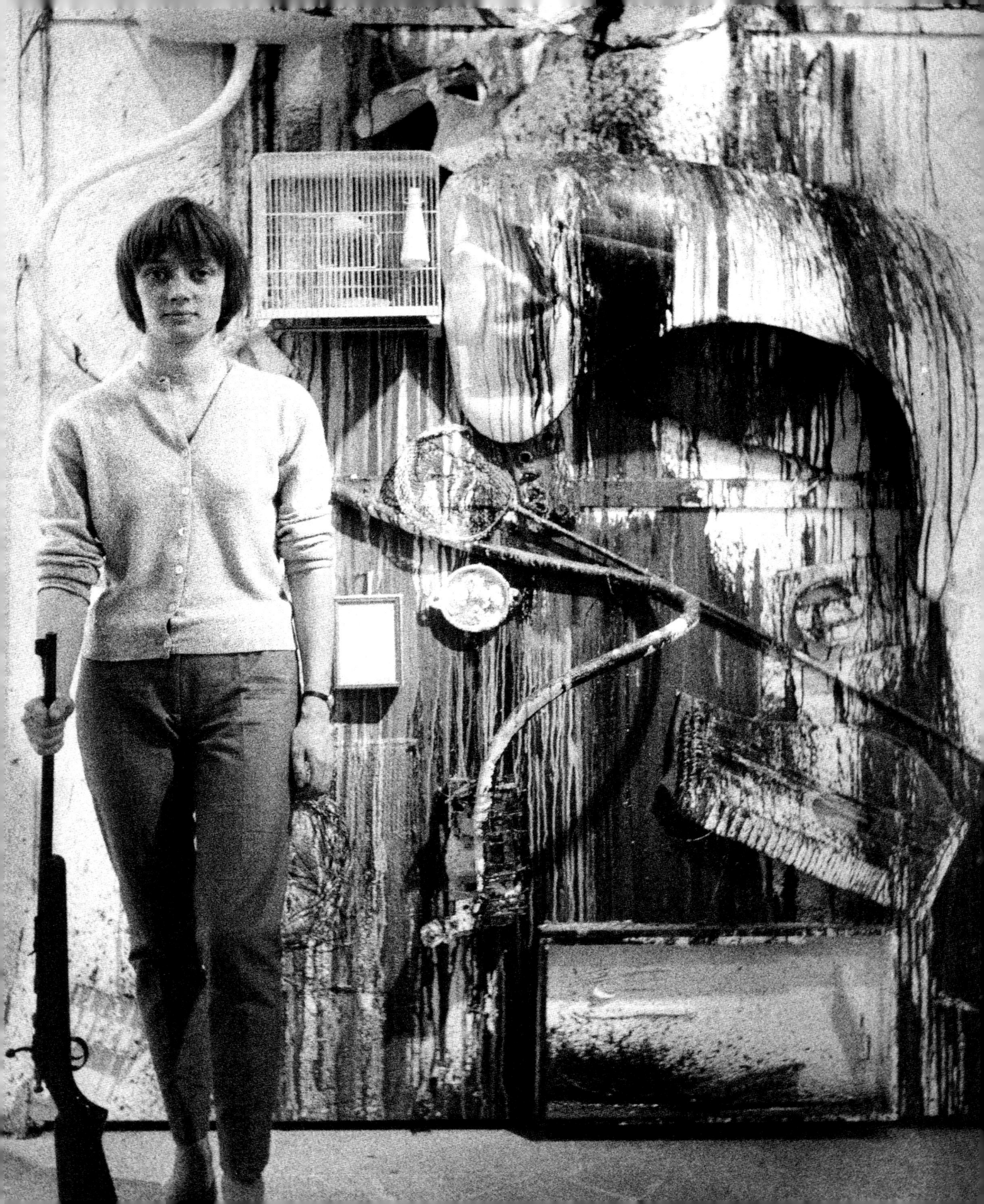

Contents

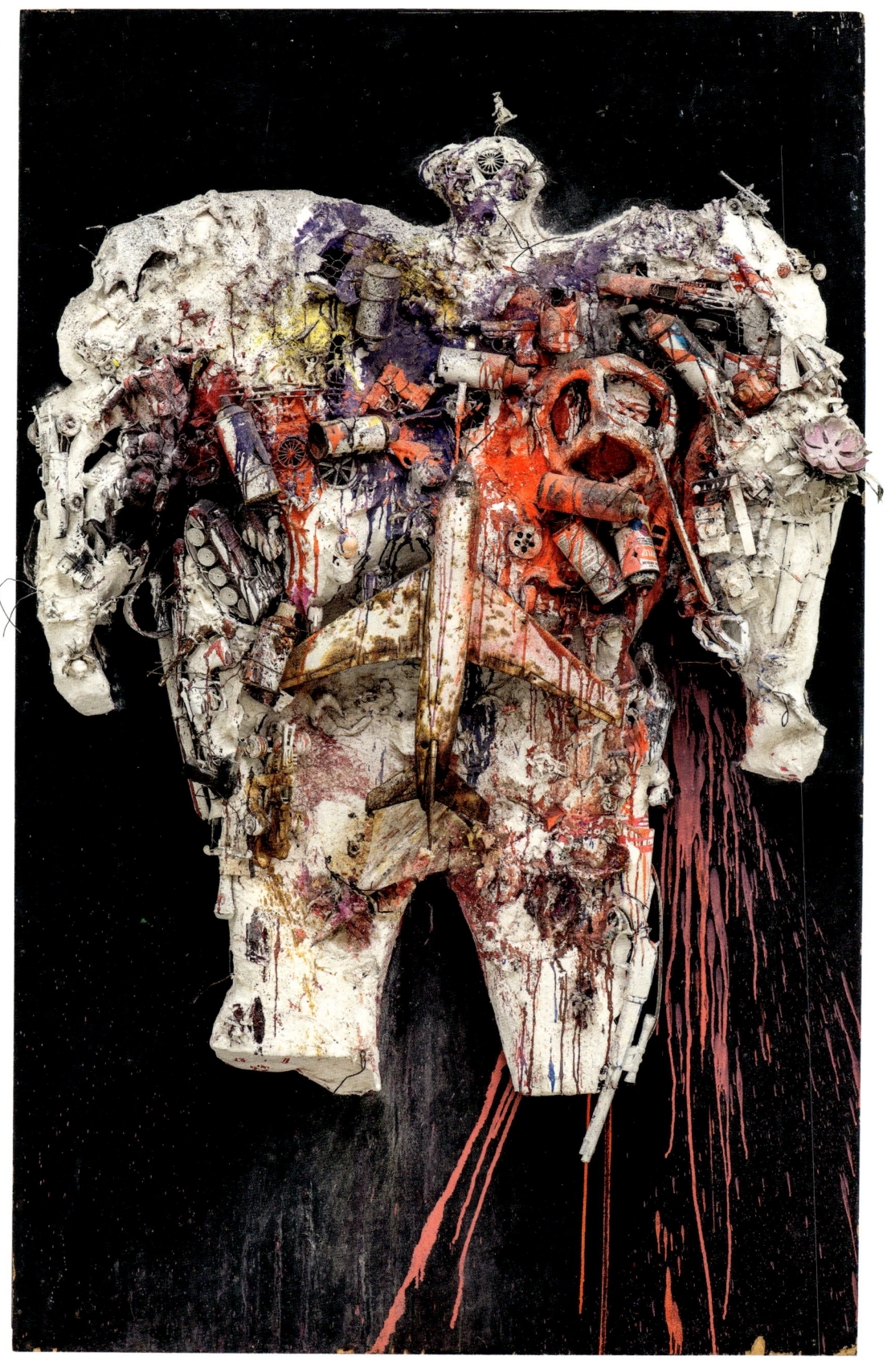

Taking Aim

Rigorously simple, *Shooting Suit* (1962, p. 9) still conjures up Niki de Saint Phalle's body. The zipped, one-piece overall of stiff white material fit her exquisitely. Its tailoring emphasized her delicate waist and curved hips. Foot straps kept the pant legs taut. Some width in the sleeves and around the shoulders allowed her to hoist the .22 rifle she used in most of her shooting works. The suit's only ornamentation is the straight line of a zippered pocket on the left sleeve. Accented with black around the neck and wrists, its quotation of functional work clothing exceeds the workmanlike. Most photos show that Saint Phalle accessorized the suit with short black boots (p. 8). The garment could have outfitted the daring female lead from an episode of the television series *The Avengers* that was popular at the time, or even a female version of Dr. No (p. 9), the nemesis from the recently released James Bond film. It was an armor suited to a modern knight errant, or a warrior Joan of Arc.

First worn for her spring 1962 appearances in California, where Saint Phalle had been invited to show her controversial shooting process in the Renaissance nightclub parking lot on the Sunset Strip in Los Angeles, as well as in the Malibu countryside in front of Hollywood folk, the suit became for a while a kind of official uniform for the then 32-year-old French-American artist. Some faint spatters on the thick, industrial-looking white fabric of the garment testify to its active use, yet the virginal or bridal white quality was important to Saint Phalle as a reference, and she maintained it. Near the end of her life Saint Phalle made sure *Shooting Suit* was preserved as an artifact in the collection of the Sprengel Museum in Hanover, Germany, one of the museums where she was able to deposit a significant number of pieces representing her life's work.

She wore the suit again in New York that same spring of 1962, under a jacket that was part of her costume as a female martial Napoleonic figure for a play. Saint Phalle's role in this play had her striding through the audience down the center aisle of the Maidman Playhouse and then firing a pistol at her sculpted version of the ancient Greek statue the *Vénus de Milo* (p. 7) that had been rolled onstage. By re-creating the white marble Venus from the Louvre Museum in Paris as an effigy in wire and plaster, into whose surface bags of paint had been secreted, the artist made a target that would bleed color when wounded.

In shooting the Venus during the play, Saint Phalle took aim at the world's most famous sculpture from antiquity, but also at the classical image of beauty

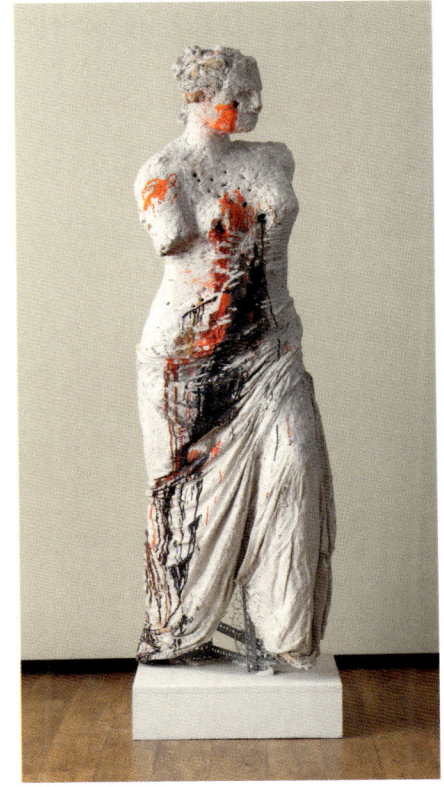

OPPOSITE
The Death of the Patriarch, 1962
Plaster, paint, various objects on wooden panel,
251 x 40 x 160 cm (98¹³⁄₁₆ x 15¾ x 63 in.)
Hanover, Sprengel Museum

ABOVE
Vénus de Milo, 1962
Paint and plaster on metal structure,
193 x 63.5 x 63.5 cm (75¹⁵⁄₁₆ x 25 x 25 in.)
Private collection

7

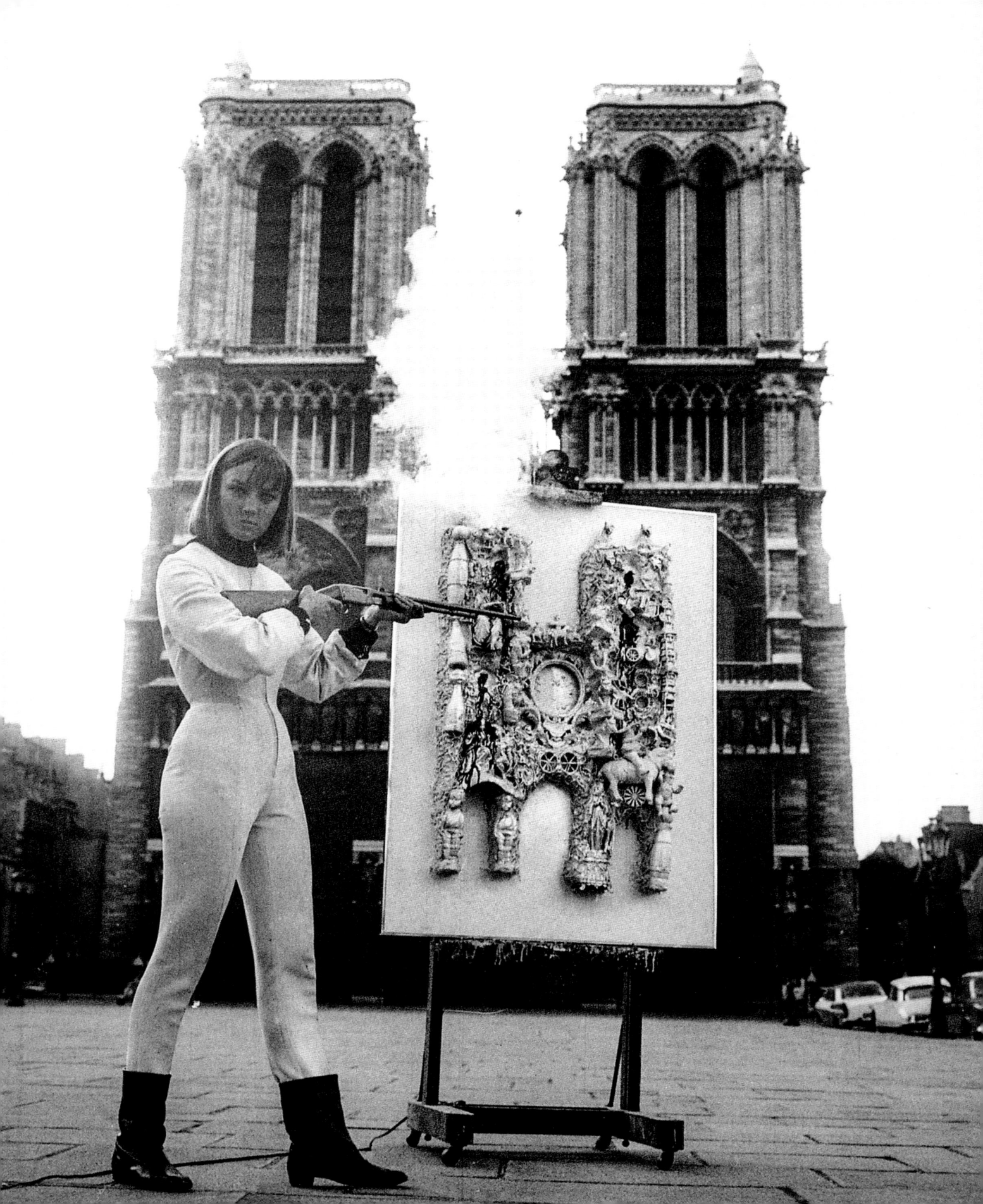

itself and of the ideal woman. Multiple targets presented themselves in this one canonical figure: the Louvre as a repository, the classical ideal in art, whiteness, the female figure as subject and object, and love and sensuality. Apparently more than a prop and not so easily dispatched, the surviving plaster Venus is included in the play's cast photo, peering over Saint Phalle's shoulder. It remained in her collection during her lifetime. The play sold out and was attended by influential figures of the avant-garde art scene like the artist Marcel Duchamp (1887–1968) and the New York gallerist Leo Castelli (1907–1999).

Niki de Saint Phalle established a distinct profile in the art world. She worked and collaborated with a network of like-minded avant-garde artists, mostly men. She had entered the art world with a spirit of passionate adventure, a woman on a mission to excel like a man.

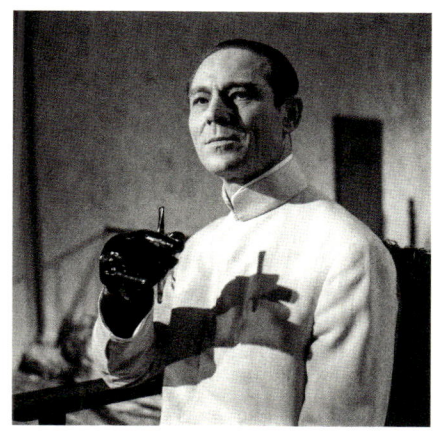

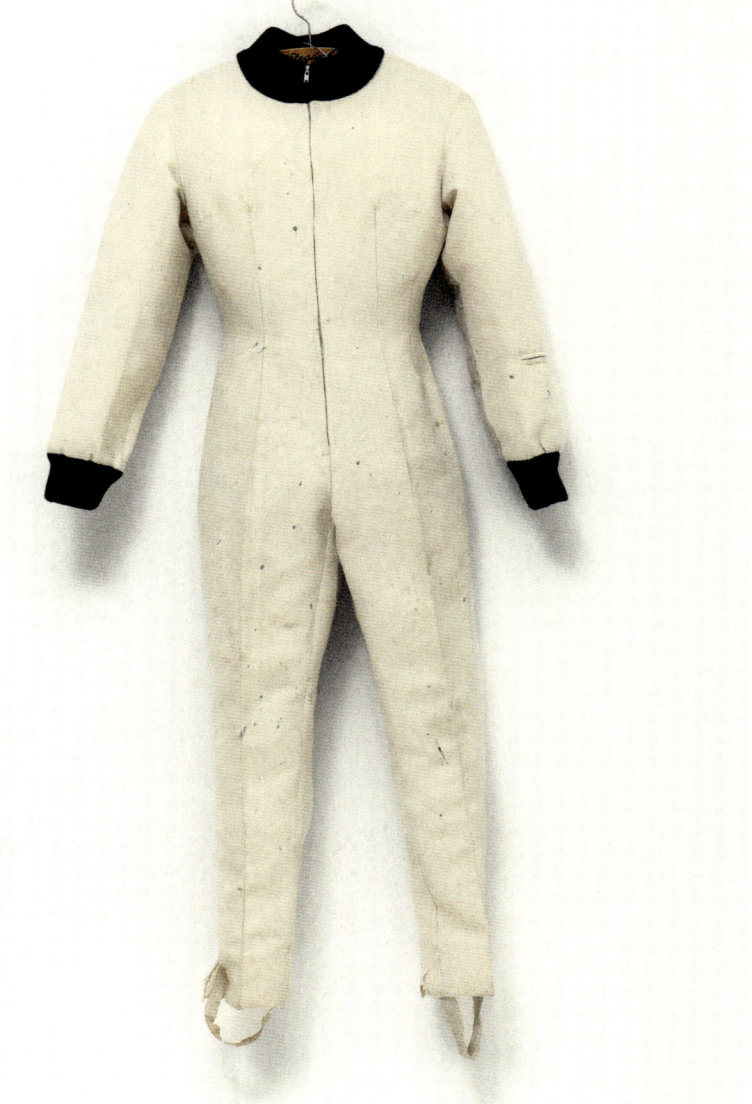

ABOVE
Joseph Wiseman as the villain Dr. Julius No, in the 1962 James Bond film *Dr. No* based on Ian Fleming's 1958 novel

LEFT
Shooting Suit, 1962
Cloth fabric, 145 x 60 x 20 cm
(57¹/₁₆ x 23⅜ x 7⅞ in.)
Hanover, Sprengel Museum

OPPOSITE
Niki de Saint Phalle wearing *Shooting Shoot* in Paris, 1962, on the occasion of the 800th anniversary of Notre-Dame Cathedral

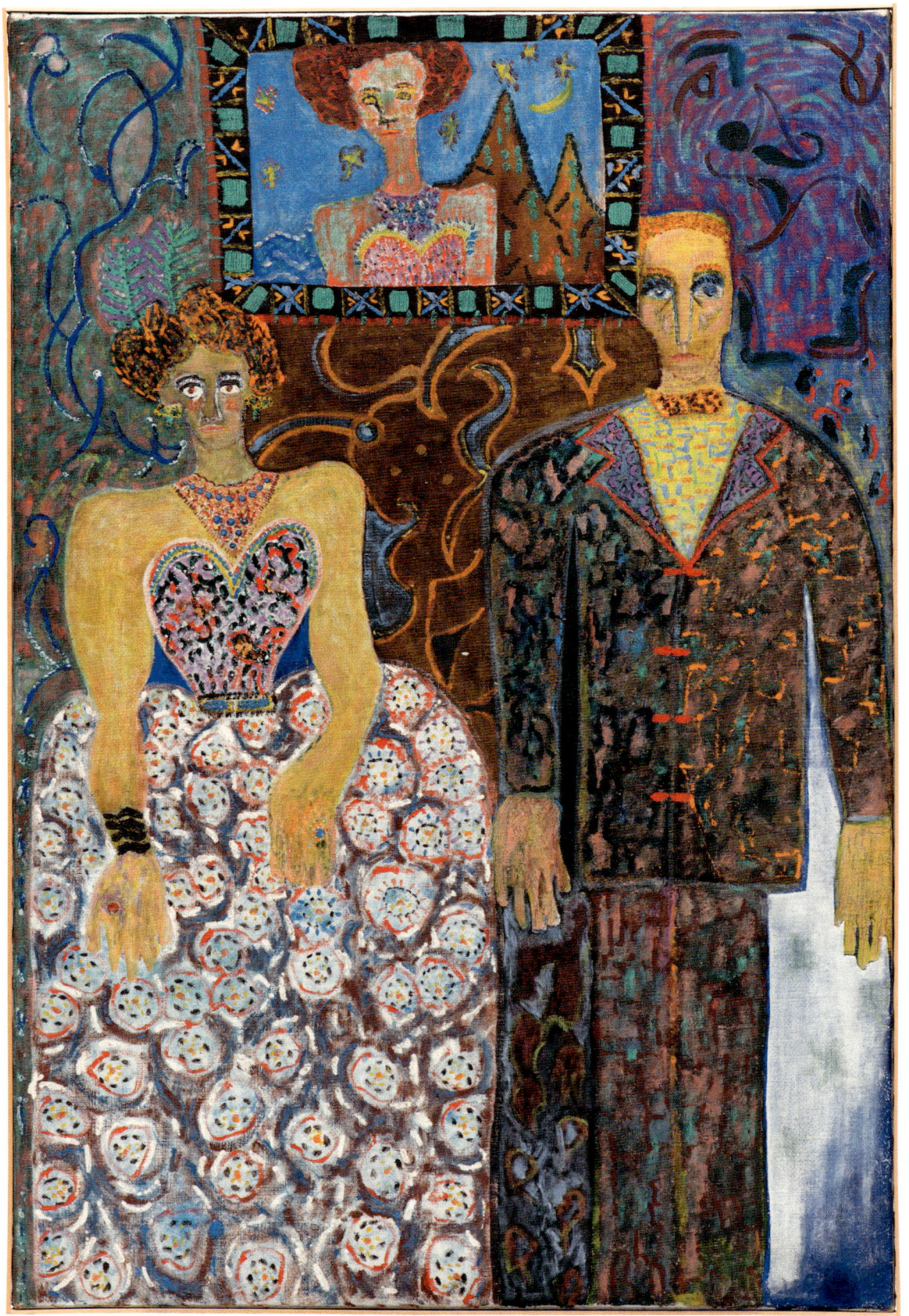

Meat Without Coupons

The future artist was born in 1930 as Catherine Marie-Agnès Fal de Saint Phalle in Neuilly-sur-Seine, a well-to-do suburb of Paris. The umbilical cord had wrapped itself twice around her neck, which she came to regard as a portent that she would be fated to have difficulty breathing later in life. Her father, the French banker and aristocrat Count André-Marie Fal de Saint Phalle (1906–1967), was detained for work at the Saint Phalle family bank in New York when she was born, and he chose her name to honor a former girlfriend, not her mother. Beautiful and wealthy, Marie-Agnès's American mother Jeanne Jacqueline Harper (1908–1978) had grown up in France and married into the Catholic Saint Phalle dynasty that traced its lineage back to the Crusades.

The couple already had a son when Marie-Agnès was born, and the family would swell to include five children in total. Her mother proved distant both physically and emotionally, moving in 1931 to live with her husband in New York. Her son came with her, while the new baby daughter stayed behind and resided in the stately chateau of her paternal grandparents in the French countryside at La Nièvre. The Saint Phalle family bank would fold that same year. Marie-Agnès was allowed to rejoin her parents and brother in the United States in 1934, as a three-year-old. After her father lost his job, the family moved for a while to Greenwich, Connecticut, where the children were cared for by a French governess nicknamed "Nana." Only then getting more acquainted with her daughter and no doubt wishing to be rid of the reminder of the count's former girlfriend, her mother rechristened her "Niki" and, from then on, the girl was known as such. Until World War II prevented it, Niki de Saint Phalle regularly crossed the Atlantic and summered with her maternal American grandparents at their beautiful Chateau de Fillerval, the gardens for which had been designed by André Le Nôtre, the principal gardener of King Louis the Fourteenth and designer of the gardens of Versailles.

As soon as possible the Saint Phalle family relocated again from Connecticut to New York City. Six-year-old Niki de Saint Phalle entered school at Convent of the Sacred Heart on East 91st Street, on the affluent Upper East Side. She especially liked her penmanship classes but wondered why nuns always wore black and if God had something against color. She disliked the ugly green uniform, and never got awarded the red ribbon for excellence. Undesirable behavior got her expelled from this school at the age of eleven. Her maternal grandparents

"I was a Depression baby. While Mother was expecting me, she discovered Father's infidelity. Once Mother told me it was all my fault. She cried all through her pregnancy. I felt those tears."
– TRACES: AN AUTOBIOGRAPHY (1999)

Family Portrait, 1956
Oil on canvas, 151.3 x 100 cm
(59⁹⁄₁₆ x 39⅜ in.)
Hanover, Sprengel Museum

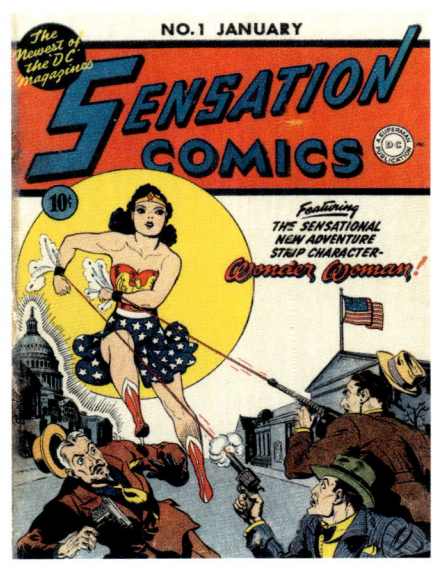

During the summer of 1941, when she and her family were staying in Darien, Connecticut, Niki de Saint Phalle worked with neighborhood children to present her first ambitious work of art—a play she came up with called *Meat Without Coupons*.[1] Saint Phalle set the play in England, which was experiencing wartime food rationing. She also assumed the leading male role herself. Tickets were sold for 10 cents to an audience of neighbors, who assembled to watch the young playwright act the part of a restaurant owner who bickers and fights with his wife. In the story the couple run the restaurant together; the husband serves the clients while the wife cooks. But the restaurant owner falls in love with his young cashier, and when his wife suspects adultery and threatens him, he strangles her. To get rid of her body he butchers and serves her in a stew replete with vegetables and spices. Because meat is scarce, the savory stew draws steady customers. The play reaches its high point when a policeman who has spent time on a cannibal island recognizes the taste of human flesh and discovers human bones in

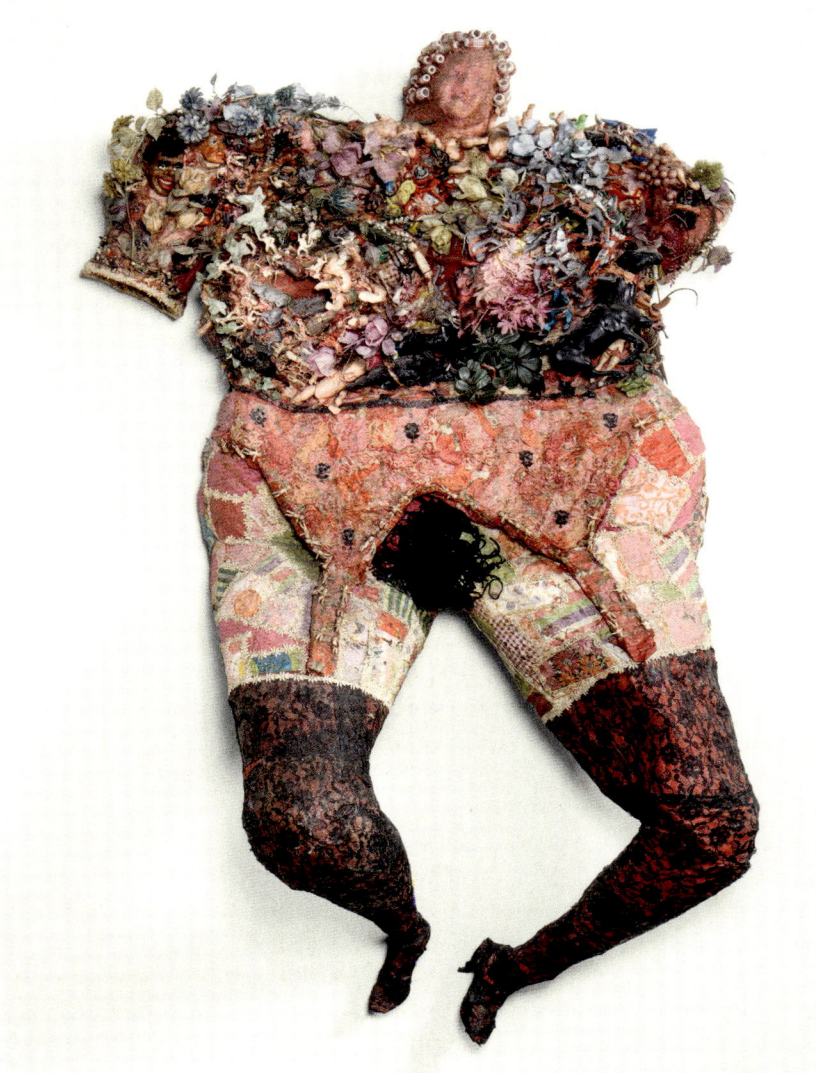

ABOVE
Sensation Comics No. 1, January 1942
Cover art by H.G. Peter and John L. Blummer

RIGHT
Leto or Crucifixion
(Leto ou Crucifixion), c. 1965
Various objects on wire mesh,
236 x 147 x 61.5 cm (92¹⁵⁄₁₆ x 57⅞ x 24²⁄₁₆ in.)
Paris, Centre Pompidou, Musée national d'art moderne, Centre de création industrielle

the kitchen. Justice prevails. The restaurant owner is accused and imprisoned. His beloved soulmate, the cashier, is left behind.

At the end of the one and only performance the shocked audience did not clap. Saint Phalle's mother appeared mortified, though her father laughed and was proud of his daughter's imagination. Aside from shining a light on her parents' marital tensions, the play aired the pubescent Niki de Saint Phalle's unhappy perception of how readily women could be eliminated, broken, consumed. To escape such a fate, she had naturally assigned herself the male power role. Her later sculptural work *Leto or Crucifixion* from about 1965 (p. 12), which depicts a helpless, armless, high-heeled, curler-headed woman wearing a pink garter belt, reveals the artist's loathing for the perceived female fate.

In 1942, Niki de Saint Phalle continued her education on New York's Upper East Side, entering the progressive Brearley School for girls, where she would last two years. There she felt encouraged to read, write, and act. She got to act, and she played Clytemnestra in the ancient Greek play *Agamemnon*. Performance appealed to her, but she also liked to draw trees. She loved birds. After going to bed, she read books and comics like *Wonder Woman* (p. 12) with a flashlight. Saint Phalle identified with characters who "saved the day." At Brearley she met another half-French, half-American girl like herself, Jackie Matisse (1931–2021), the daughter of the New York gallerist Pierre Matisse and granddaughter of the artist Henri Matisse. Jackie's divorced mother would later marry Marcel Duchamp. Both girls were bilingual and felt kinship in their bi-national status. The pair would become lifelong friends and both would become artists as adults. During the war, the Saint Phalle family rented houses on Long Island or in Connecticut during the summer instead of traveling to Europe. As a child Niki de Saint Phalle got used to changing residences and feeling quite rootless.

Niki de Saint Phalle's father André had always had extramarital affairs and dalliances with his wife's friends or with house servants on Sundays when his family attended church. However, in 1942 he extended his erotic reach to include his own daughter. She became the victim of sexual abuse when her father, the Catholic count who was then 35 years of age, sequestered her in a shed during a supposed search for a fishing pole, explored her body with his hands, and forced himself on her. Saint Phalle wrote, "Shame, pleasure, anguish, and fear wrenched my chest. My father said, 'Don't move.' I obeyed like an automaton, then with violence and kicks I freed myself from him and ran into the field of cut grass until I was exhausted."[2] The traumatic event changed her life. The abuse continued that summer; the child spoke to no one about her father. When they ceased, she gradually repressed the experience. Much later, at the age of 64, she revealed and explored her feelings about the abuse in her artist's book *Mon Secret* (p. 89). In the book, written for her daughter, she considers that she might have been an 11-year-old who looked more like 13. She writes that her father fondled her and placed his penis in her mouth. In a letter he later called the abuse "when he tried to make her his mistress."

During this molestation period, she acted out again in school. More attentive adults might have tried to get to the bottom of the problem, but the adults in her life failed her. By 1944, Saint Phalle was ripe for what she later called imaginative revenge. She and her deskmate at school collaborated in painting red all the fig leaves of the Greek statues at the Brearley School. The school insisted both girls see a psychiatrist, or they would be expelled. When Saint Phalle's mother told her she was not like other little girls, Saint Phalle worried for the first time in her life that she might be insane. In her artist's book *Traces*, a moving autobiography

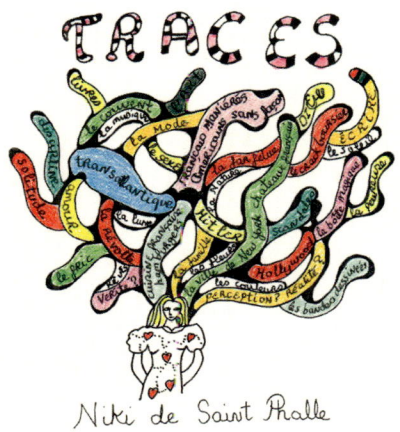

Traces: An Autobiography, 1999
Cover for artist's book, 26.1 x 22.2 cm
(10¼ x 8¾ in.)
Published by Acatos, Lausanne

"I was faced with the enormous problem of reinventing and re-creating myself. I had no clear national identity. I felt half French, half American. I also wanted to be half man and half woman."

– TRACES: AN AUTOBIOGRAPHY (1999)

La Classe de ballet (The Ballet Class), 1953–55
Oil and tempera on canvas, 80.3 x 99.6 x 2 cm
(31⅝ x 39¼ x ¹³⁄₁₆ in.)
Stockholm, Moderna Museet

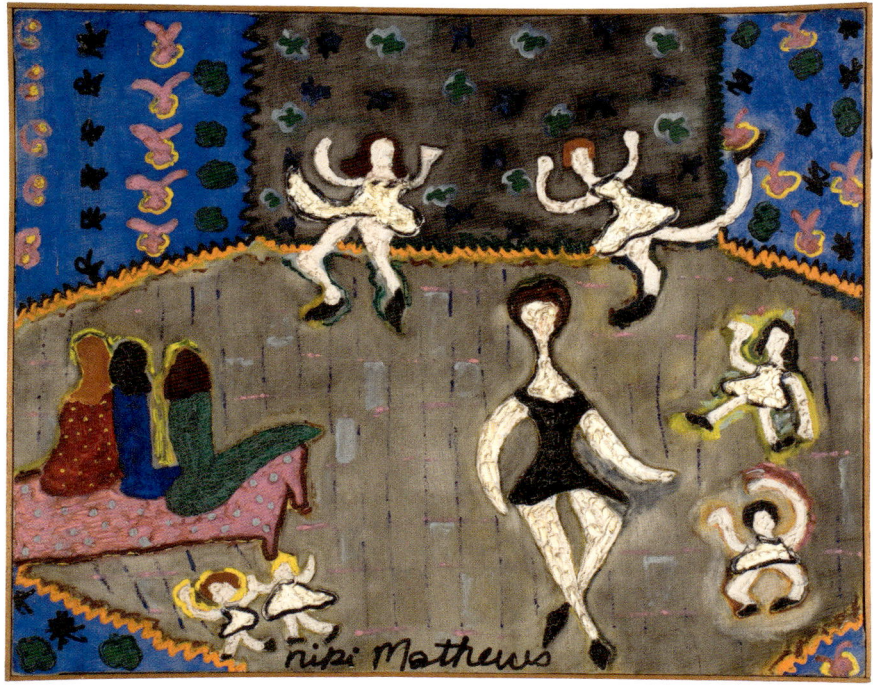

of the first 19 years of her life published after the death of her parents, she relates many details that reveal abusive parenting on the parts of both her mother and her father. She was not the only sibling to feel destabilized by her family. Two of her younger siblings—her sister Elizabeth and her brother Richard—would take their own lives in adulthood.

After being expelled from Brearley, Saint Phalle switched to a convent school in Suffern, New York, where she did not remain very long. She had become an atheist. A 1946 summer trip to Paris—now that the war was over, travel had become easier again—introduced Saint Phalle to the Louvre Museum, and she met relatives. An aunt helped her finish her secondary education in the Old-fields School in Glencoe, Maryland, by 1947. That year she not only completed high school but also took a class in the dramatic arts. Perhaps she was considering acting as a profession—Saint Phalle certainly had the looks of an ingenue. She went to dances and parties, and in 1948 she met a talent scout who asked her to model for his agency. The idea appealed to her. She started modeling, which she did on and off until she was about 26 years old. She appeared in fashion magazines like *Harper's Bazaar* and *Vogue,* and a month before her 19th birthday she was pictured dressed in an evening gown as a post-debutante on the front cover of the national magazine *Life,* as well as inside the magazine modeling elegant "separates" on page 92. Her wage of $15 an hour seemed fantastic to her and must have offered a sense of independence from her family. Her resolve to leave her parents' house as soon as possible was getting closer. Yet, from the beginning, Saint Phalle did not bank on remaining a model.

When she encountered one of her elder brother's friends on a fateful 1948 train ride to Princeton, she no longer presented as the goofy kid sister she used to be. Harry Mathews (1931–2017), then serving in the U.S. Navy, hailed her with, "Niki, you look beautiful!" The two teenagers—each adrift in their own way—very quickly parlayed a mutual attraction into an elopement attended only by two witnesses. To please their parents, the young couple married again the following year in the French Church in New York in a ceremony appropriate to their social standing. German-born photojournalist and portraitist Hans Namuth (1915–1990) took the wedding pictures. Namuth later became famous for documenting Jackson Pollock's (1912–1956) painting method as well as for photographing many other Abstract Expressionist artists in their social and work settings. He shot Niki de Saint Phalle as bride a few years before she herself began to include brides as subject matter in her art.

While Harry Mathews transferred to Harvard to study music, the young woman now named Niki Mathews experimented with painting. Both partners felt drawn to the arts. She soon became pregnant with their first child, a daughter, Laura, who was born 1951. Despite having just become new parents, the Mathewses decided to leave postwar America for Europe. Harry Mathews graduated Harvard, and in fall 1952 the family of three moved to Paris, supported mainly by Mathews family money, but also by Niki Mathews's modeling. After arriving in France, the Mathewses traveled to Spain and Italy to visit cathedrals and museums.

The young couple continued their respective educations in Paris and absorbed the cultural offerings of the city. They regularly visited the Louvre, looking carefully and methodically at the collection, section by section. They attended modern plays. Around this time Niki Mathews read Simone de Beauvoir's *The Second Sex*, which had been published in 1949. The book could have made any recent bride feel qualms about her decision to get married.

La Fête (The Party), 1955
Oil on canvas,
127 x 178 x 3 cm (50 x 70¹⁄₁₆ x 1³⁄₁₆ in.)
Hanover, Sprengel Museum

The boat passengers' highly colored and at times deformed faces recall the expressive way James Ensor (1860–1949) crowded masks and people together in works like *Christ's Entry into Brussels in 1889* (1888), where he caricatured a society hardly worth its salvation. Later, in her book *Harry and Me: The Family Years*, Saint Phalle dedicated a handwritten page to her *La Fête* painting, with a reference to Ensor's influence.

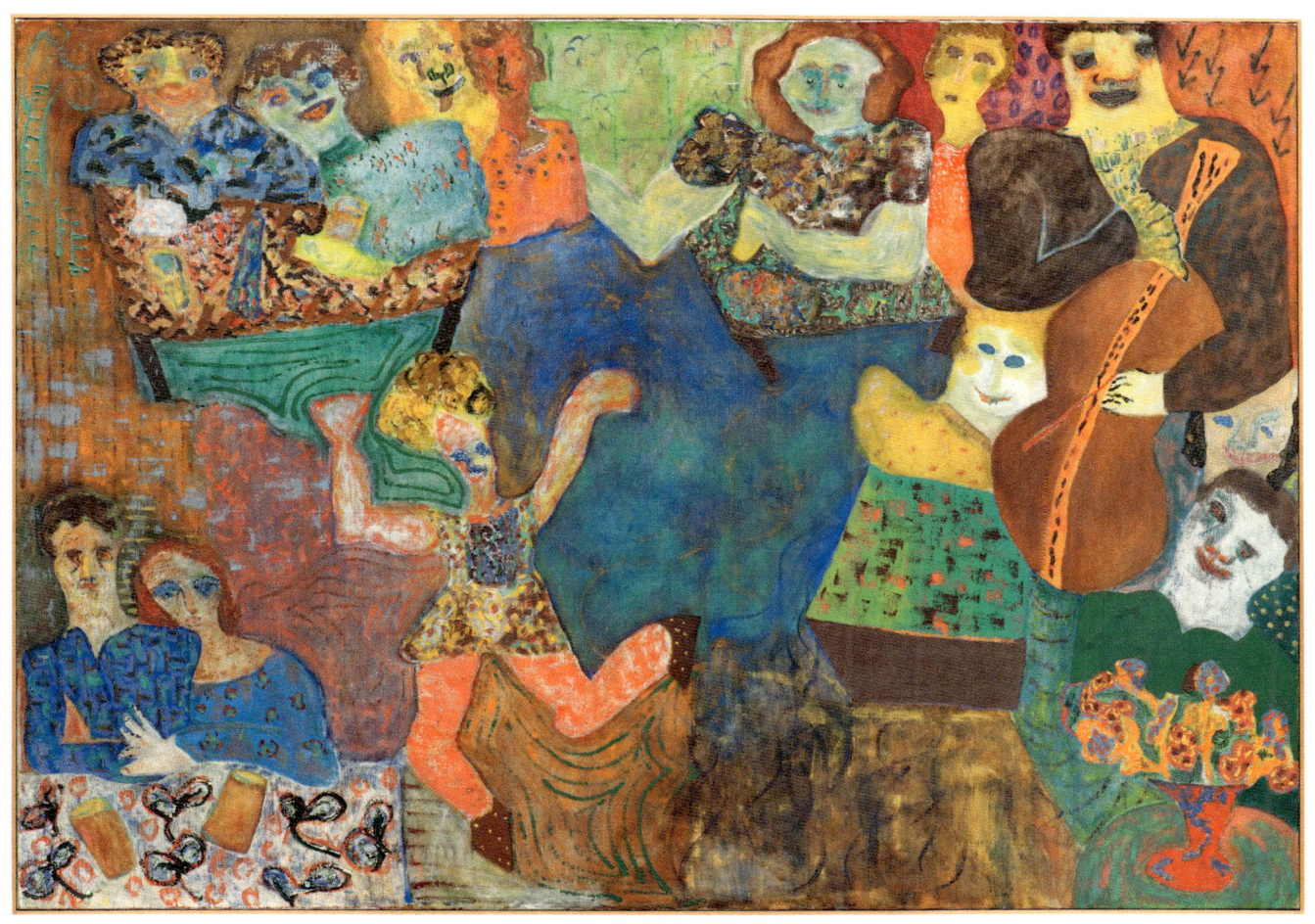

Beauvoir (1908–1986) wrote that women were socialized into behaving as they did, and that they were forced to conform to a world in which men held all the power. Chapter by chapter, she discussed the subordination of a woman through her life stations, from childhood to old age. Luckily for Niki Mathews, her husband Harry believed in women's rights, and he willingly helped with household chores and childcare, as Saint Phalle would later describe in her autobiographical book *Harry and Me: The Family Years* (published posthumously in 2006, p. 87). The couple assumed an arts-centered, unconventional lifestyle, with Harry Mathews stepping up as an active father.

There were pressures on the young couple, however, such as Niki Mathews's health issues with autoimmune thyroiditis, mutual infidelities, and Niki's eventual nervous breakdown in 1953. After attacking Harry's girlfriend and swallowing a bottle of sleeping pills, she was hospitalized in Nice, where she received electroshock and insulin treatment. The treatment was successful, although she remained fragile. Tony Bonner, a family friend, visited Niki Mathews during her six-week stay in the Nice clinic and admired some artwork she had spontaneously made there. Following her instinct to physically order things she found around her, she had picked up twigs, pebbles, and leaves from the hospital grounds to collage with glue. The friend returned with more conventional art supplies—gouache paint and paper. Creating drawings and collages in the medical facility became her therapy, and she resolved to become an artist.

Upon their return to Paris from Nice, Harry and Niki Mathews both assumed a new creative focus. Encouraged by his wife, Harry Mathews began to see himself as a writer and poet, and Niki Mathews put acting and directing classes aside in favor of painting. The aesthetic of Art Brut or "raw art," established by the Surrealists and French artist Jean Dubuffet (1901–1985), reigned in certain circles and helped create a broader acceptance for self-taught artists and non-traditional art materials. An acquaintance of Niki Mathews in Paris, the American painter Hugh Weiss (1925–2007), who also worked in a naive style, became a mentor to Mathews for the next five years. Weiss recognized something promising in how Mathews's work had developed within the context

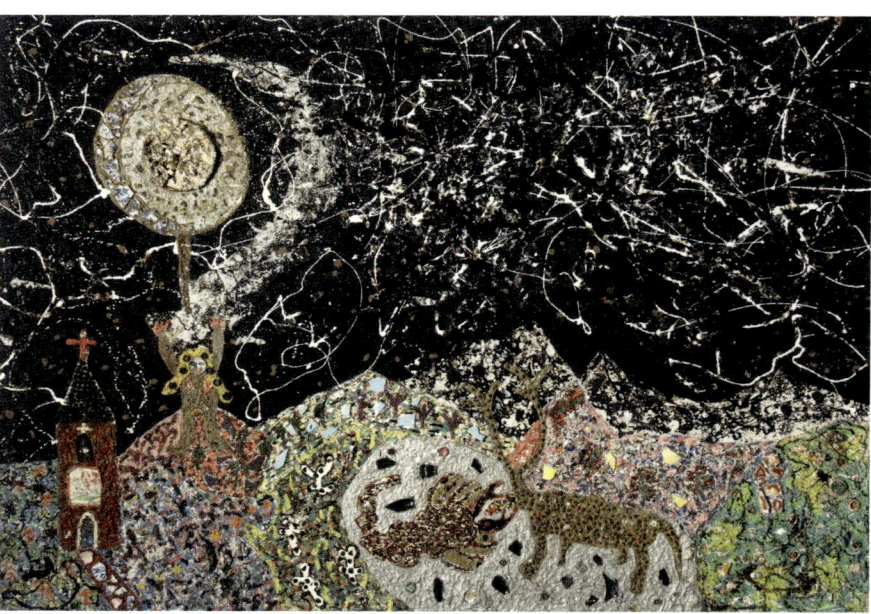

Scorpion and Stag, 1956–58
Oil, various small objects on plywood,
140 x 200 cm (55⅛ x 78¾ in.)
Nice, Musée d'Art Moderne et
d'Art Contemporain (MAMAC) Collection

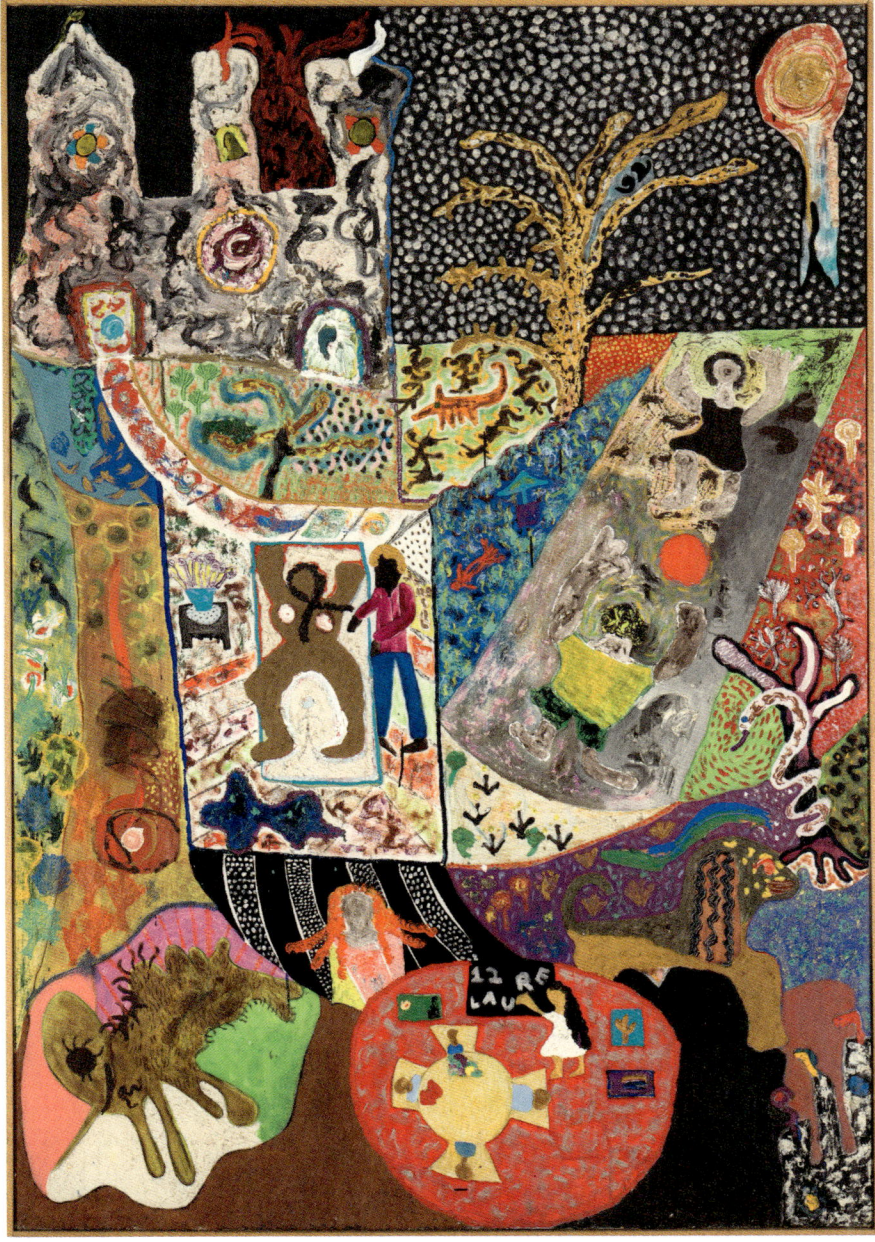

Composition, 1956
Oil on canvas, 190 x 130 cm (74^{13}/$_{16}$ x 51^{3}/$_{16}$ in.)
Stockholm, Moderna Museet

of the French postwar avant-garde. He encouraged Mathews not to go to art school, but to follow her instincts. She wrote about reading Jean Dubuffet's poetry and art writings. It must have been reassuring to know Dubuffet found the art of those who experience mental health problems impactful, expressive, and psychologically revealing, and that he even collected it.

Rather than being stigmatized by a mental breakdown, a contemporary artist could use his or her raw state as a touchstone or a natural point of departure for their work. In his essay "L'Art brut préféré aux arts culturels" from 1949, Dubuffet starts by saying: "What country lacks its small clique of cultural arts: its troop of careerist intellectuals? It is obligatory. From one capital to another, they ape each other marvelously; they practice an artificial, Esperanto art tirelessly copied everywhere. Is art the right word? Does it actually have anything

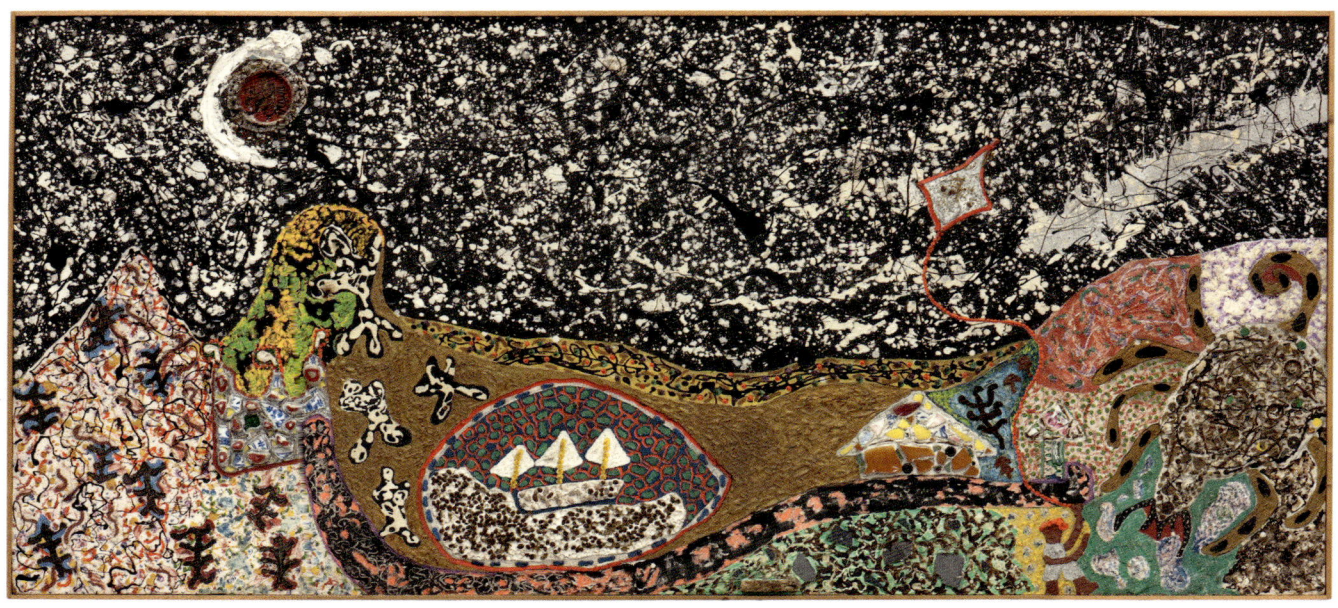

Bateau, n/d
Oil, various small objects on plywood,
222 x 102 x 7 cm (87⅜ x 40⅛ x 2¾ in.)
Hanover, Sprengel Museum

to do with art?" Dubuffet felt human society deserved better: "True art is never where it is expected to be: in the place where no one considers it, nor names it. Art hates to be recognized and greeted by its name."[3]

Meat Without Coupons really was possible in the art world of the 1950s—that is, cooking something up, creating by obeying one's gut feelings instead of laws, serving up whatever experiences, materials, and characters lay closest to hand, as rough as that might be. Artistic training and the apprenticeships of bygone centuries became optional. Skill gave way to expression. Sanctioned modernisms seemed flavorless to many. To sacrifice the past made a future possible. The door was open for outsiders and rulebreakers.

An early painting about Saint Phalle's daughter Laura's dance class, titled *The Ballet Class* (p. 14)and dated to the years 1953–55, is signed prominently "Niki Mathews" near to the middle of the lower edge. It depicts seated and sidelined mothers watching their bright young daughters dance on what might be an octagonal wooden dance floor. Little girls pirouette and pinwheel around their teacher, who shares the center of the painting with the artist's signature. One of the teacher's black dance shoes touches the "s" of Mathews's name. Thus while the mothers watch their children, at least the artist connects with the real main performer, the teacher. The dance class becomes a microcosm where a professional female figure takes charge of her world, working, moving to music, unencumbered by the kind of street clothing that encases the mothers. They seem to not have legs or arms and appear pressed together in an anonymous bank of bodies. The artist cannot depict the proportions of human anatomy accurately, and she does not care too much about this. She cares more about repetitive marks patterning the walls and the lines of the floorboards that stripe up instead of receding in Renaissance-type perspective. Her painting style appears raw and unschooled. The figures are outlined like Henri Matisse (1869–1954) did with his dancers. They exist as textured drawings without color gradations that would suggest depth. The size of the canvas is not unambitious—about 31 x 39 inches (80 x 100 cm), which is comparable to or exceeds that of many of Edgar Degas's ballet pictures. This size canvas would be appropriate for purchase by an upper-middle-class family with apartment walls large enough to accommodate it, and Niki Mathews would have gladly sold the work. Although it was shown in her first gallery show at the Gallery Gotthard in St. Gallen, Switzerland, in 1956, no one purchased it.

Other early works shown in 1956 appear simultaneously reminiscent of paintings by both Henri Matisse and Pablo Picasso (1881–1973), such as her lost gouache painting *On the Beach* from around 1952–54, which borrowed from a painting like *On the Beach* (1937) by Picasso, as well as Matisse's *Dance* of 1909. Paul Klee's (1879–1940) way of exploring color relationships through gridded painting surfaces, such as in *Castle and Sun* (1928) or *Static-Dynamic Gradation* (1923), is recalled by the early Niki Mathews painting *Where is the Man* from around 1952–54. The location of this gouache painting, too, is unknown. The Swiss gallerist who showed these early works in St. Gallen in 1956 did not return all the paintings he had borrowed, just the ones he exhibited. One painting sold. The remaining works—were they forgotten in the back room?—were either sold later without the artist's knowledge, lost, or given away and might still be found. Niki Mathews was young, busy, just starting out; such an oversight had no repercussions for the gallerist.

La Fête (p. 15) stands out among these early works especially because it includes a self-portrait of Niki Mathews, huddled with her husband Harry in the lower left corner, while their daughter Laura dances to party music on board a *Rheinfahrt*, a sightseeing boat trip along the Rhine River. In contrast to their child, Harry and Niki Mathews in their blue sweaters appear desolate and shrink away from the beefy, joyful passengers that pack the upper right diagonal of the painting. Laura dances with expansive gestures, like Saint Phalle's future sculpted *Nanas* will do.

Niki Mathews continued to evolve in her style, inspired by cultures from other eras. She loved ancient Egyptian art, for example, as well as the work of contemporary artists. Several key encounters left a lasting legacy. She and Harry belonged to an active network of friends and acquaintances involved in the arts—poets, writers, visual artists, and musicians—and word got out about where to travel, what to see, who to meet. The urban neighborhoods with affordable rents and spaces that could be used as studios funneled artists into nearby bistros and cafes. As a result of their physical adjacency, they would

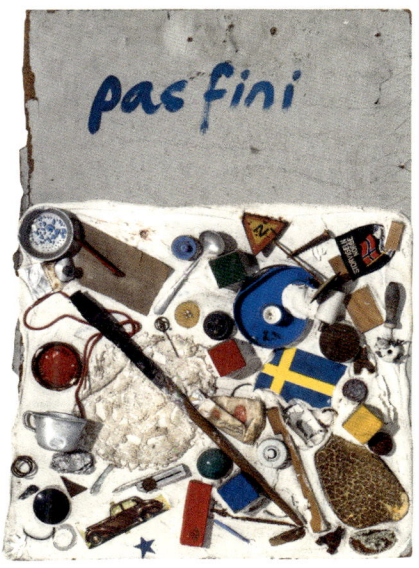

ABOVE
Untitled (pas fini), c. 1959–60
Oil, various small objects on plywood,
62 x 40 cm (24½ x 15¾ in.)
Nice, MAMAC Collection

BELOW
Nightscape, 1959
Plaster, paint, various objects,
wooden door, plywood,
216 x 82 x 11 cm (85 x 32¼ x 4⁵⁄₁₆ in.)
Hanover, Sprengel Museum

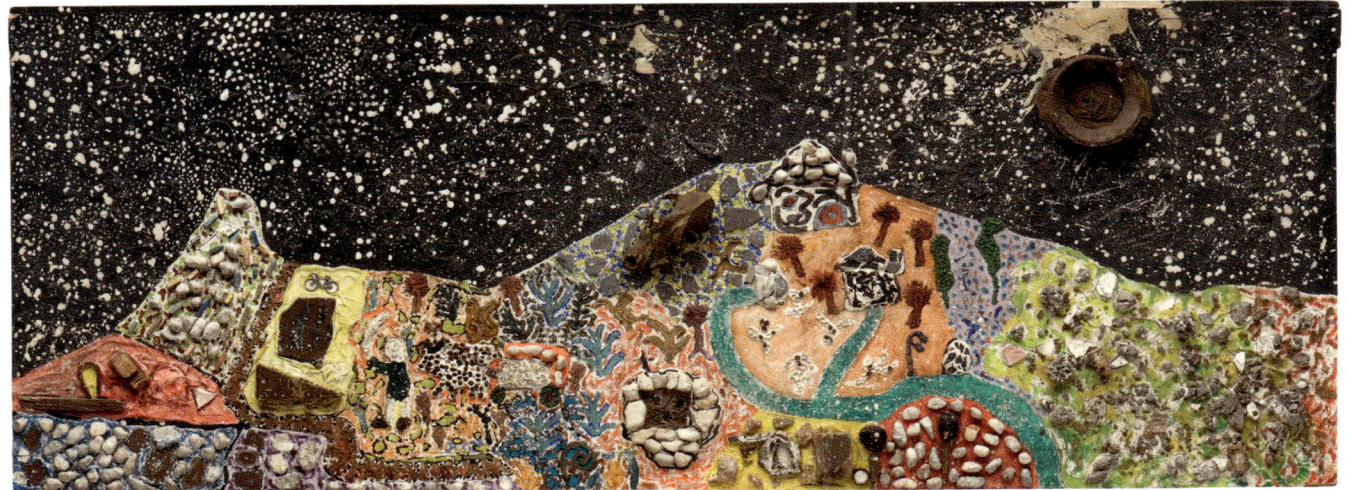

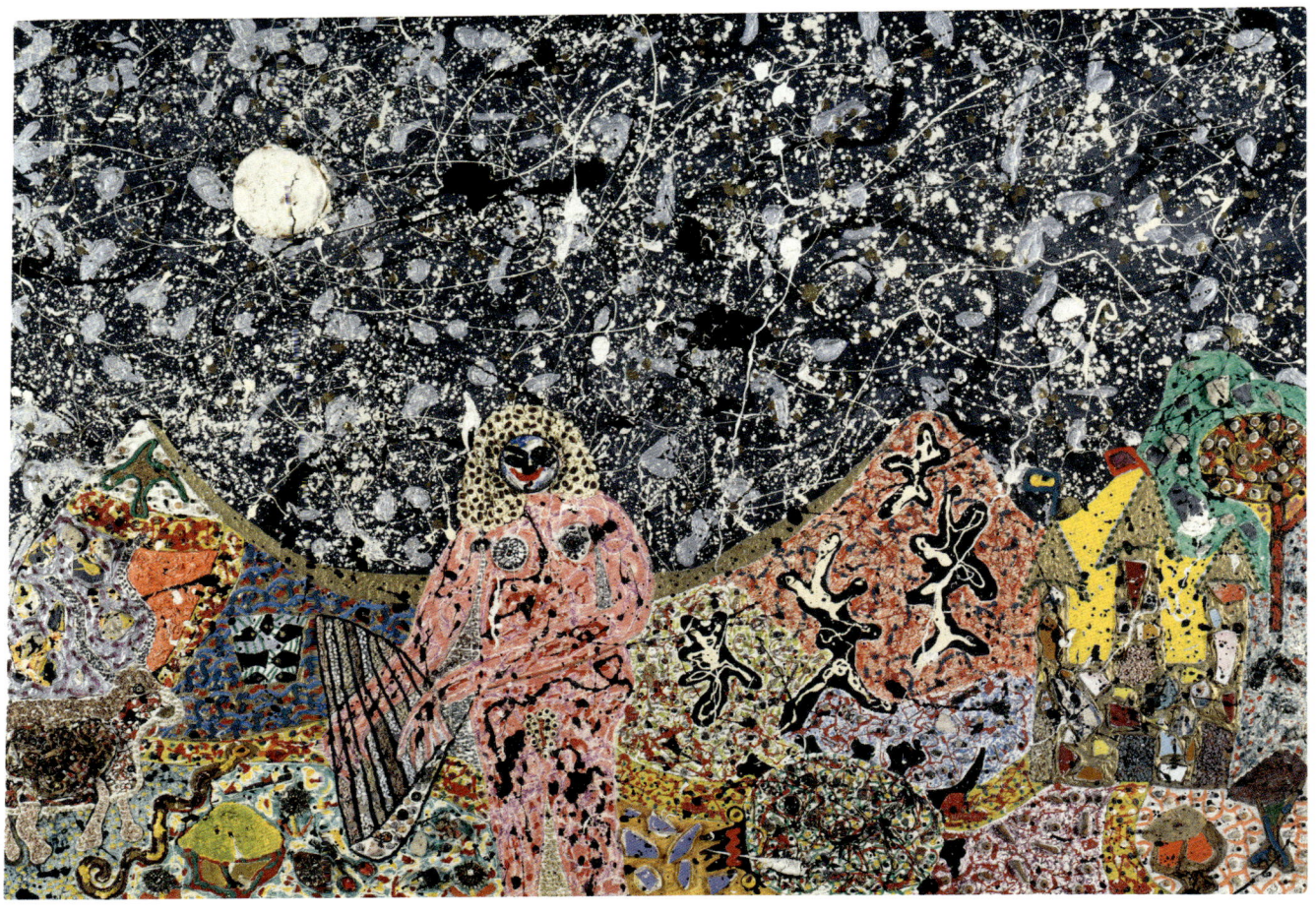

Pink Nude in Landscape, 1959
Oil and found objects (crockery fragments,
pebbles, coffee beans, buttons, beads, nails,
shells) on wood, 201 x 141 cm (79⅛ x 55½ in.)
Santee, Niki Charitable Art Foundation

Symbolic creatures populate this imaginary
sphere and call forth animals and the elements.
A snake (the underworld), a long-horned ram
or a bovine animal (earth), a bird (air), and fish
(water) appear in a visual tangle that is hard to
read as a narrative. The artist set her rough style
and textural mixed media in jarring contrast to
the subject of paradise or an ideal landscape.

frequently go out at night for a drink or a meal, which in turn led to friendships
and collaborations, the formation of artist groups, and further introductions.

A good example of this kind of communication and influence was the
Mathews family's decision to move to the island of Mallorca, Spain, home to the
little village of Deià. On a trip to Madrid from Deià with her family in 1955, Niki
Mathews visited the Prado Museum and absorbed the liberating art of Francisco
Goya and Hieronymus Bosch, who both treated their subject matter in innovative, even subversive and shocking, ways. The Mathews family moved on from
Madrid to Barcelona, where they saw Park Güell, created between 1900 and 1914
by the visionary architect Antoni Gaudí (1852–1926). Gaudí invented highly
unusual architectural forms inspired by nature. What would conventionally be
built with right angles or straight lines instead might curve, meander, dissolve,
or bulge. His buildings seemed to have grown rather than to have been constructed. His work also has a playful, inventive feel in its decoration. For example, he cemented broken china dish shards and glass to mosaic the surfaces of
walls, benches, and applied sculptures. *Trencadis* is the name of this decorative
technique, and the word means "broken up" in the Catalan language. Besides
broken crockery, traditional *trencadis* may incorporate buttons and shells. After
her visit to Park Güell, Niki Mathews resolved to someday design a park of her
own. The permanent polychromy of *trencadis* mosaic left a lasting impression
on her, and while at first she only painted patterns that resembled it, she would
later incorporate broken dishware into mixed media assemblages. A work like

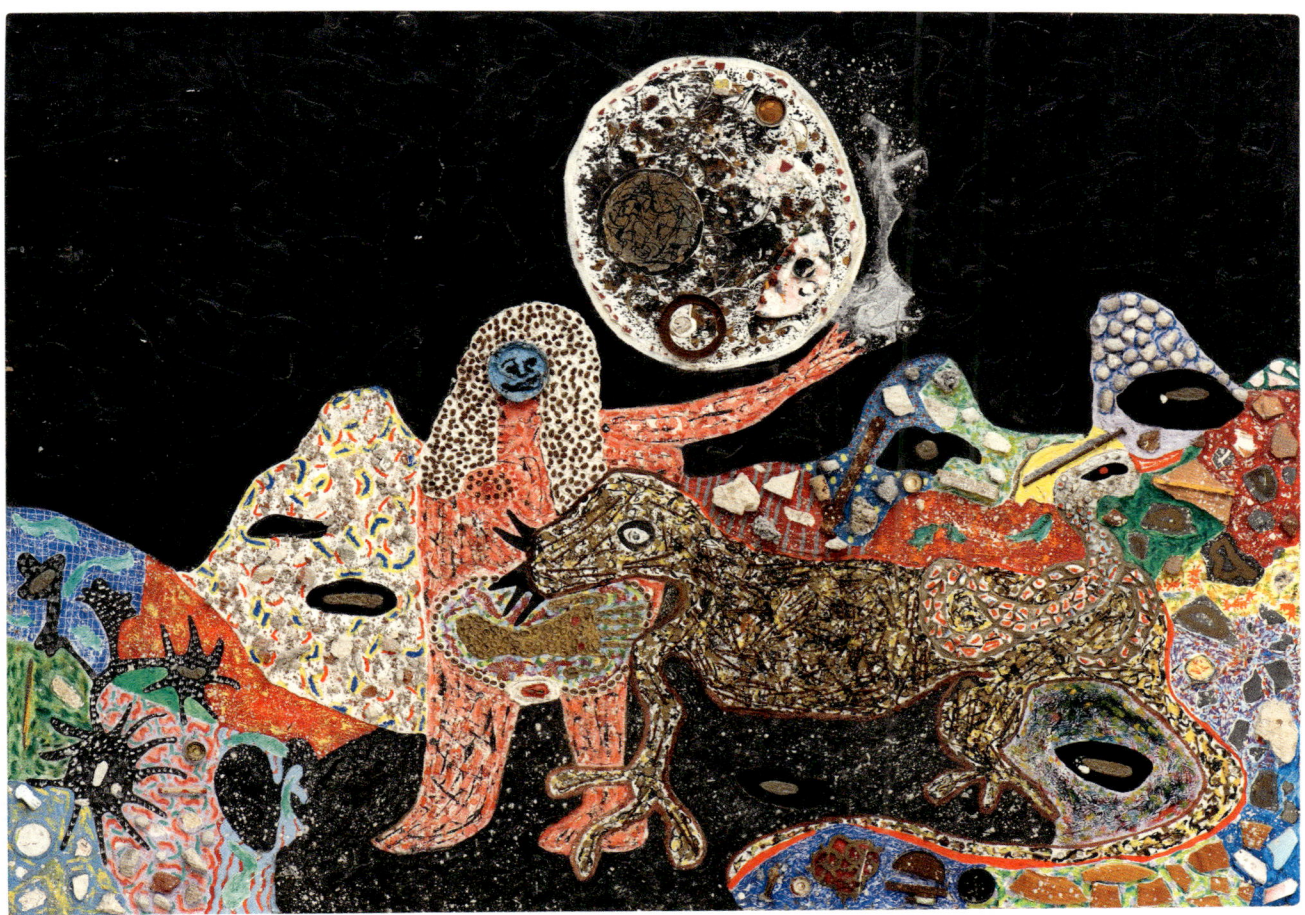

The Round Room (1956–58) grew out of her experience of Gaudí's Park Güell, both in its curving forms and its small, colorful patterns.

In May 1956, while living in Deià, Niki Mathews had a second child, a son called Philip, who was named by the poet Robert Graves in honor of Saint Philip's feast day. Like many female artists with small children, Niki Mathews did not have a work studio separate from her living quarters, and at times allowed her daughter to paint with her, even onto some of her works. A small strip of canvas near the lowest edge of *A Woman Between the Town and the Flower* was allotted to Laura Mathews's small landscape. Her style does not look appreciably different to her mother's. When this painting was made (the dating is approximate), Laura was between five and seven years old. Niki Mathews was in her late twenties.

In *A Woman Between the Town and the Flower*, the main female figure wears a dress and holds a bouquet or multi-headed stalk of red blossoms. Her dark green face has no features, just a head of orange-red hair, a color Niki Mathews sometimes dyed her own hair at this time. Dark, muddy tones complicate the painting's center and dissolve the easy readability of its subject matter. The fleshy pink of the open sky in the upper register leaks into the woman's dress and balances against Laura's clear blue sky along the bottom edge. Some sharp green tent shapes brighten a muddy patch and could be distant pines, but their pointy shapes also echo the spelling of the word "Mama." A thick, dark, round shape rises behind the tall standing woman. It reads as a sunflower, a shining sun,

Pink Nude with Dragon, 1958
Oil, various small objects on plywood,
143.5 x 200 x 6 cm (56½ x 78¾ x 2⅓ in.)
Hanover, Sprengel Museum

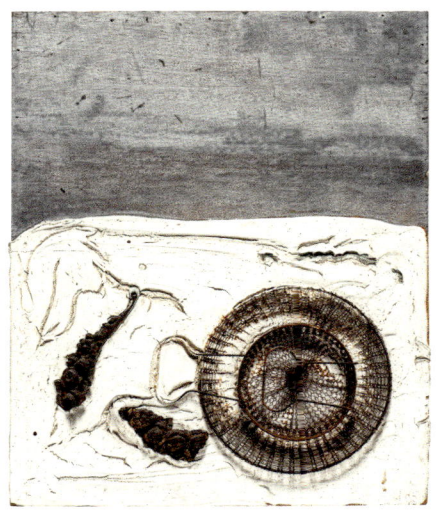

ABOVE
Winter Landscape, 1960/61
Paint, plaster, objects on plywood,
62 x 50 x 2.6 cm (24⅜ x 19¹¹⁄₁₆ x 1 in.)
Hanover, Sprengel Museum

OPPOSITE
Untitled (Abstract after Jackson Pollock)
[Sans titre (Abstract à la Jackson Pollock)], 1959
Paint and various objects (beads, buttons, shells)
on wooden door, 197 x 80 cm (77⁹⁄₁₆ x 31½ in.)
Santee, Niki Charitable Art Foundation

some other star, or a planet. Variations of such a round, radiating presence recur in several paintings of this era. The scale of the two worlds in this painting—the upper one of the mother and the lower one of the child—separates them into distinct realms. The woman caught in between the town and flower, as the title says, stands on the line separating the little girl's world from herself. A green-winged creature lifts up and escapes away into the sky over the woman's head.

In August 1956, the Mathewses left their children in Mallorca and traveled to Paris, where they stayed for three months in the apartment of an absent friend in a dead-end alley named Impasse Ronsin. Located in the neighborhood of Montparnasse, in the 15th arrondissement, the Impasse Ronsin's shabby architecture and overgrown street and gardens had housed artists before. Max Ernst once had a studio there, and Constantin Brâncuși still worked there. In the Impasse Ronsin Niki Mathews met the Swiss artists and married couple Jean Tinguely (1925–1991) and Eva Aeppli (1925–2015) for the first time. Aeppli had just started making life-size doll-like figures of cloth, while Tinguely incorporated motion and mechanics into his work.The Mathewses soon found a larger place to live in Paris and moved in with their children. Niki Mathews decided to disguise a non-functioning fireplace in her children's bedroom with a tree sculpture. Apparently starting to get interested in collage and assemblage, she wanted the surface of the plaster tree to have objects embedded in it, such as toys, Coke bottles, plastic flowers, fishing lures, and more. Mathews asked Tinguely to help her by welding an armature to hold this sculpture upright, and he was happy to assist, even though he had never welded before. The tree came to life—it was her first sculpture and her first collaboration with Tinguely. Unfortunately, this work has been lost.

By 1958, both Niki Mathews and her son Philip faced severe health problems, which stretched the family's emotional resources and led Harry to function as the main caregiver for the children. Niki Mathews's thyroid condition sidelined her often, and her medical care proved hit and miss. A doctor's recommendation that she move to the mountains resulted in Harry buying a house in the southeast of France in the mountain village of Lans-en-Vercors. Nearby in Hauterives stood the Ideal Palace (1879–1912) made by Joseph Ferdinand Cheval (1836–1924). The whole family traveled to visit this monument, together with the American poet and art critic John Ashbery (1927–2017).

Cheval was a letter carrier who one day tripped on an unusually eroded stone and decided to build something with it. He collected more river-washed stones, which he gradually built into a fantastic palace over a 33-year time span, completely on his own. Although a self-taught artist, Cheval's use of the rocks that he picked up and wheelbarrowed to the site of his bold, large-scale architectural and sculptural structure made a deep and lasting impression on Niki Mathews, just as Gaudí's park in Barcelona had done. She would later dedicate a New York exhibition to Cheval, with one work's title specifically mentioning him.[4]

She painted a series of imaginary nightscapes in which the dark sky opens up to space, and the spattered dots become constellations. Nearly five feet (141 cm) long, *Assemblage Landscape* (1959) includes such points of light. Real objects like a can, broken dish shards, a ball of string, a long paintbrush, and an oyster shell stick out. Paint gobs and trickles, plus plaster, encrust these objects onto the canvas, building depth as a disordered texture on the surface. The viewer could be standing in a rough desert and facing its horizon. A full moon weighs heavily in the sky, stabbed by a paintbrush and pliers. Or, if the viewer is willing to interpret mechanics and motion, they may see a large, horseshoe crab-shaped satellite shooting diagonally through the sky from left to right.

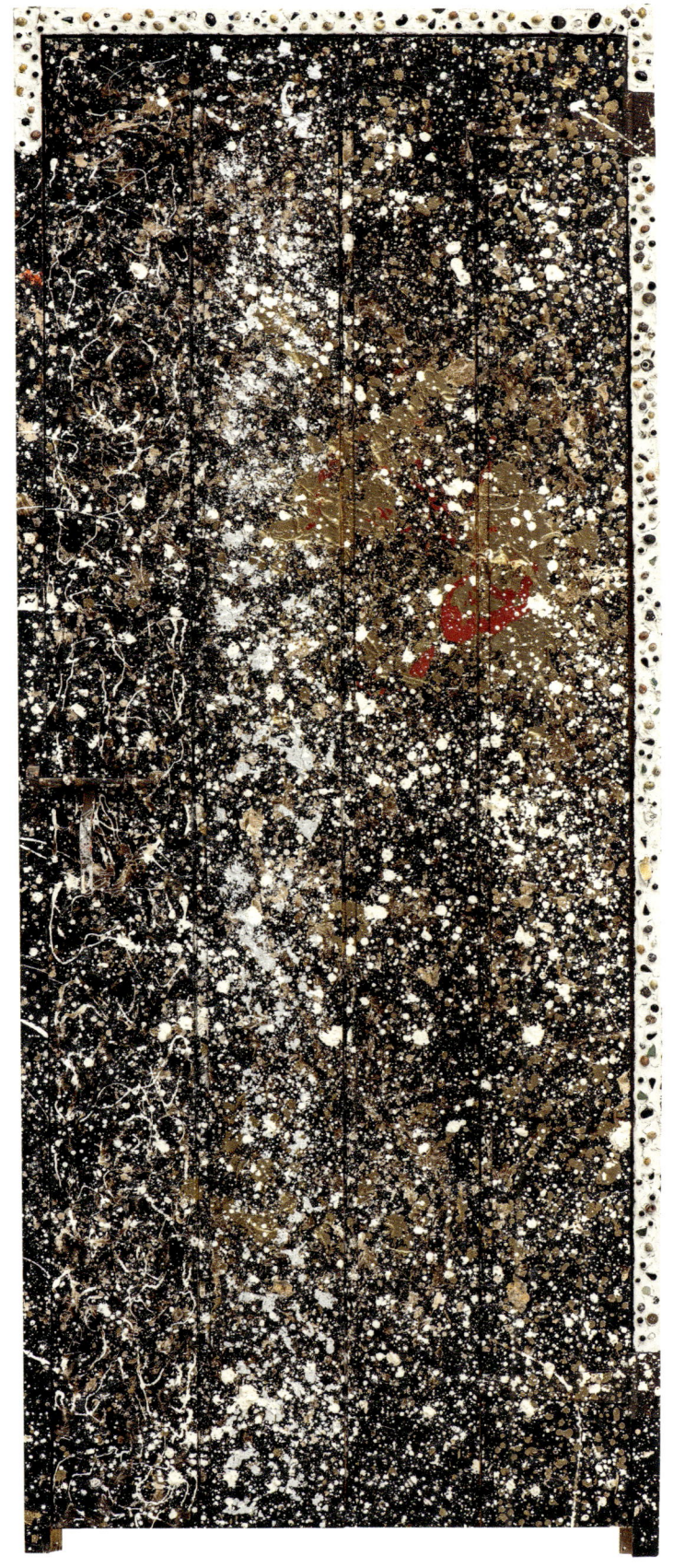

As a number of unfinished canvases from this period show, the artist began such works by constructing the lower part of the assemblage first, pressing objects into plaster on the bottom two-thirds of the plywood panel. The unfinished works show her search for adequate encounters between objects as she experimented with assemblage during her stylistic evolution. She played with placement, contrasting round forms like a paint can lid or saucer with more aggressive shapes like a pointy screw or the long handle of a paintbrush, or indeterminate, evocative forms like those of a crushed cup or rolling pin handle. Pollock had guided paint spontaneously, sometimes energetically, letting it drip or flinging it as he moved around his canvas flat on the ground. Niki Mathews worked similarly on a flat surface where she created the energy fields and relationships between her chosen objects. The last third of the plywood that became sky was quicker to execute, and was painted comparatively thinly and then spattered, streaked, or left a solid dark color. Taking a cue from Pollock, Niki Mathews had switched away from oil paint to gloss paint.

Pink Nude in Landscape (1959, p. 20) shows how easily a borrowed Jackson Pollock sky blends with and overtakes a Gaudí-inspired *trencadis* landscape. Real coffee beans, pebbles, buttons, nails, tacks, and shells figure into the surface texture. A smiling pink nude stands off-center on the wood panel, where she plucks a lyre to bewitch some animals, but not a male human partner.

Art historian Ulrich Krempel, formerly the director of the Sprengel Museum where *Pink Nude in Landscape* resides, has identified tacks forced in from the back of the work that protrude in the breast and genital areas, sharp side out, weaponizing the sexual parts of the figure's body.[5] The scale of the work is ambitious: nearly five by over six feet (141 x 201 cm) and distinctly larger than, say, something like the Venetian Renaissance *Pastoral Concert* in the Louvre Museum, painted by Titian around 1509, which features nude females and dressed male courtiers in an outdoor concert setting. In Saint Phalle's painting, a revolving ring of nearly abstract black-and-white dancers disport to the nude's lyre music on the hillside behind her. They recall Matisse's background circle of nude dancers in *The Joy of Life* (1905–6). By using subject matter akin to that of a Renaissance painter like Titian or the Fauvist Matisse, Saint Phalle harkens back to art history's established tropes. At the same time, the proximity of the long-horned animal and the lyre suggest inspiration as unexpected as the lyres of Ur from ancient Mesopotamia, which had been exhumed in the 1920s from the Royal Cemetery at Ur and revealed a belief system in which women were provided musical instruments to play in the landscape of the afterlife. The lyres had been dug up in a gravesite more than 4,500 years old that contained the bodies of 10 royal women, one of whom even had her fingers placed where the strings would have been. Art history resides in *Pink Nude*. It betrays layers of the artist's aesthetic allegiances as she searches for a way forward.

A darkened sky automatically suggests night, or a psychologically dark place; however, the artist's dark sky landscape series could reflect the inauguration of the space race during the late 1950s by the Soviet Union, that quest to understand and control the unknown. Niki Mathews may have studied the thin, black-and-white catalogue printed in French that accompanied the 1959 exhibition about Jackson Pollock and new American painting. In that catalogue, Abstract Expressionist painter Robert Motherwell's words resonate with Mathews's exploratory *Assemblage Landscape*: "Traveling in the night, without knowing where, aboard an unknown ship, an absolute conflict with the elements of reality."[6]

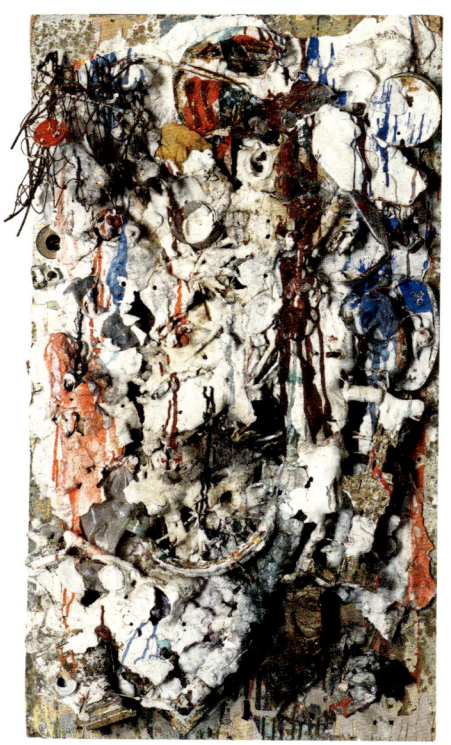

Tir première séance – deuxième séance shooting session, 1961
Oil, various small objects on plywood, 130 x 73 x 28 cm (51³⁄₁₆ x 28¾ x 11 in.)
Nice, MAMAC Collection

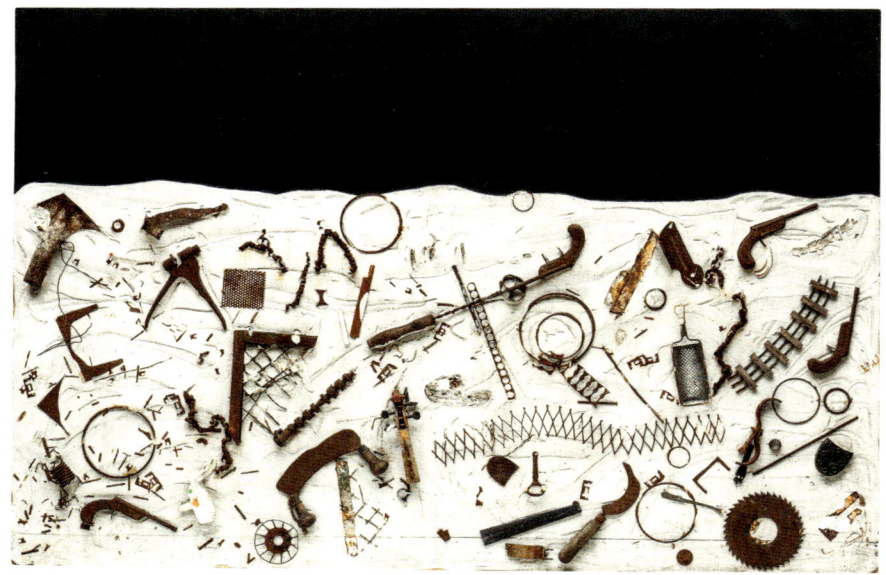

Night Experiment, *c.* 1959
Metal objects, wooden objects, plaster,
paint on wood, 130 x 196 x 13 cm
(51³/₁₆ x 77³/₁₆ x 5⅛ in.)
Hanover, Sprengel Museum

In October 1959, Niki Mathews attended the first Paris Biennial. Her acquaintance Jean Tinguely had been invited to participate in the prestigious show. There she saw the work of the American Robert Rauschenberg (1925–2008), among others, with whom she would later collaborate. Mathews felt her own art deserved respect. Her ambition had been fired up by a scathing comment made during a shared meal by American painter Joan Mitchell (1925–1992), who was living in Paris at the time. Well known as an Abstract Expressionist painter who had established herself among her male peers, Mitchell intentionally talked down to Mathews, calling her "one of those writer's wives that paints."[7] She repeated similar comments on several different occasions. Quite stung, Mathews resolved to be taken seriously and not seen only as a housewife that painted. When her husband Harry refused to put her name on the deed of the house in which they both lived in Lans-en-Vercors, something shifted.

Despite being for the most part satisfied with her husband and loving her children, Niki Mathews needed to leave her nuclear family for the sake of her own mental health. She suggested to her spouse that they undergo a trial separation for a year so that she could dedicate herself only to art, a move she would make in 1960. However, she could not and would not go back. Unable to reconcile her work as an artist with the societal expectations of being a wife and mother, Mathews suffered from the unhappiness that Betty Friedan (1921–2006) would identify as the "problem that has no name" in her 1963 book *The Feminine Mystique*. The last sentence of chapter one reads, "We can no longer ignore that voice within women that says: 'I want something more than my husband and my children and my home.'"[8]

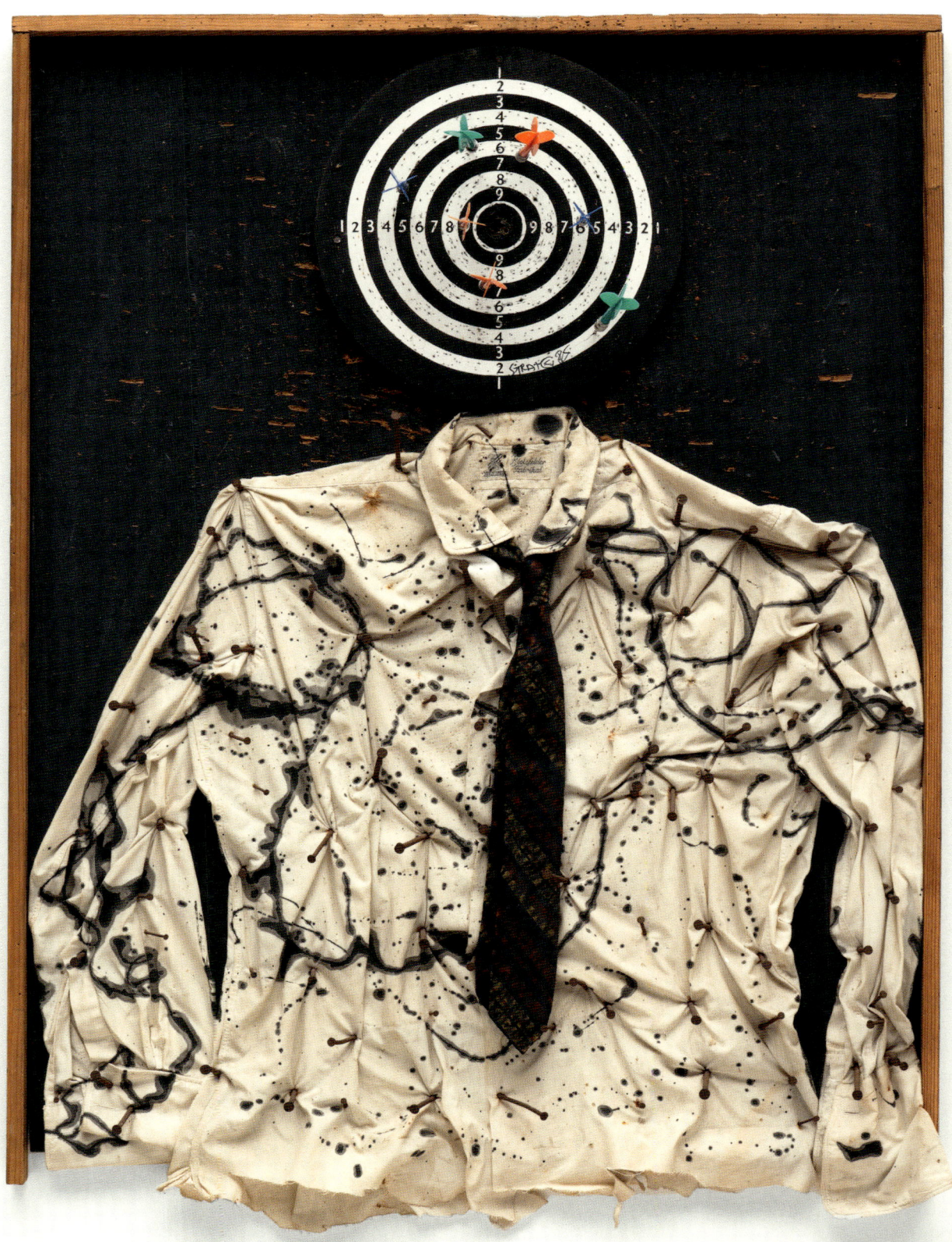

The Assemblages
and the Shooting Paintings

Facing an unknown future and determined to survive after separating from her husband in 1960, Niki de Saint Phalle reassumed her maiden name, partly to annoy her family. She instinctively explored the cultural forces of her time. The developing post-World War II art market, the changing museum and gallery world, growing networks of curators and like-minded artists, and even the shift in news distribution from newspapers and radio to television and the proliferation of popular magazines—all of these factors came into play. In a remarkable pivot, she managed to go from being a little-known, untrained naive painter, encumbered with the baggage of being a wife, mother, and the beautiful model daughter of an aristocratic banker, to establishing herself as someone to be taken seriously by the art world. By 1961, she was seen as an exciting, even notorious artist. How did this happen?

Her accomplices were a group of young artists working in Paris in the 1950s and 1960s who scavenged or selected real objects instead of working with traditional art materials. Although quite unique in how they each worked, all of the artists connected art to actual life by instrumentalizing household items, trash, machine parts, and even food as their media. At the heart of this work was the idea that objects contain exploitable social meaning. In 1960, the critic Pierre Restany (1930–2003) united their work under the umbrella term *Nouveau Réalisme* (New Realism). Anti-elitist in intent, New Realism's unconventionality drew a line in the sand. The public either loved it for its humor and surprise factor or hated it because it defied their expectations of what art should be. Saint Phalle's friend Jean Tinguely, whose career had flowered, belonged to the original group. So did Restany, Yves Klein, Arman (1928–2005), François Dufrêne (1930–1982), Raymond Hains (1926–2005), Daniel Spoerri (1930–2024), and Jacques de la Villeglé (1926–2022), all men. A few others would soon join them, including Saint Phalle herself as the only female.

Often joining forces on projects and making common cause, the New Realists especially loved assemblage and collage, showing allegiance to Cubist collage and Dada objects as well as Marcel Duchamp's readymades. Because of Saint Phalle's adoption of assemblage as a major artistic mode, it is useful here to explain more about Duchamp's influence on the art world at the time. A French artist living in New York, Duchamp had established the idea of the readymade in art—that is, the selection of an industrially manufactured object to which the artist simply

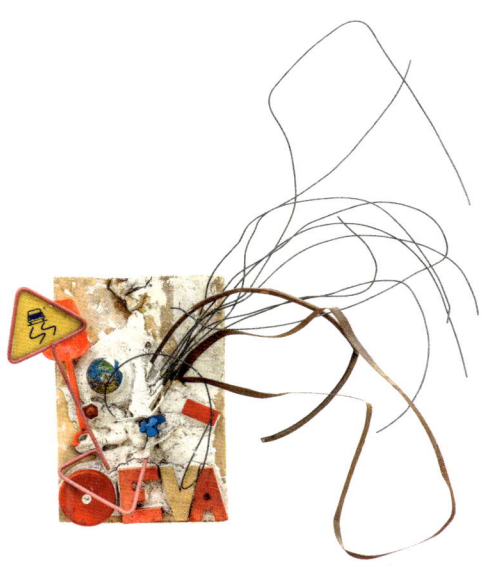

OPPOSITE
Saint Sébastien or Portrait of My Lover, 1961
Dartboard, arrow, shirt, tie, paint on wood,
100 x 74 x 15 cm (39⅜ x 29⅛ x 5¹⁵⁄₁₆ in.)
Hanover, Sprengel Museum

ABOVE
Eva, 1960–61
Plaster and various small objects on plywood,
50 x 58 x 30 cm (19¹¹⁄₁₆ x 22¹³⁄₁₆ x 11¹³⁄₁₆ in.)
Hanover, Sprengel Museum

27

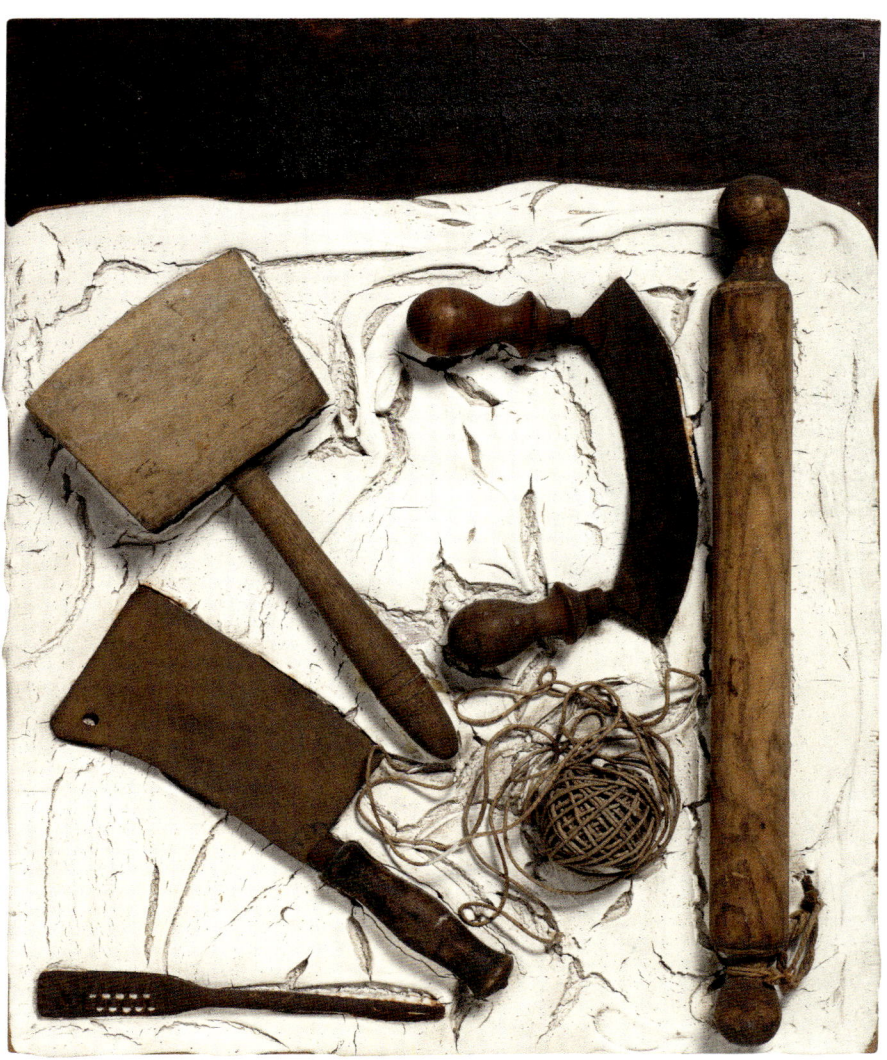

Cleaver (Le Hachoir), 1960
Color, plaster, objects on wood,
61 x 50 x 9 cm (24 x 19¹¹⁄₁₆ x 3⁹⁄₁₆ in.)
Hanover, Sprengel Museum

attached a newly invented idea. The choosing of the object usually included
the particularity of the object's presentation. For example, in 1915 Duchamp
chose a snow shovel from a hardware store. He suspended the shovel from the
ceiling; hanging on a wire, it would shift slightly in the air currents of a room
and thus come alive, its long silhouette and wide blade evoking a sauntering,
elegant female flapper. (Or not, if this is not what the viewer sees: to this day,
the snow shovel still stops visitors to the Museum of Modern Art in New York
in their tracks.) The artist named the work *In Advance of the Broken Arm.* With
works such as this, Duchamp rejected painting and sculpture as mimesis and
advanced the use of real objects in art. Along with his concept of the readymade,
Duchamp had also ushered in wordplay in his sometimes abstruse titles and in
the naming of his invented female alter-ego, Rrose Sélavy, pronounced "Eros,
c'est la vie," or "Eros, that's life." His playful adoption of a second gender for artistic purposes also teased the art world.

Duchamp, by now in his early 70s, showed up at New York and Parisian
art openings, museum panels, and happenings, and his work was increasingly
included in exhibitions. He had married Alexina "Teeny" Matisse, mother
of Niki de Saint Phalle's girlhood friend Jackie Matisse. When Jean Tinguely

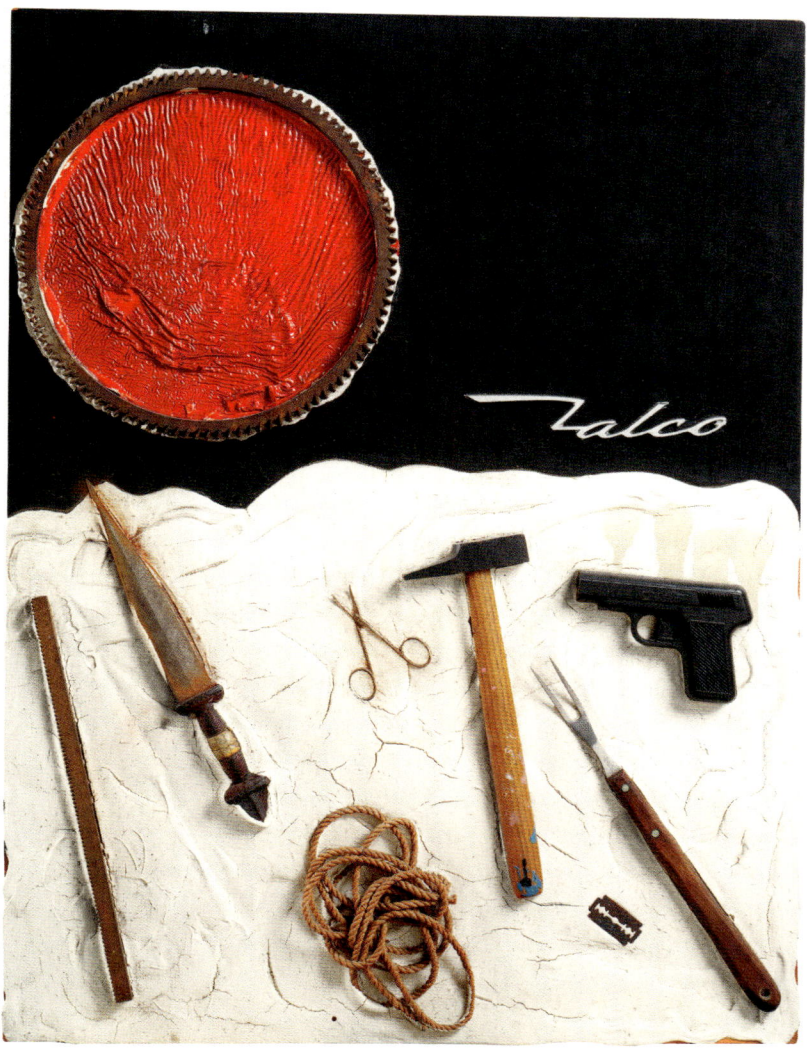

Tu est moi (Paysage de la mort), 1960
Objects, wood, plaster, and paint,
79.5 x 60 x 3 cm (31⁵⁄₁₆ x 23⁵⁄₈ x 1³⁄₁₆ in.)
Princeton University Art Museum

came to New York for the first time in 1960 to attend his own opening in a gallery there, Duchamp was a person Tinguely wanted to meet again. Former Dada artist and then New York psychiatrist Richard Huelsenbeck, who put Tinguely up in his home, made sure the two men got together. Huelsenbeck also introduced Tinguely to Robert Rauschenberg, Jasper Johns, and others lighting up the New York art scene, whom Tinguely would later introduce to Saint Phalle. Tinguely networked effectively.

Although she remained back in Paris, Niki de Saint Phalle was well acquainted with Tinguely by the time he got invited to New York, having briefly lived in the same street as the artist and bought one of his works in the 1950s. As Tinguely gained prominence, Saint Phalle was working at becoming an artist in Paris and lived in the apartment vacated by her husband and children. Paris art events brought Saint Phalle and Tinguely into continual contact in 1960, and through him she met many other artists and curators. While mutual attraction was building, Tinguely's friendship and his personal interest in her helped Saint Phalle at this time in her career. He gave her confidence in her ideas. Tinguely introduced Saint Phalle to Pontus Hultén (1924–2006), the director of the Moderna Museet in Stockholm, who would include her in important

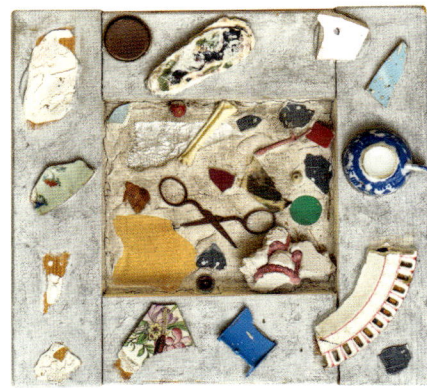

Paire de ciseaux (Scissors), 1960
Oil, various small objects on plywood,
32 x 33.7 x 7 cm (12⅝ x 13¼ x 2¾ in.)
Nice, MAMAC Collection

exhibitions, make early purchases of her work, and become a lifelong supporter of her art.

Saint Phalle initiated working relationships with several of the New Realists. In the beginning, Daniel Spoerri's tabletops intrigued her; they were meant to assassinate life and reality. Saint Phalle recalled their relationship as particularly productive: "I would say the one person who really influenced me with my early collages, by pushing me to go farther, more directly, was Spoerri, not Jean, because Spoerri was involved with collage."[9]

Niki de Saint Phalle first adapted her Gaudí-inspired broken ceramics technique to assemblage under the influence of Spoerri. She reduced narrative and color, which had both been important to her early paintings. At times the distant aerial perspective of her early landscapes continued, but when the landscape horizon line disappeared, the plywood ground became a flat field of scattered objects. Saint Phalle introduced qualities of anger, sharpness, danger, and consumption into the assemblages with tools, forks, grates, files, knives, scissors, and even firearms. She said the violent connotations of these objects harkened back to her mental breakdown, when she had hidden small weapons in her purse and under her bed to ensure a sense of protection for herself. They also complied with a New Realist tendency towards aggressive materials and processes, itself a reflection of a general sense of anxiety in a society that had survived a world war and entered an age of armament that could enable mutual destruction. Saint Phalle's assemblages took on an edgy, disturbing presence.

According to Saint Phalle, Spoerri and Tinguely competed for her attention as she hung out with the artists, critics, and curators she was meeting through her association with the New Realists.[10] However, after she left her husband, despite Spoerri's initial artistic influence and friendship, it was she and Tinguely who

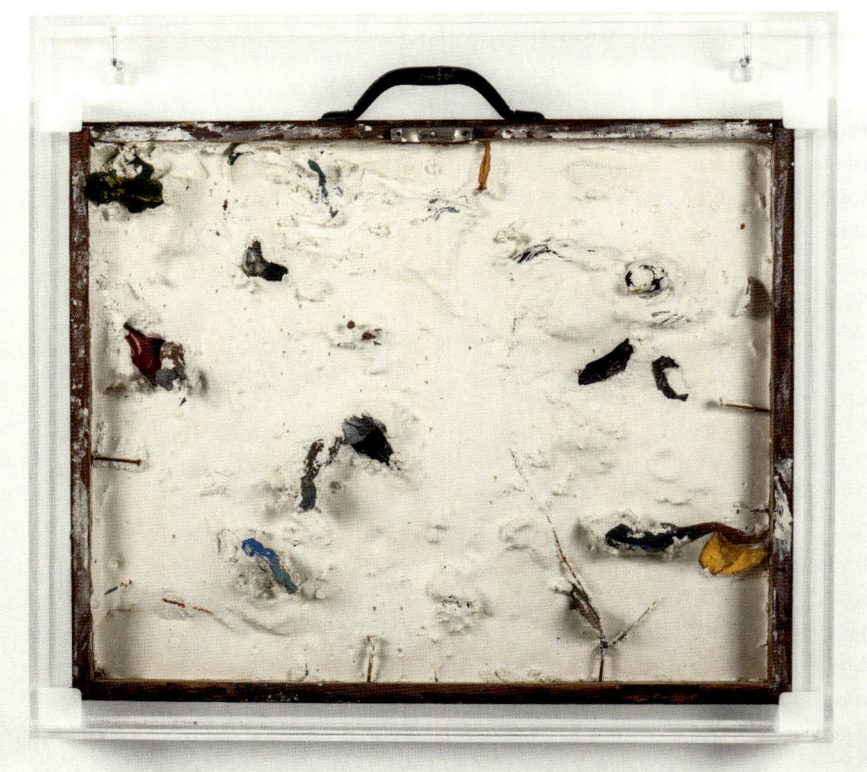

Tir (non tiré) dans valise, c. 1960–61
Oil, various small objects in suitcase,
47.5 x 55 cm (18¹¹⁄₁₆ x 21⅝ in.)
Nice, MAMAC Collection

quickly became a couple. Saint Phalle moved back to the Impasse Ronsin, where they lived together until the street was torn down to accommodate the expansion of the nearby hospital whose coal Tinguely had stolen for heat during his poorer years. In 1963, they bought and relocated to a former inn outside of Paris, in L'Essonne, where curators, artists, and critics often visited them, and where they worked and stored their art. Saint Phalle and Tinguely would remain in creative dialogue for the rest of their lives as collaborators, competitors, allies, and friends, and even marry in 1971, despite—or maybe because of—their intense personalities and shifting romantic interests in other partners.

Significantly, because of her New Realist connection, one of Saint Phalle's assemblages was included in an exhibition in the Museum of Modern Art in New York. Seen by the public in New York from October 2 through November 12, 1961, *The Art of Assemblage* also traveled to Dallas and San Francisco. Among other artists, Duchamp was represented by 13 works, Tinguely by two, Spoerri by one. The assemblage by Saint Phalle that curator William Seitz chose for the show demonstrated a Duchampian wordplay in its title, *Tu est moi* (1960, p.29), which is ungrammatical French and in English means *You Are Me (Landscape of Death)*. The title's wording, however, reflects several meanings when spoken: *Tu est moi* also sounds like the French words for "You and me" ("Tu et moi") as well as the imperative "Kill me," or "Tuez-moi." The ready-made items Saint Phalle chose and embedded in plaster for her assemblage suggested some kind of death: a steel gear, a toy pistol, a hunting knife, a steel file, a hammer, a cooking fork, nail scissors, a razor blade, and rope. By playing with multiple meanings of the phonetics in the title, Saint Phalle mirrors a Duchampian tendency to provide for more than one understanding of a work. Who is to say that Saint Phalle is not playing with the idea of *la petite mort*, a French euphemism for orgasm, since, as Duchamp said, "Eros is life"?

While numerous Saint Phalle assemblages feature weapons, not all do. At times she included children's toys in her work, and the colors brightened. *Get Well Soon (Valentine)* (1960–61) features a Dutch get well card and a teddy bear, a paint lid, wire, a small container, a paintbrush loaded with white paint, and a red disk that looks like a radiating sun. One can only speculate on how this type of work may have reflected her pain at leaving her children and seeing them less often. A very famous lost Dada assemblage of 1920 by Francis Picabia had made fun of famous painters "aping" reality by relating them to a toy monkey, and Saint Phalle includes a toy monkey in one work, *Monkey* (c. 1960–61). In contrast, *Two Guns and One Knife* (also 1960–61, p. 37), includes a kitten-heeled woman's pump-style shoe gooped with plaster, two guns, and a knife embedded in plaster. All of these are adhered to a wood block, with the shoe standing as if on the ground, and the weapons sticking up into the air. Additionally, the plaster bristles with small, sharp metal points.

In *Hors d'oeuvre (Portrait of My Lover/Portrait of Myself)* from 1960, Saint Phalle set up a "portrait" of her anonymous lover by pressing his shirt into plaster on plywood and placing a target where his head would be. She added some buttons and small objects, and dabs of blue paint. (This work is almost the same format and size as Jasper Johns's 1955 *Target with Four Faces*.) When this work was shown publicly, Saint Phalle set up a tabletop of darts nearby for gallery visitors to throw, thus suggesting they change their passive viewing into action. The darts could be removed from the target and reused multiple times as in a game. The artist issued a playful invitation to punish the boyfriend, but because she put herself into the title as co-victim, the blame and the suffering was shared. Here

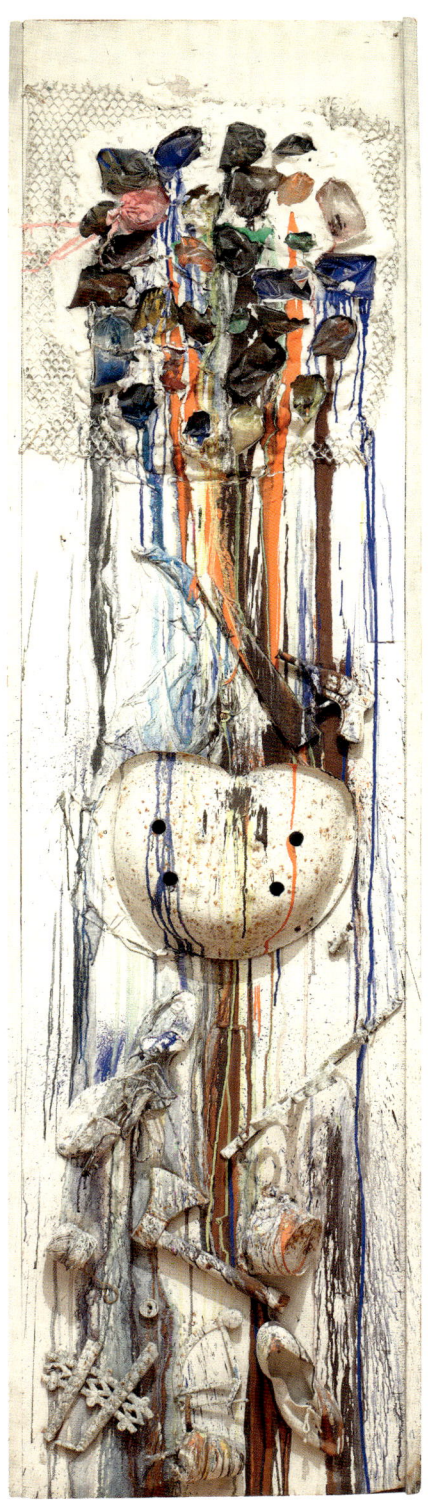

Shooting Painting (American Embassy), 1961
Oil, various objects on plywood,
222 x 102 x 7 cm (87⅜ x 40⅛ x 2¾ in.)
New York, The Museum of Modern Art

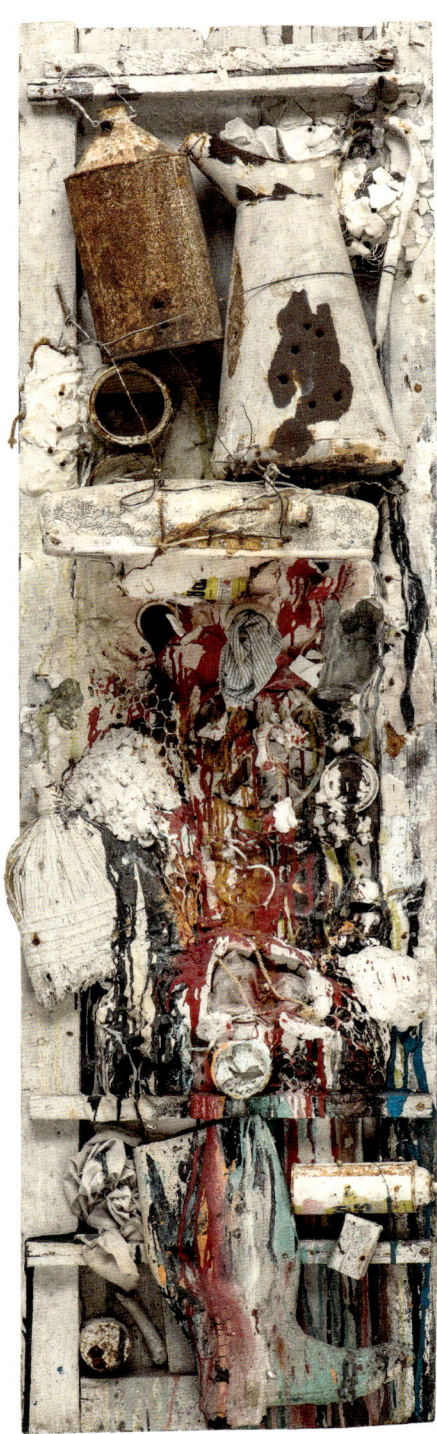

Homage to Bob Rauschenberg
(shot by Rauschenberg), 1961
Paint, plaster, various objects on a wooden
shutter, 186.5 x 56 x 41 cm (73⁷/₁₆ x 22 x 16⅛ in.)
Hanover, Sprengel Museum

Saint Phalle demonstrates the antinomy so often seen in her work. She does not blithely purify human situations into innocent and faulty behaviors. In this case, men and women love and hurt each other, and each are the target of the other, so mutual damage appears unavoidable.

Another slightly smaller dartboard work, *Saint Sébastien or Portrait of My Lover* (1961, p. 26), changes several elements. Saint Phalle more powerfully nailed the drip-painted man's shirt to the plywood backing, making the pierced male body recall the martyr Saint Sebastian, whose body was stuck with arrows. Saint Phalle would have been familiar with the imposing *Saint Sebastian* (1480) by Andrea Mantegna in the Louvre, and she would know the homoerotic appeal of most Saint Sebastian depictions. At the time she was excited by what she considered a glamorous relationship between Rauschenberg and Johns, and this work may have referred to her friendship with them at the time. The instinctual layering of sexuality, play, joy, pain, blame, and revenge reveal themselves in several of Saint Phalle's early works, and in her later films. Around March or April of 1961 Saint Phalle executed *Dart Portrait*, another work that used a circular dartboard with what is now one green dart mounted above a striped Breton sweater on a bright green background. *Portrait on Roller Skates*, made together with Tinguely, imbues the proportions of the target assemblages with playful self-portraiture and potential movement. *Revolver and Red Paint Lid* takes the viewer back to a sun setting into a horizon, while simultaneously mirroring the deflated, anonymous corpse of a target-man. Both works are from spring of 1961.

After having established herself as an assemblage artist, Saint Phalle's major innovative move in early 1961 related directly to the art scene at the time. She answered the major players in Paris with her *Tirs*, or *Shooting Paintings*, inspired by the New Realists' ever more spectacular gestures and welcoming of public participation. Her new idea evolved from her targets. After looking at a white relief painting by Dutch artist Bram Bogart displayed next to one of her dart pieces, she wondered what it would be like to see a painting's imperturbable surface actually bleed. In contrast to the Abstract Expressionist technique that spattered a canvas from above or from the outside, Saint Phalle conceived of the painting ground as a woundable body that erupted when fired upon with a gun. To get this to happen, she prepared plywood panels with sacks of paint and other soft materials covered over by plaster, making them appear initially as monochromatic reliefs. Not fixated on permanency, she even embedded foodstuffs she had on hand, like eggs and spaghetti, likely a nod to Daniel Spoerri, but which also added texture and goop as interior organic materials gushed forth.

The first shooting session happened in Impasse Ronsin on February 12, 1961. Photos of the session make it look casual, less a performance than a wintery outdoor studio experiment. Nonetheless, two photographers were invited, Harry Shunk and János Kender, and several New Realist friends attended. Jean Tinguely made sure there was a good group. Vera and Daniel Spoerri came, as did the gallerist of the new Galerie J, Jeanine de Goldschmidt, and her husband, the critic Pierre Restany, who would spontaneously invite Saint Phalle to join the New Realists as an official member after this event. Just like the dart boards, the *Shooting Paintings* allowed others to participate. Those attending probably hoped to join in from the start. The Niki de Saint Phalle catalogue raisonné suggests at least four works were finished at the first session, of which only grainy black-and-white photos still exist.[11] Within two weeks a second session had produced seven more finished *Tirs*. Word got out. By April, the Office de Radiodiffusion-Télévision Française had broadcast Saint Phalle shooting at plaster objects mounted on rods that contained ink, tomatoes, shampoo, and more. Televised, the aristocratic model with a gun became a national, and then international, sensation.

To an audience, Saint Phalle's virgin picture surface looked pale, bumpy, or rough, more like a relief or an assemblage studded with small objects. White plaster covered the unknown. Exactly what colorants had been concealed, and where, was anyone's guess. Chance, noise, and surprise reigned during

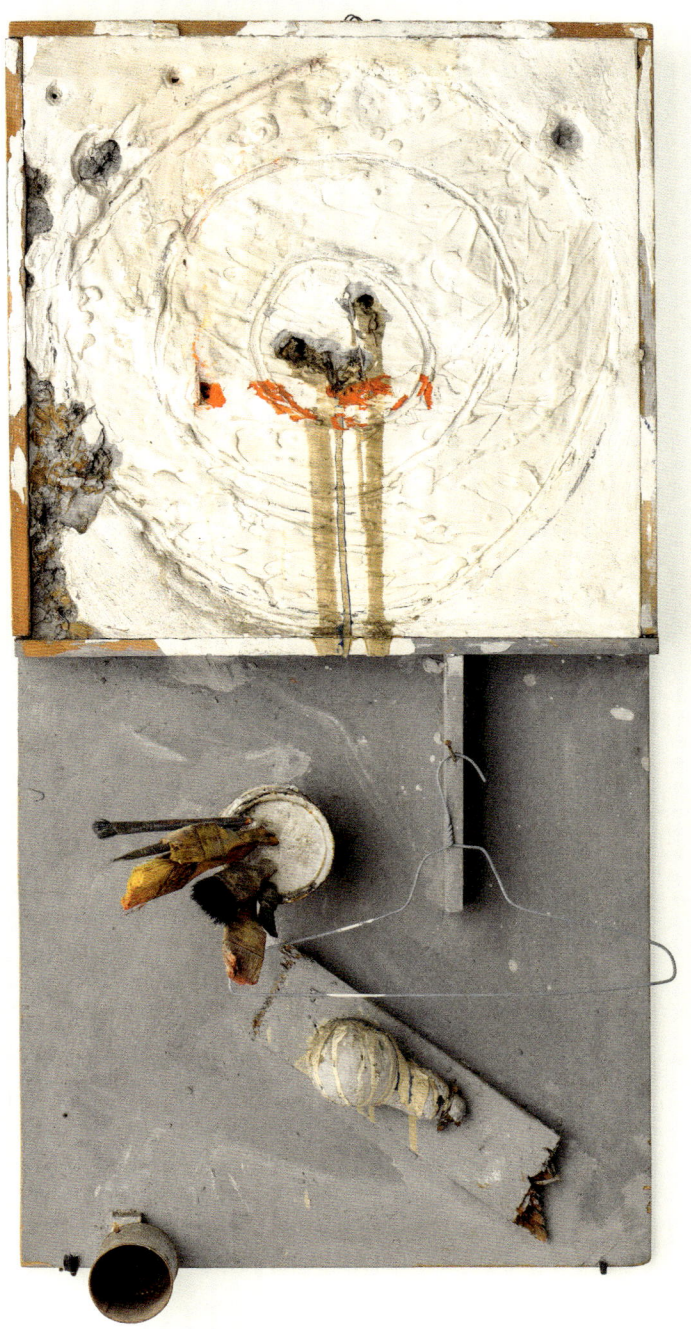

"Oil painting is finished. It's finished now because we are concerned with other problems. We are concerned with death; we're concerned with objects … we want to find a new way."
– SAINT PHALLE IN AN NBC INTERVIEW, 1962

Tir de Jaspar Johns, 1961
Paint, plaster, wood, metal, cement, newspapers, and glass, 119.5 x 59 x 26 cm (47 x 23¼ x 10¼ in.)
Stockholm, Moderna Museet

BELOW
Niki de Saint Phalle, with Jean Tinguely and
Jim Metcalf, at shooting and exhibition opening,
Feu à Volonté (Fire at Will), June 1961
Paris, Impasse Ronsin

OPPOSITE
June 26 Shooting Session
(Tir, séance 26 juin 1961), 1961
Plaster, metal, acrylic, and various
small objects on wood, 322 x 210 x 35 cm
(126¾ x 82¹¹⁄₁₆ x 13¹³⁄₁₆ in.)
Nice, MAMAC Collection

the shooting. When the public participated, a work could get shot to pieces as the participant tried for more and more color. Such a shooter might need to be stopped at some point—the artist might intervene. Or a shooter might take a long time deciding what to aim for and be satisfied with minimal shooting. Johns, for example, who was visiting Paris at the time, shot only after great deliberation and then minimally at a work assembled as an homage to his subject matter. Did the shooter decide when the work was "finished"?

A vertical work assembled on a wooden shutter in homage to Rauschenberg, and which the artist himself shot, shows numerous bullet holes but only one main red splatter. After the first red burst Rauschenberg shot again, hoping for more red to emerge, to no avail. Saint Phalle herself by all accounts had a good aim. A fair amount of unpredictability governed the final result. By so instigating splattering and dripping, Saint Phalle hyperbolized Abstract Expressionism's style. She took authorship away from the heroic artist and gave it back to chance and the public who came to watch and maybe shoot with their varying degrees of aptitude and lust.

In the 2015 Grand Palais, Galeries Nationales Paris, and Guggenheim Museum Bilbao catalogue about Saint Phalle, art historian Sarah Wilson has pointed out how similar the French word "Tir" sounds to the English "tear," a drop of water

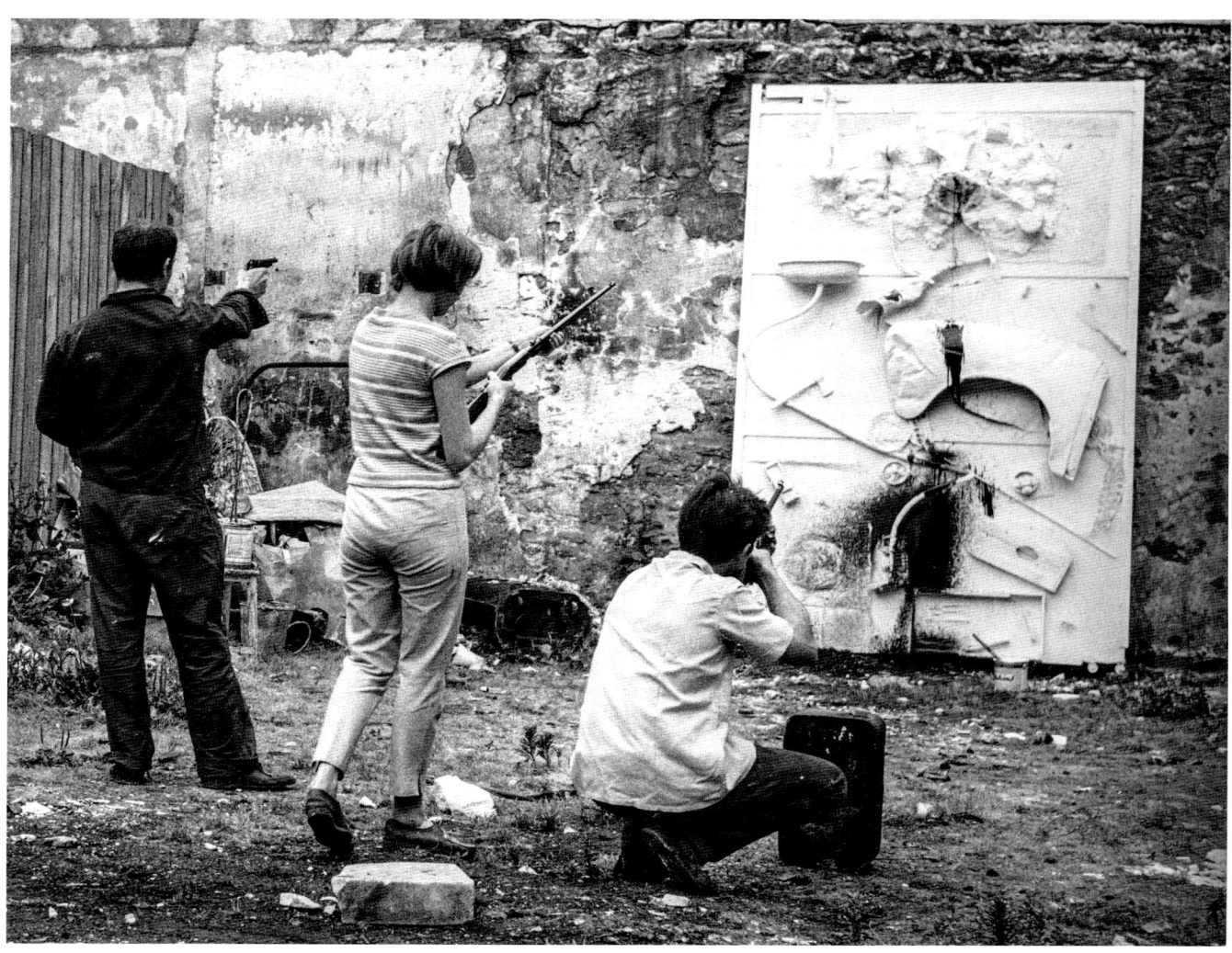

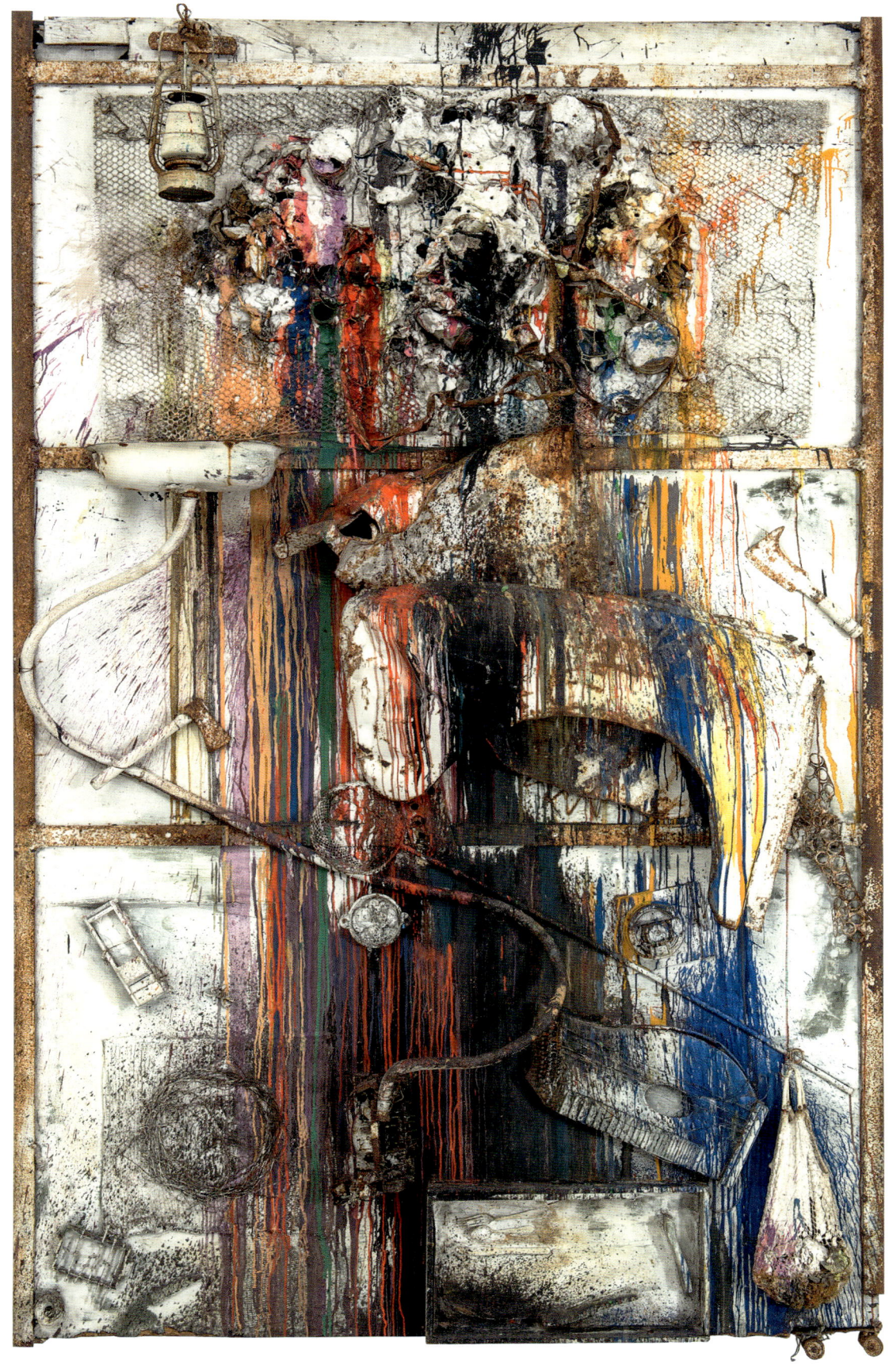

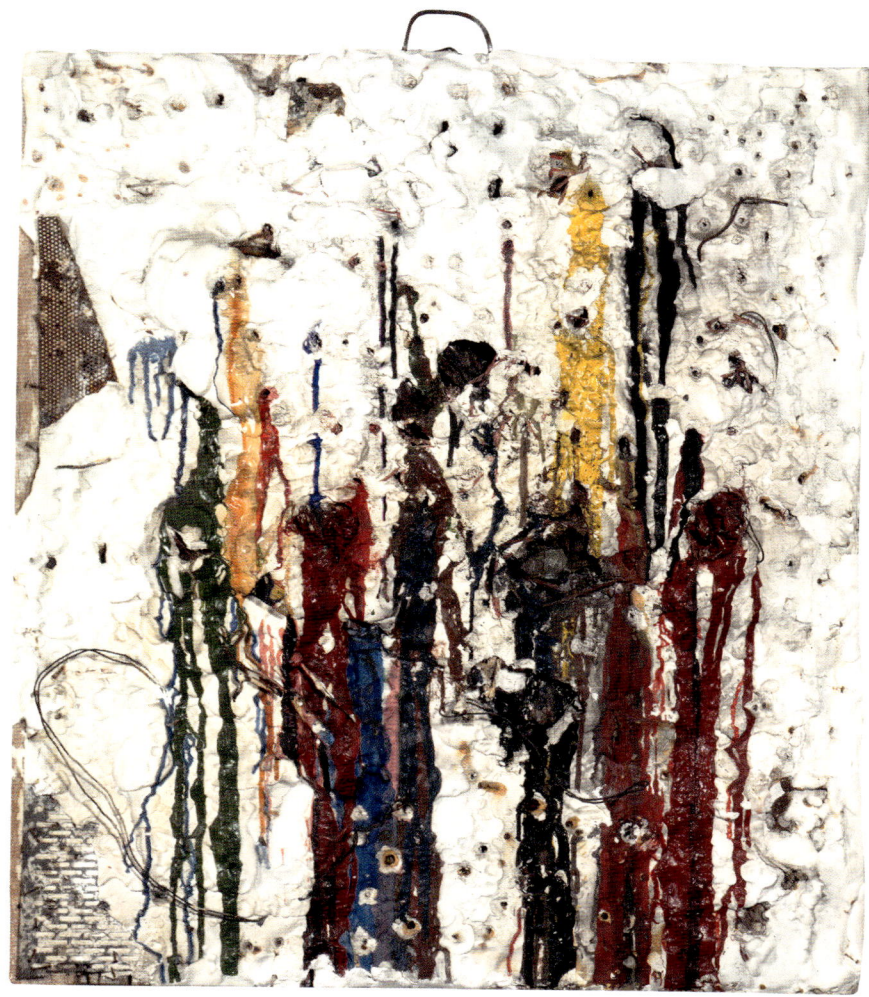

Tir – séance Galerie J, 1961
Plaster, acrylic paint, acrylic glass (hood) on
wood, 96 x 79 cm (37¹³/₁₆ x 31⅛ in.)
Kunsthalle Mannheim, On loan from the
Förderkreis für die Kunsthalle Mannheim e.V.
since 1998; donated by Hans Bichelmeier on the
occasion of his 65th birthday in 1998

that runs down a cheek, evoked by sorrow or anger. In her books and drawings,
Saint Phalle often pictured a woman's head with tears tracking down her face. She
once even designed a pendant necklace called *Medusa Crying* in which a female's
tears assemble into a glistening bib. Since the *Tirs* proved a kind of release for
Saint Phalle as a reaction to her suffering and anger, the idea of crying tears adds
a nuanced layer to the series. Saint Phalle operated from a position of unfenced
emotional vulnerability.

The evolved weapons and the plague of mass shootings that ushered in the
21st century, particularly in the United States, may make Saint Phalle's concept
seem over-the-top, surreal, and dangerous. However, in 1961, barely 17 years after
Paris was liberated from the Nazis, those attending a shooting sometimes covered
their ears or regretted the spattering of a Chanel suit, but they did not fear an
untoward event. The French accepted Saint Phalle's use of a .22 rifle as they would
a shooting stand at a fairground. Indeed, the first *Tir* event in the Impasse Ronsin
borrowed the rifle from just such a Paris amusement park.

Saint Phalle explored formats for her shootings, and she clearly considered
what the shooting itself could signify in various contexts. For example, for her
June/July 1961 solo show at Galerie J, Tinguely built a small shooting range so
that the public could participate indoors daily for two weeks from 5 to 7 p.m.
Saint Phalle prepared a group of *Tirs* staged within gilded, ornate, small- and
medium-sized old master-type frames that came from flea markets. This format

choice suggested she was aiming at conventional bourgeois salon art. The title of the Galerie J exhibition, *Feu á Volonté (Fire at Will)*, issued a command. Saint Phalle and her volunteers literally became the assassins of painting. When met with bullets, the prepared surfaces poured forth their innards. Their picture fields thus wounded, the ornate frames bore witness to impact and leakage. Ever since Dada and Futurism, the avant-garde had been talking about killing the art of the salons and museums, and finally a woman artist and her crew actually took aim. Interestingly, a few of the works prepared for the gallery remained "non tirée" or "not shot." Listed in Saint Phalle's catalogue raisonné, they took various ingenious forms. One was enclosed in a briefcase, one was an "old master" format, while another had been built upon the headboard of a bed.

Saint Phalle was ambivalent, though, about destroying painting per se. She may have loved the excitement of shooting, but she also loved paint and the run of color. Some of the *Tirs* are beautiful. Saint Phalle planned for seductive color variation and painterly color contrasts. Some colors appear sparingly. Some are subtle, others less so. Gravity guided paint downward as it meandered over the bumps of embedded objects, yet she placed those with intent. The paintings often have a natural edge; that is, the plywood remained unframed. Textured mesh ground holding the plaster shows through in places. Saint Phalle later sought new effects by including spray paint cans that could explode when punctured. The explosions added a hissing acoustic effect during the shooting, too. Even if she could not entirely control the results, aesthetic considerations held sway.

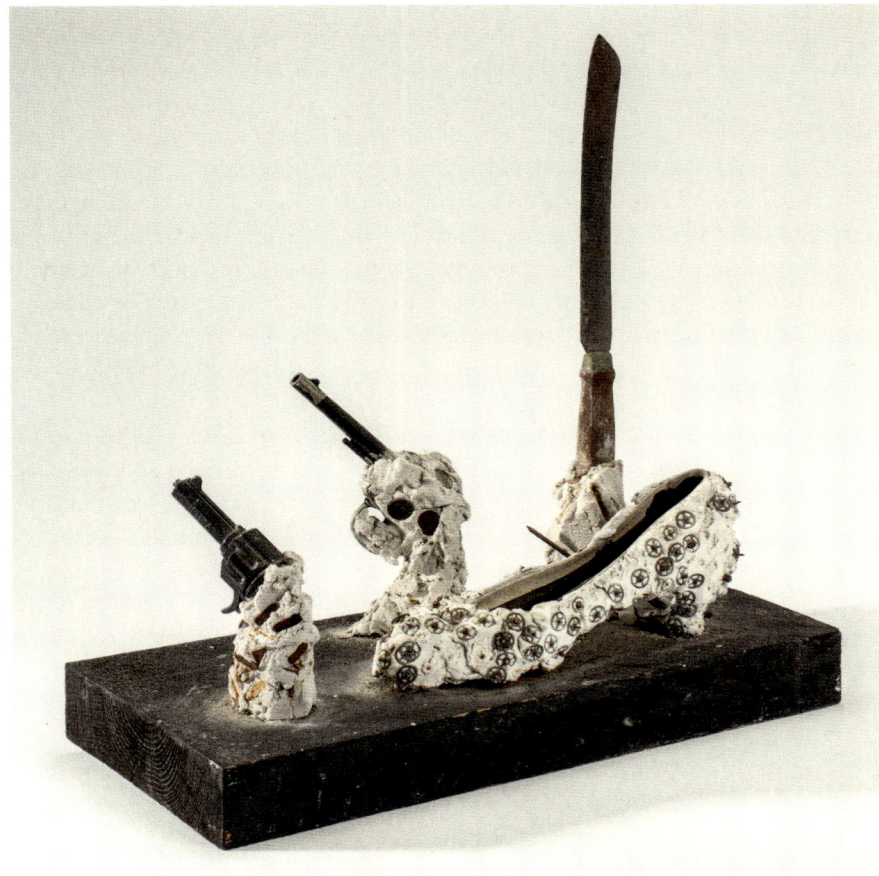

Two Guns and One Knife, 1960–61
Cement, metal, plastic, leather, and wood,
43.2 x 44.3 x 20.3 cm (17 x 17⁷⁄₁₆ x 8 in.)
Stockholm, Moderna Museet

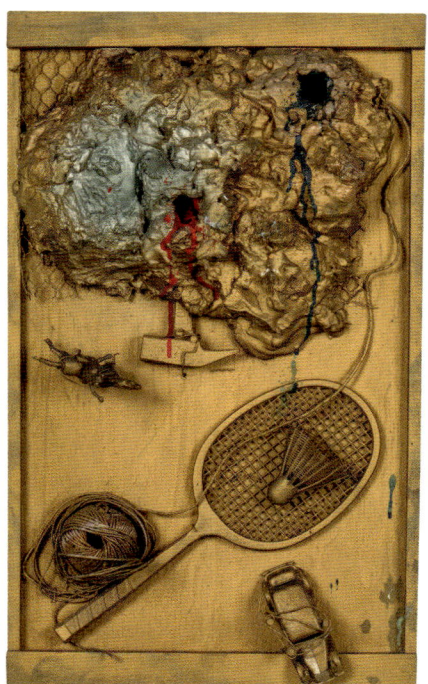

Tir à la raquette – Séance galerie J, 1961
Oil, plaster, wire mesh, and objects on plywood,
355 x 59.5 x 9 cm (139¾ x 23⁷⁄₁₆ x 3⁹⁄₁₆ in)
Nice, MAMAC Collection

OPPOSITE
Grand Tir Galerie J Session, 1961
Paint, plaster, and various objects on
conglomerate panel, 143 x 77 x 7 cm
(56⁵⁄₁₆ x 30⁵⁄₁₆ x 2¾ in.)
Stockholm, Moderna Museet

American painter Joan Mitchell, a permanent resident in France since 1959, had been a thorn in Saint Phalle's side with her cutting comments about the artist being "one of those writer's wives that paints." Yet a work such as Saint Phalle's tall *Rifle Tir* (1961) from the Galerie J session bears comparison to a painting like Mitchell's landscape format *To the Harbormaster* (1957). Both works play with variations of the primary colors against a white ground. Several shades of mostly blue marks, punctuated by red and orange tones, provide for a welter of strokes in Mitchell's painting, and a cascade in Saint Phalle's *Rifle Tir*. Saint Phalle leaves a dark crush of material suspended from the bottom corner of her plywood ground, as if it hangs on for dear life. In Mitchell's composition, earthy tones coalesce right of center in a dense presence.

Saint Phalle roughens her surface with the bullet holes, but also with string, a cloth, and other small items that are hard to identify given the thickness of the plaster and paint covering them. Mitchell creates an energy field of strokes that approach each other from the right and the left, coming and going, while the paint, thinned, succumbs to gravity. At least one red dot in *To the Harbormaster* approximates a puncture wound. Niki de Saint Phalle's shooting painting and Joan Mitchell's Abstract Expressionist painting—are they estranged sisters?

After shooting sessions in Paris, Stockholm, Berlin, and near Amsterdam, some of them even nationally televised, a gallery on the West Coast of the United States beckoned Saint Phalle to come. In February 1962, she and Tinguely traveled to California together. Upon their arrival in Los Angeles, the couple made sure to visit the Watts Towers (1921–54) by Sabato ("Simon" or "Sam") Rodia (1879–1965), which became the third outsider architectural monument to impact Saint Phalle, after Gaudí's Park Güell in Barcelona and Cheval's Ideal Palace in Hauterives. William Seitz had written eloquently about the Watts Towers in the catalogue for the 1961 *Art of Assemblage* show that had included works by both Saint Phalle and Tinguely. A pilgrimage to the towers was a must for them because the naive monument embodied Rodia's pure self-reliance and creative drive. Untrained as an architect, he built the towers over decades using only found materials.

Saint Phalle had been invited by the Everett Ellin Gallery in Los Angeles to demonstrate her *Tirs*. The event happened outdoors in a parking lot on Sunset Boulevard, not many miles from Hollywood. More conscious than ever of her image, Saint Phalle changed the nature of the performance. Wearing her white jumpsuit publicly for the first time, Saint Phalle did not include the public in the creative process, but instead did all the shooting herself.

After the Sunset Boulevard event, the artist Edward Kienholz helped to organize a second American shooting session, this time in the Malibu Hills overlooking the house of gallerist Virginia Dwan (1931–2022). The prepared works were ambitiously scaled. A young, hip audience assembled. Among others, the actor Jane Fonda, who was 25 years old, as well as Henry Geldzahler, the curator who would bring contemporary art to the Metropolitan Museum of Art in New York, were in attendance. Photographs of Niki de Saint Phalle at the event silhouette her against the Hollywood Hills, while the audience relaxes in the grass and on chairs outside. Kienholz assists with the shooting by handing her loaded rifles so that she does not need to continually reload for the event to proceed smoothly. Dwan purchased one of the finished paintings created on her property for $2,500. Displayed for a while in the Dwan Gallery with a caged live bird next to it, the painting was later moved back to Dwan's home, where it was hung near her swimming pool. Over time it decayed; remarkably, Dwan did not safeguard the work.

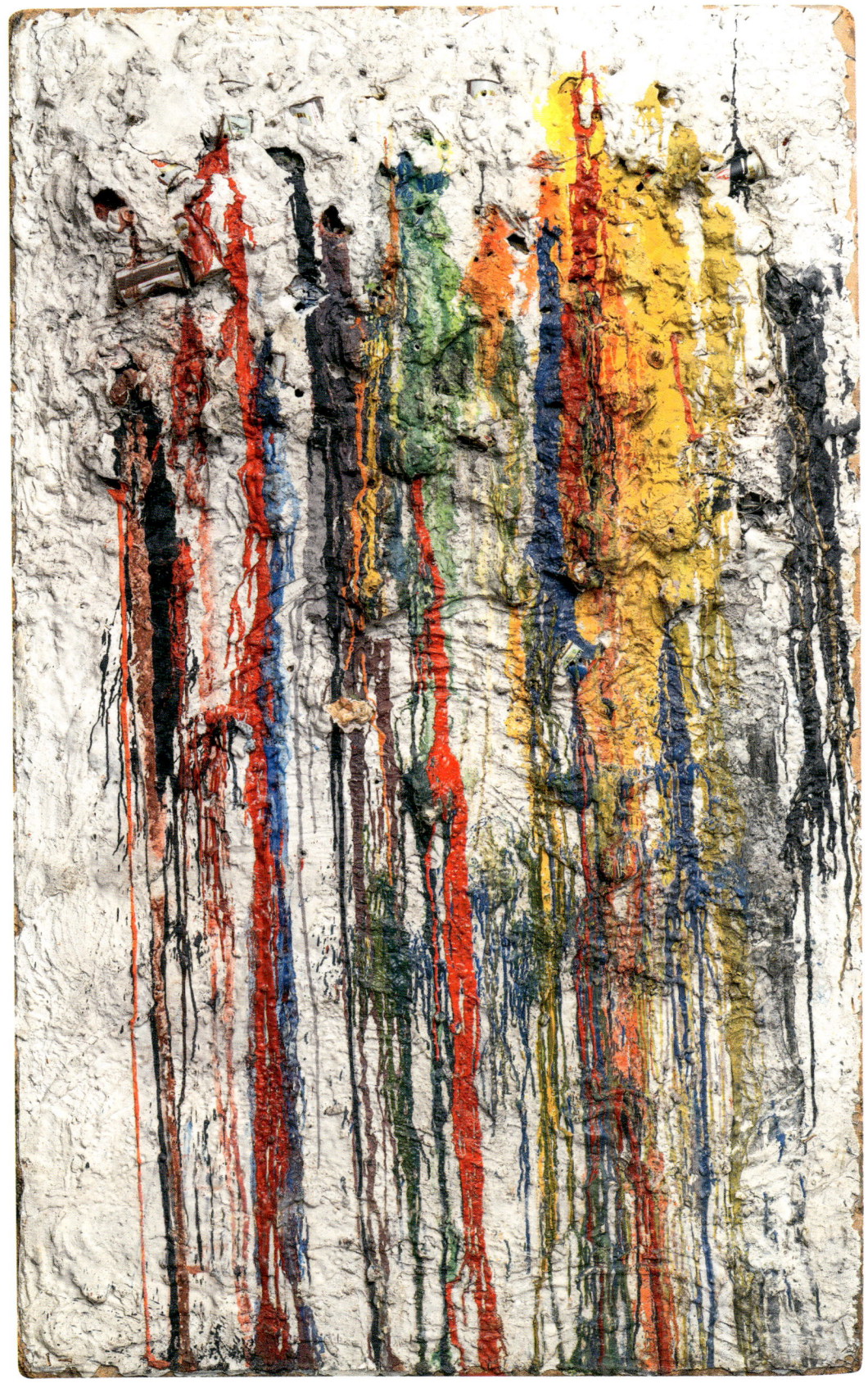

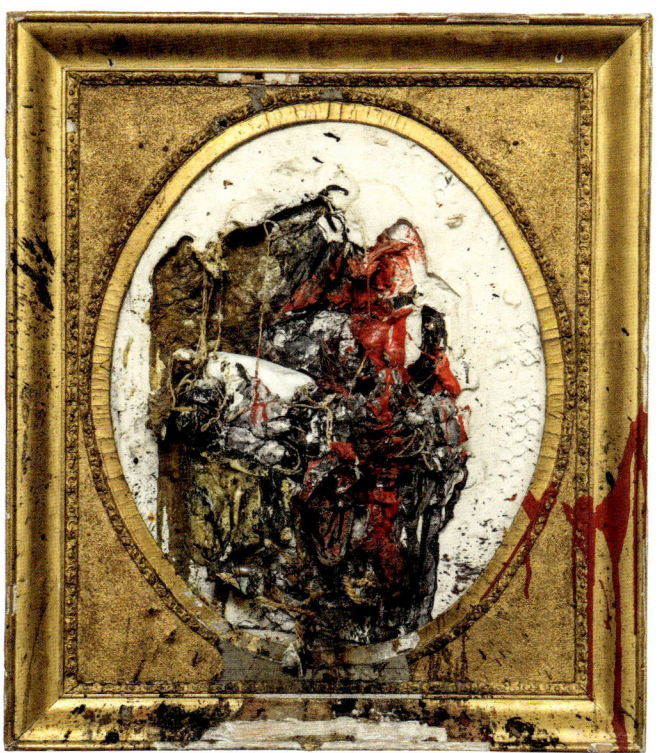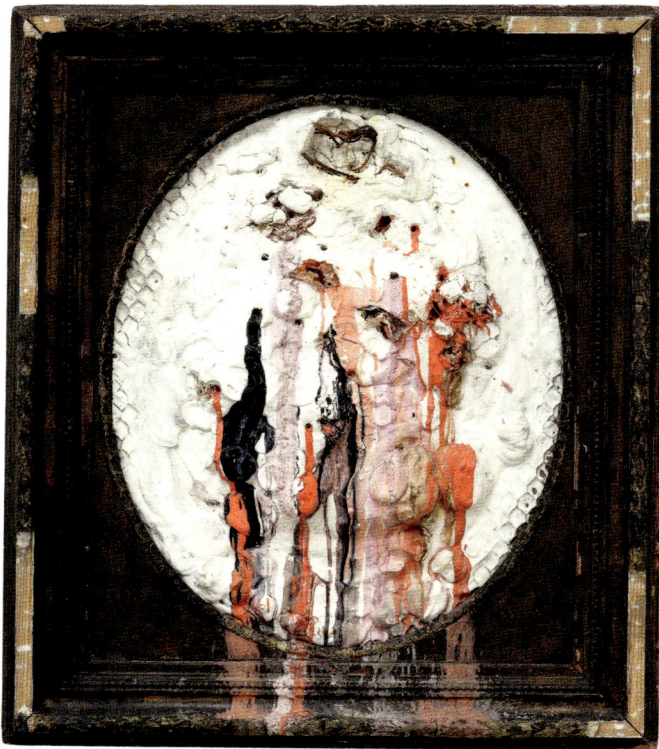

In May 1962, Saint Phalle and Tinguely arrived in New York to participate in a play that Saint Phalle had asked Kenneth Koch (1925–2002) to write for them. She knew the author through her first husband, writer Harry Mathews. Koch called it *The Construction of Boston.* The plot did not follow a logical narrative, but had oblique references to current events. During this short performance—the entire play is said to have taken about 15 minutes—Tinguely, cross-dressed as a female sex worker, built a wall across the stage using concrete blocks. (The Berlin Wall had been built in August 1961.) Using a device he fabricated, Tinguely also fired ping pong balls from a feather duster. Rauschenberg "made weather" by activating a rain machine, which dumped water on stage. The playbook emphasized Saint Phalle's beauty and her redemptive function. Wearing a Napoleonic coat over her white jumpsuit, she entered the play's action through the audience's center aisle, accompanied by three soldiers. Saint Phalle then fired at the *Vénus de Milo,* which had been wheeled on stage (p. 7). After the resounding shots, red and black paint gushed out of the statue.

Perhaps because they were not professional actors, or perhaps because they did not feel up to memorizing Koch's text, the artists had their lines spoken for them by proxies or projected to be read by the audience. Saint Phalle was the only one of the participating visual artists who had had any actor's training, but Maxine Groffsky still spoke her lines for her. Geldzahler, like Tinguely clothed as a flamboyant female, read lines for Tinguely's character. The painter Frank Stella read lines too. Dancer and choreographer Merce Cunningham directed, at least officially and much to his own chagrin, as he did not have much influence over the behavior of the other artists. For part of the play he did enlist some of his dance troupe to make breakfast and brush their teeth on stage. Unrehearsed, a cannon shot meant to re-whiten the *Vénus de Milo* backfired and the cannon nearly dropped offstage into the front rows of the more-than-sold-out theater.

Marcel Duchamp attended, as did Marian Javits, an arts patron, bon vivant, and proto-feminist who even dragged along her husband, Jacob Javits, the New York Republican politician. The one-evening-only event brought New York art world insiders together in a playful collaboration that must have been exciting, funny, and confusing both to bring to stage and to see.

That summer, Saint Phalle and Tinguely traveled to Spain's Costa Brava; it was her third trip to the country. The couple met up with Duchamp, who connected them to Salvador Dalí (1904–1989) and his wife Gala (1894–1982). A celebration in tribute to Dalí was scheduled at a bullring in Figueras, and Duchamp suggested that Saint Phalle and Tinguely participate, so they constructed a paper and plaster bull, stuffed it with fireworks, and blew it up in Dalí's honor at the bullring. When it exploded, blood red liquid poured out, and a white dove, which was calculated to survive the explosion, flew out. No doubt the inclusion of a living animal in such an art project would no longer be considered ethical; at least the plaster bull did not sacrifice a life.

The spectacular, daring, unpredictable quality of events like these emboldened Saint Phalle to fabricate more ambitiously scaled structures. In Paris and in Copenhagen she exhibited large works to shoot apart, and then shared the pieces with the public. At this point in time, the end products of the shooting events were sometimes treated more like ephemeral relics or souvenirs than works of art. Saint Phalle shifted to formulating topical themes in her work. She constructed altars to contemporary culture that took on her conservative Catholic background and the political tensions of the day. One good example of this is an assemblage which she did not actively shoot, but which does feature rows of handguns aiming in, out, and up. The *O.A.S. Altar* (1962, p. 41) is over eight feet

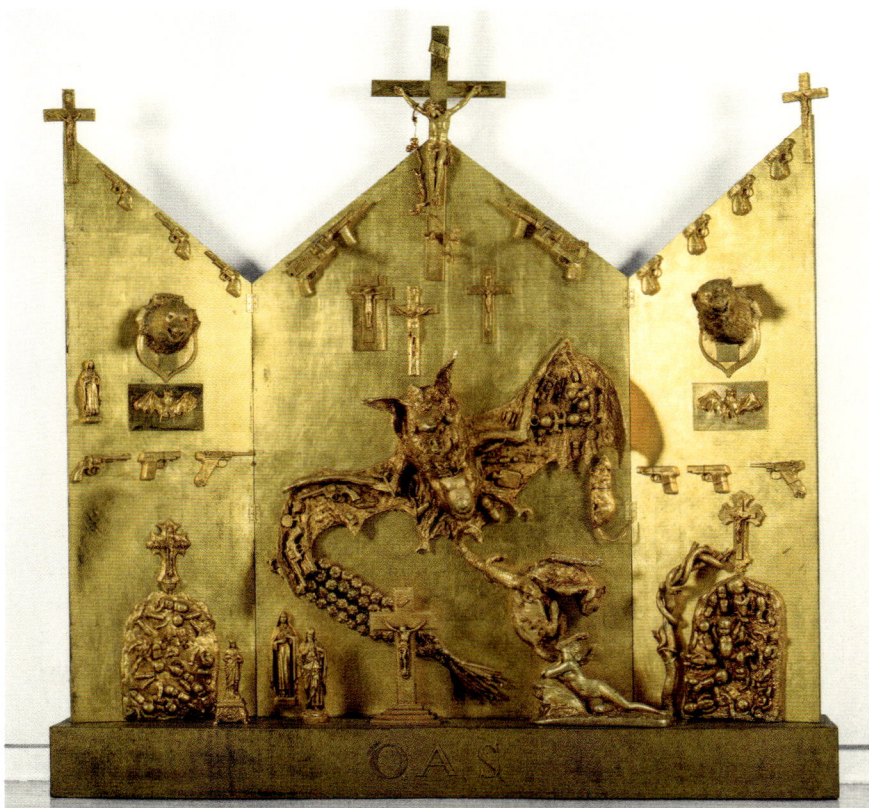

O.A.S. Altar (Autel O.A.S.), 1962–92
Bronze, 252 x 241 x 41 cm (99¼ x 94⅞ x 16⅛ in.)
Nice, MAMAC Collection

Later, *O.A.S. Altar* was cast in bronze in an edition of three, in a version that measured about a foot higher. The decision to reproduce this work indicates its long-term significance for the artist.

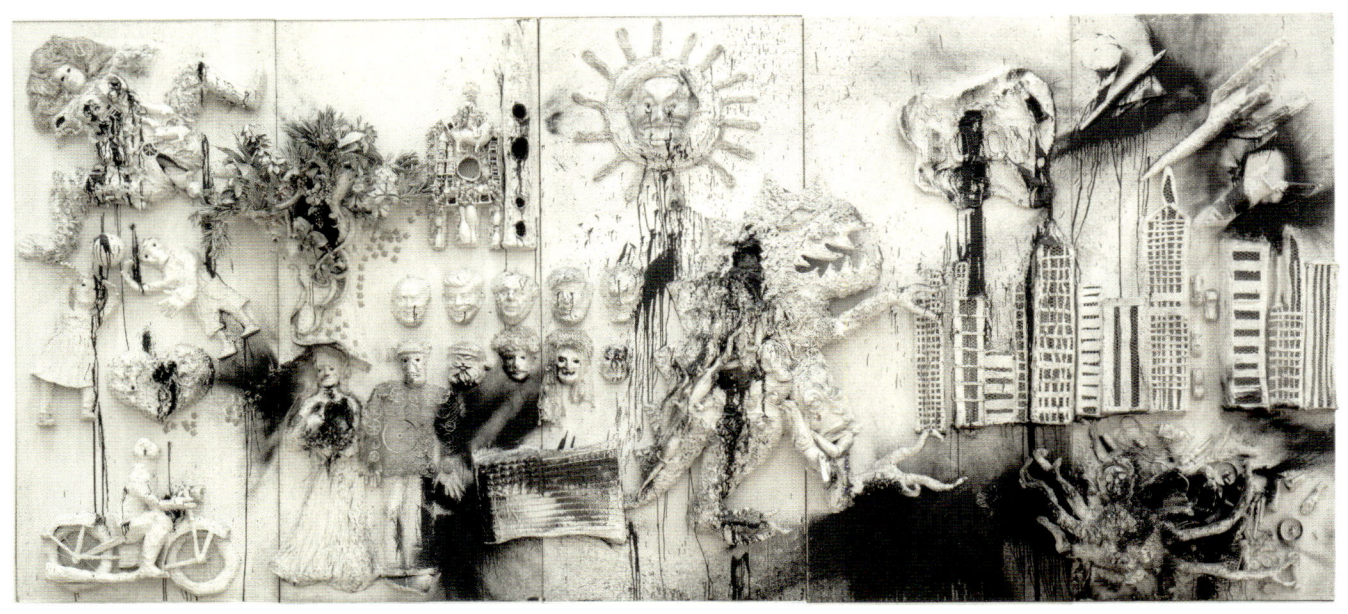

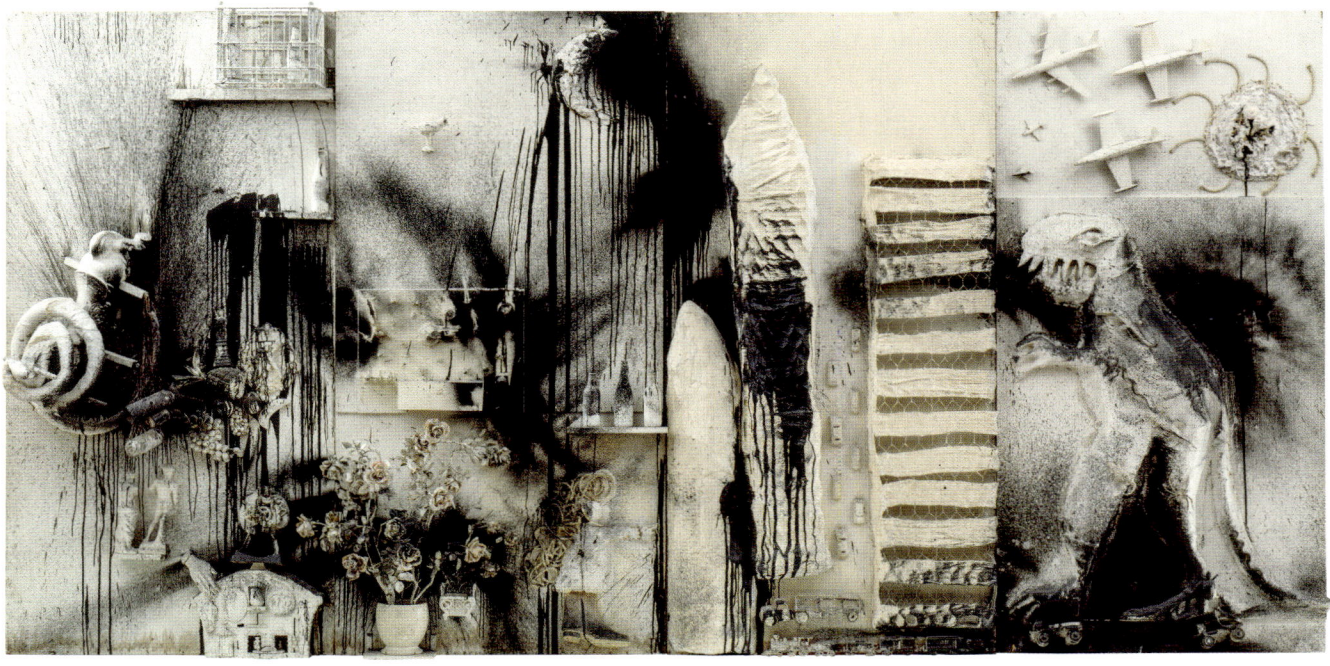

high and nearly as wide, and almost two feet deep (222 x 240 x 41 cm). It incorporates Christian religious symbols and taxidermied animals: flying bats large and small, an alligator, a dead cat, a rat, and what may be two snarling Tasmanian devil heads. In addition, Saint Phalle included toy airplanes and tombstones embedded with the body parts of naked dolls. Static Christian symbols of salvation, including the central crucifix, passively accompany the forces of evil. A small, voluptuous, nude European female with an upward gaze snuggles on a cliff, gentle and unfearful. Either she poses naively as a tidbit for the large bat, or she has been granted special protections because of her beauty and race.

The initials O.A.S. can be interpreted as an acronym of "oeuvre d'art sacré" ("sacred work of art"), since this is an altar, but also as a reference to the Organisation Armée Secrète (Secret Army Organization), a French right-wing terrorist group formed to combat Algerian independence from French colonial rule. The nationalist O.A.S. committed bombings and murder. With this "altar" Saint Phalle tackled a major political issue that had roiled France and Algeria since 1954, while conflating the Catholic church with the conservative French values of a terrorist organization.

Saint Phalle exhibited ten works, shooting paintings and altars, including *O.A.S. Altar*, at a solo show in Paris at the Galerie Rive Droite in 1962. On the strength of this exhibition, with its new focus on specific themes like the *O.A.S. Altar*, Alexander Iolas (1908–1987), a New York gallerist, offered Saint Phalle her first show in New York. Saint Phalle relocated for a time to New York to produce work for the exhibition. She and Tinguely moved to the Chelsea Hotel, a well-known haven for artists of all stripes. There she made *Gorgo in New York* (p. 42), a shooting painting that cites the 1961 British monster movie *Gorgo*, directed by Eugène Lourié. As art historian Cécile Whiting has discussed in her article "Apocalypse in Paradise: Niki de Saint Phalle in Los Angeles," picturing catastrophe became an artistic trope during the late 1950s and early 1960s, caused by the heightened anxiety brought about by the destruction of urban centers Hiroshima and Nagasaki and the postwar nuclear arms race.[12] Tinguely's humorous, mechanical, self-destructing *Homage to New York* at the Museum of Modern Art from two years earlier had referenced an end-of-the-world scenario, and that may have been in the back of Saint Phalle's mind when she transplanted the monster Gorgo from the British Isles to New York. In a drawing that accompanied the publication for the Iolas Gallery exhibition, reptilian monsters fight in front of a cathedral, and the artist's handwriting reveals an atomic bomb exploding. A bubble containing the word "Boum!" adds acoustic effect.

In the work, which is nearly eight feet (243.2 cm) high, Gorgo rumbles in from the right, nearly as tall as the tall skyscraper she will attack. Gorgo is a mother! Her young were abducted by humans and she comes calling, entering about 16 feet of white urban landscape assemblage spread out on four panels. Saint Phalle has kept the palette minimal, with black splatters released by shooting. Gorgo appears cartoonish, only minimally annoyed by an air force above: that is a good thing, because here in the painting, as in most such monster movies, the audience becomes attracted to the not-very-convincing monster and is on her side. Overweening human behavior unleashed that monster in the first place. In Gorgo's case, her motherly instincts got the better of her. Saint Phalle professed to love watching monster movies, and Gorgo's fate clearly resonated with her.

In fall 1962, Saint Phalle opened her first one-woman exhibition in New York at the Iolas Gallery. The exhibition itself was dedicated to the letter carrier and outsider artist Cheval, and a work called *Homage to Le Facteur Cheval*

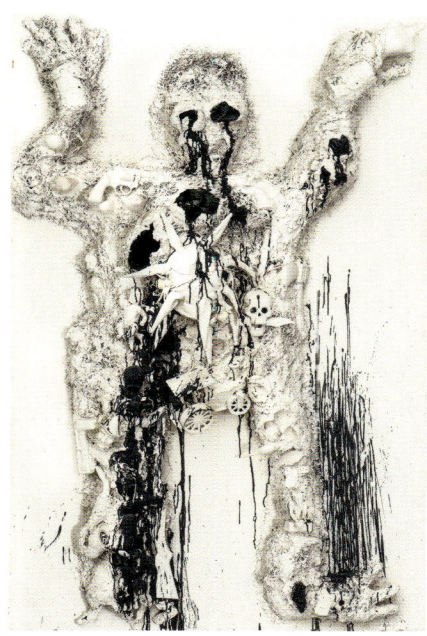

Drôle de mort ou Gambrinus, 1963
Oil, plaster, various objects on wood,
182 x 120 x 27 cm (71⅝ x 47¼ x 10⅝ in.)
Nice, MAMAC Collection

OPPOSITE ABOVE
King Kong, 1962
Mixed media, relief, 276 x 611 x 47 cm
(108¹¹⁄₁₆ x 240⁹⁄₁₆ x 18½ in.)
Stockholm, Moderna Museet

Under the row of Nikita Khrushchev, John Kennedy, Charles de Gaulle, Fidel Castro, and Abraham Lincoln appear less distinguished individuals, including an evil-looking elf, a hag, and ghouls, all floating disembodied over the American flag.

OPPOSITE BELOW
Gorgo in New York, 1962
Paint, plaster, wire, and found objects,
243.2 x 490.2 x 49.5 cm (95¾ x 193 x 19½ in.)
Museum of Fine Arts, Houston, Museum purchase funded by D. and J. de Menil

The Children (study for King Kong), 1963
Paint, plaster, various small objects on plywood,
200 x 150 x 30.3 cm (78¾ x 59¹/₁₆ x 11¹⁵/₁₆ in.)
Nice, MAMAC Collection

was available at the opening for the public to "paint" using a spillage mechanism devised by Tinguely as an alternative to gun shooting. The *Homage,* which looks to have featured a large, rearing serpent and whose exact dimensions are unknown, is no longer extant. Although it was destroyed, a single panel was saved as a fragment and today is owned by the Niki Charitable Art Foundation. Saint Phalle's first exhibition in New York also included the finished *Gorgo in New York* (p. 42), as well as some of Sant Phalle's cathedral series.

"Boom" is written in the sky of what is sometimes called Saint Phalle's last shooting painting, *King Kong* (1962, p. 42), the work she considered to be her finest—another monster picture depicting the destruction of a city with New York skyscrapers. Saint Phalle made many studies for this huge assemblage before she made the final five panels that assemble to a work over nine feet high and 20 feet long, with a depth of 19 inches (270 x 611 x 48.2 cm)—a King Kong of a painting. The title misleads. King Kong does not appear, but instead Gorgo shows up again, or someone who looks a lot like Gorgo, perhaps Godzilla, looking to fight King Kong to the detriment of their surroundings. Of course, King Kong was the main character in the 1933 blockbuster film, and his name calls up the Hollywood film industry, and likely stands in for any popular culture monster unleashing its cataclysmic strength.

King Kong sums up a lot of Saint Phalle's biography and assemblage work until this point, in 1963: the birthing mother, a little girl and boy playing ball around a heart, a symbolic Tinguely speeding in on a motorcycle (which also looks like a toy from George Brecht's Fluxus assemblage meant for use, *Repository* of 1961), a church or cathedral, a bride standing with a long-skulled groom under a tree of life, accompanied by masks of heads of state past and present. Humorously, the painting's upper corners mirror each other, with the birthed child shooting into the scene like the supersonic airplanes from the other side, female and male contributions to the maelstrom. Nothing is serious here, though the content is certainly disturbing. Does the sun wear an Aztec face, hinting at blood sacrifice? Saint Phalle has shot across the entire work, but the assemblage is not badly disfigured. Spurting black paint lightly enhances the detail and mostly darkens the monster's radius. The little girl's head is spattered. This is a landscape of death. *Tu et moi, Tu est moi,* or *Tuez-moi.* "You and me," "You are me," or "Kill me."

Tir (fragment), 1962
Oil, plaster, and various small objects
on plywood, 120 x 93 x 12 cm
(47¼ x 36⅝ x 4¾ in.)
Nice, MAMAC Collection

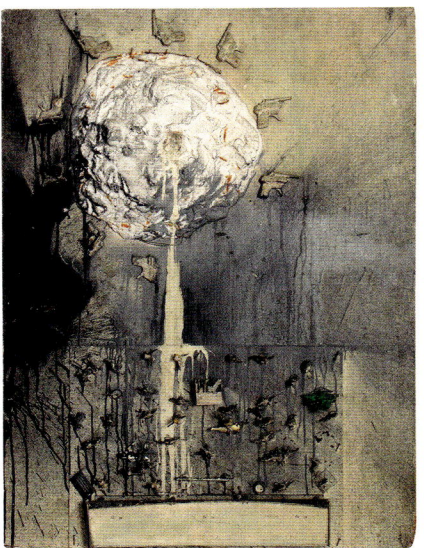

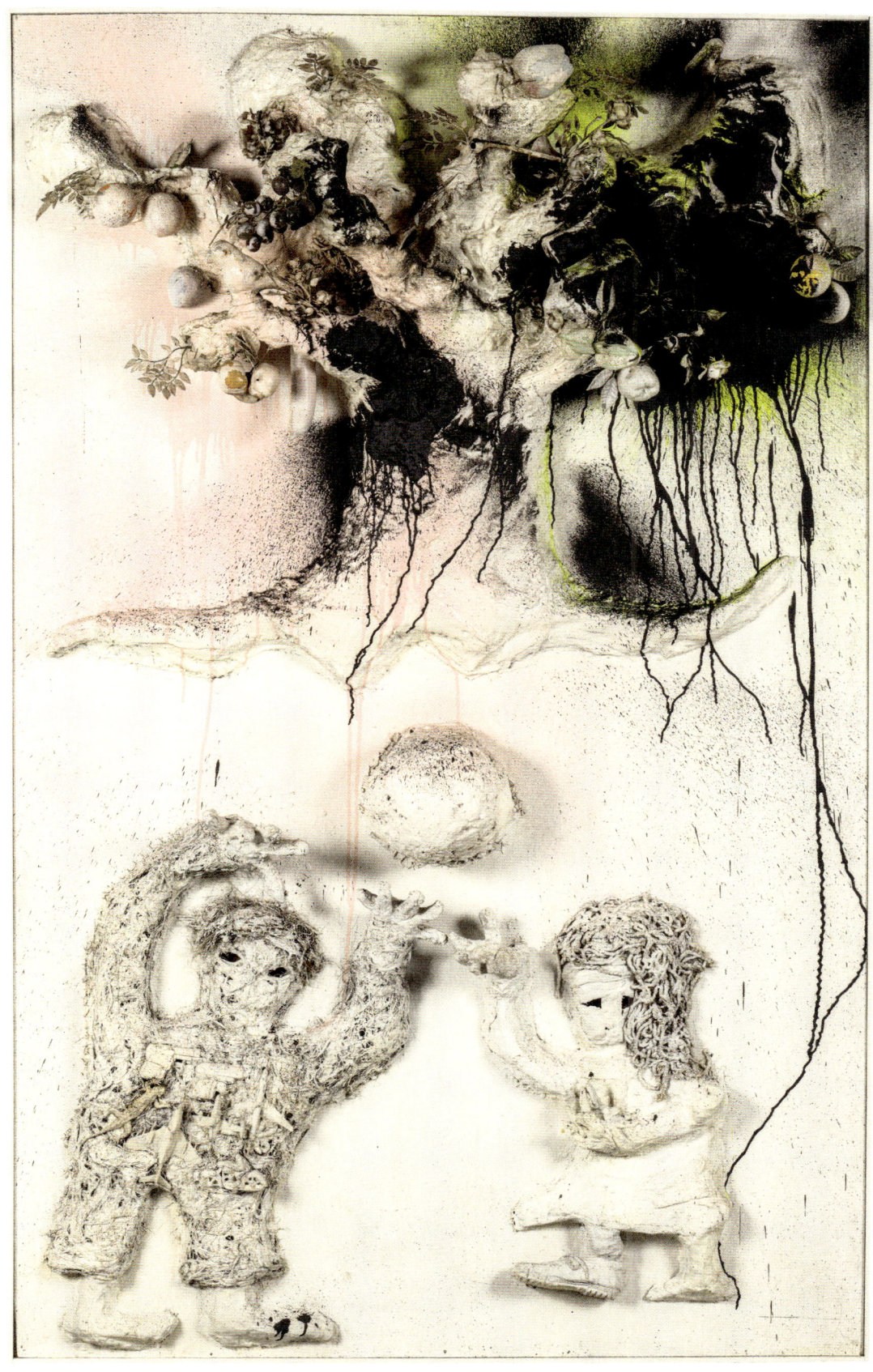

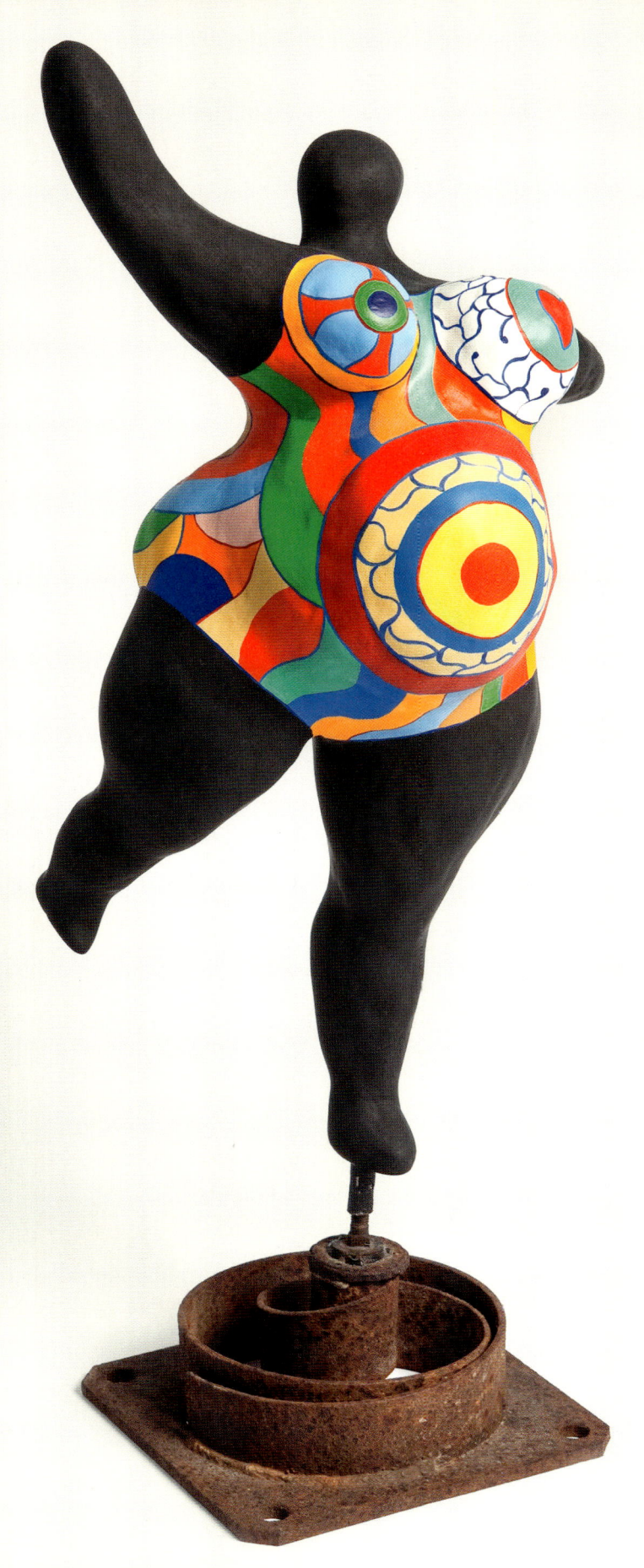

Saint Phalle and Her Women

After about three years of experimenting with the *Tirs*, Niki de Saint Phalle decided to halt the shooting, which felt addictive. The fun of pulling the trigger and watching the paintings "bleed" did not justify her working like this forever. She did not love guns, for one thing, or war, or killing sentient beings. Later, in 2001, she made a print that took on the American gun industry, which she saw as insufficiently regulated. Although she did subsequently return to the process of shooting assemblages on occasion—like when Pierre Restany called for works to commemorate the 10th anniversary of New Realism in Milan (1970), and she responded with *Altar*, which she also shot in front of the public—by 1963 she was ready to move on. She felt disinclined to continue with destruction as a creative mode.

Female figures abound in the subject matter of her early paintings. Her assemblages instrumentalize three-dimensional dolls, kitschy erotic statuettes, or figures of the Virgin Mary. She had reproduced the *Vénus de Milo* as a sculpture in-the-round for a performance. As a speculative study for the shooting work *King Kong*, or as a byproduct of it, she fabricated an assemblage showing a female with two male heads. *Kennedy–Khrushchev* (1962, p. 48) features purchased masks of Cold War opponents American President John F. Kennedy and Soviet Premier Nikita Khrushchev. Their heads flower from the stalk of a woolly-headed woman, dressed in superheroine boxing shorts and short black boots that may have once belonged to the artist herself. The work relates to the failed American invasion of the Bay of Pigs in Cuba the year before, which was an attempt to rid the country of Fidel Castro, its Communist leader, as well as to the subsequent Cuban Missile Crisis. The United States resented and feared Khrushchev's good relations with Cuba, especially when the Soviet premier sought to install medium-range nuclear missiles in Cuba, close to the Florida shore. The inevitability of mutual annihilation expresses itself perfectly in Saint Phalle's artwork in a two-headed dominatrix. *La guerre*: in French, war is feminine. As Saint Phalle made this work, the United States was still negotiating for hostages taken by the Cubans.

Unafraid of envisioning the female body darkly, Saint Phalle made a series of large-scale works that seem the personification of nightmares. Abject women's anatomies become the landfill of civilization and its follies, the depository of all the forces and expectations that can attach to a woman, eat into her, or

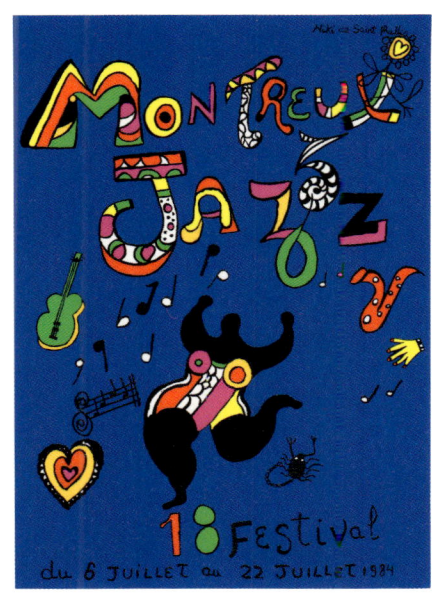

OPPOSITE
Pregnant Black Nana, 1968
Polyester and fiberglass on a steel base, 77 x 36 x 28 cm (30⁵⁄₁₆ x 14³⁄₁₆ x 11 in.)
Mannheim, Kunsthalle Mannheim, Acquired with funds and donations from the museum store on the occasion of Manfred Fath's 60th birthday

ABOVE
Poster for Montreux Jazz Festival, 1984

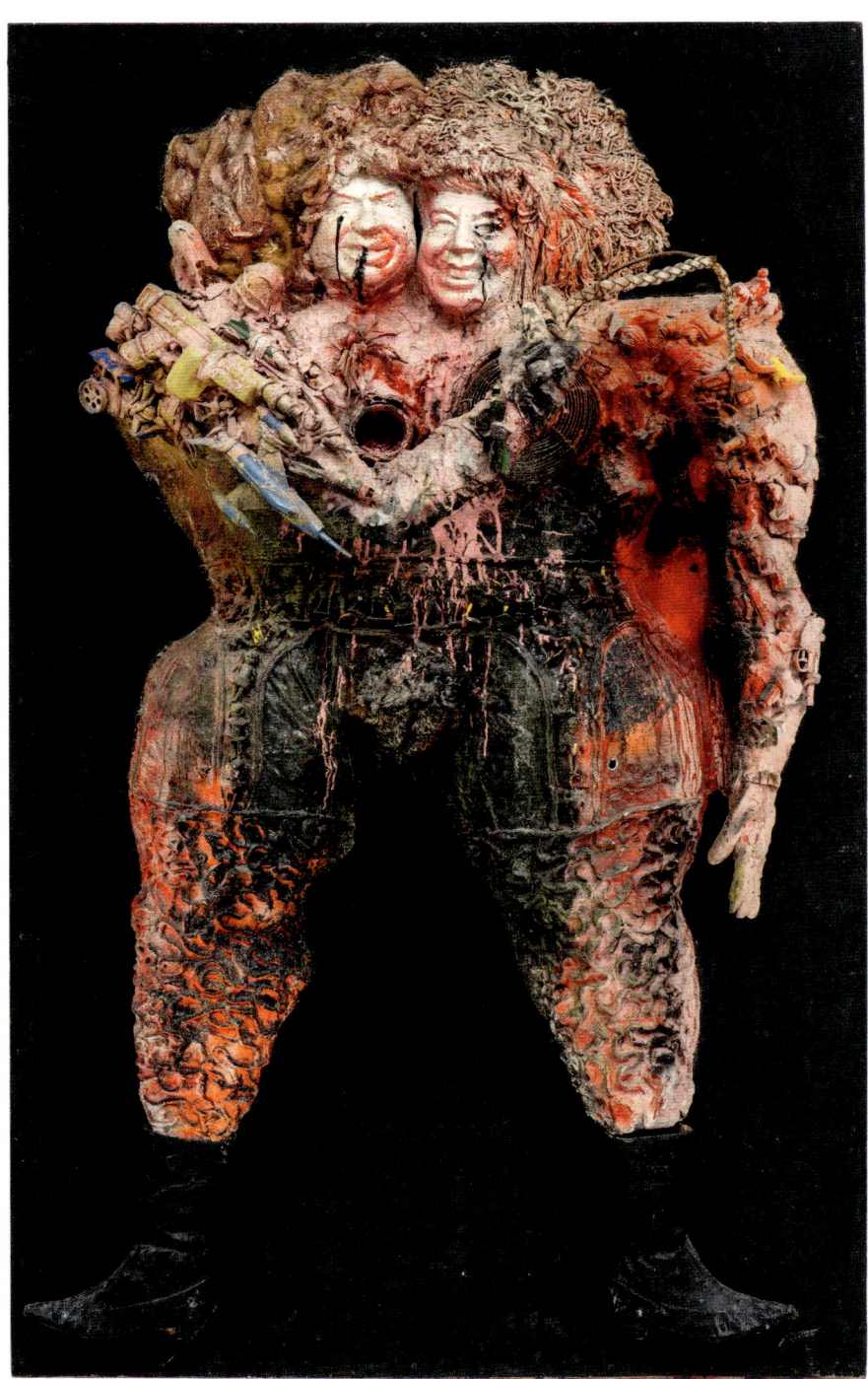

Kennedy-Khrushchev, 1963
Plaster, rabbit wire, various objects on wood,
202 x 122.5 x 40 cm (79½ x 48¼ x 15¾ in.)
Hanover, Sprengel Museum

Small objects sticking to the female's outfit connote war and battle—among other things, she has a belt of toy soldiers and a gun mounted on one of her shoulders. Pink and red splatters disfigure face and body; she wields a whip for self-laceration.

erupt from her core. These works are hard to look at. A nude, *Pink Birth* (1964), becomes a microcosm of toy animals, birds, airplanes, insects, and people, which colonize the over seven-foot-high (219 cm) torso like so many scavengers on the picking grounds of her body. The body's structure truncates at the knees and is embedded on a neutral, rectangular background. It shares the same proportions as some of the assemblages that Saint Phalle had just made as part of a series, such as *Petite Cathédrale (Small Cathedral)* (1962, p. 49). The body's parted thighs correspond to a cathedral portal. An ancient Egyptian immobility of form

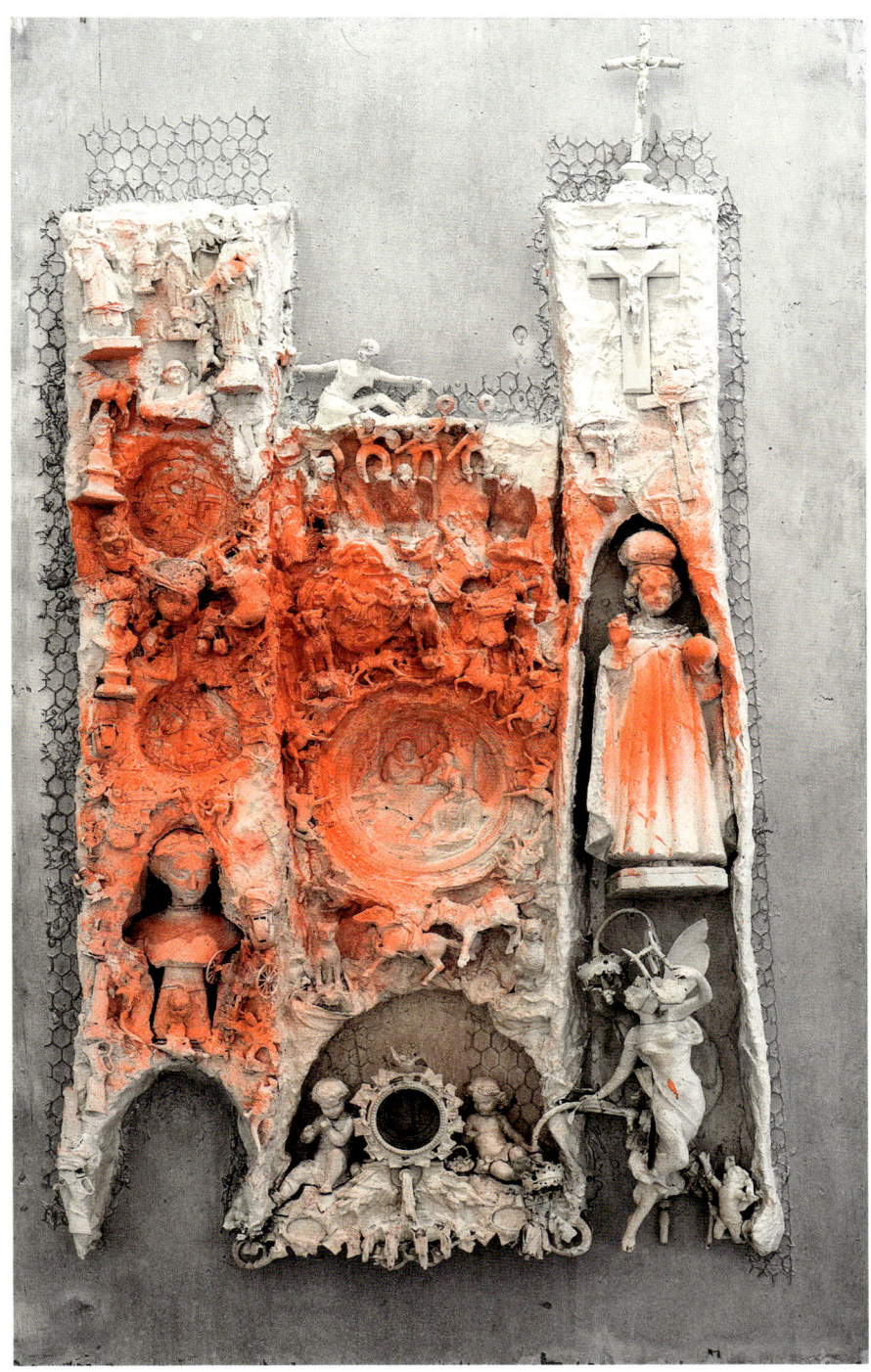

Petite Cathédrale (Small Cathedral), 1962
Paint, plaster, wire mesh, and various objects on
wood, 200 x 122 x 27 cm (78¾ x 48 x 10⅝ in.)
Nice, MAMAC Collection

infuses the pink woman's frontal pose and wedge of heavy hair that, as well as forming a coiffure, thickens and deadens the area above her shoulders with its texture. The figure's mouth is open. Holes open up in her thigh, hip, and breast, from which flowers burst. A baby drops headfirst out of her open vagina, still attached and hanging down like a large penis, making the figure a kind of man-woman. As a symbol of power, the birthed baby becomes a woman's penis.

Over six feet (198 cm) tall, *The Red Witch* (1962), aware of her powers, plots revenge for her sisters from her place of darkness. Her legs akimbo, she gestures with a black left hand towards her sex, above which, sunken into a bodily cavity, a reddened Madonna demurely holds a bouquet of lilies. In traditional Christian iconography lilies symbolize purity, yet the Virgin resides in the witch. A woman is many things. In her autobiography *Traces*, Saint Phalle expressed the fear that she too might end up like her father, with his lusts and abusive behaviors. *The Red Witch* is a bad woman; Saint Phalle wants to see how far she can go in negating beauty, health, socially ideal behavior, virtue. A woman has lusts of her own and can be angry. At the turn of the 20th century, male Symbolist painters showed woman as a dangerous seductress, and later the Surrealists sometimes showed a festering, obscene female body. In contrast, Saint Phalle's *Red Witch* emphasizes power and strength in the transgressive female.

Around this time, Saint Phalle began to feel the limits of the picture plane. She had always started with a wooden board background for her assemblage pictures, but she began to shift gradually into free-standing sculpture. She conceived figures on plinths, supported by a metal rod, riding a horse, or lying under a tree. We encounter the works as roughly our equals in size, or slightly larger than life. *Almost Married* (1963) presents a strange, truncated bride from the waist up and is one of the early works Saint Phalle later chose to cast in bronze. The almost married young woman is encased by the bodice of a straggly wedding dress enhanced with diverse objects and white paint on wire mesh. The artist gave her an ungainly quality by lengthening her arms beyond natural proportion in the puffy sleeves. With its bride exuding passive sadness, *Almost Married* could even be said to recall a genre of Renaissance sculptural bust that depicted young women, usually as posthumous portraits meant for a tomb, such as *Bust of a Princess* (1485–1500) by Francesco Laurana in the Louvre.

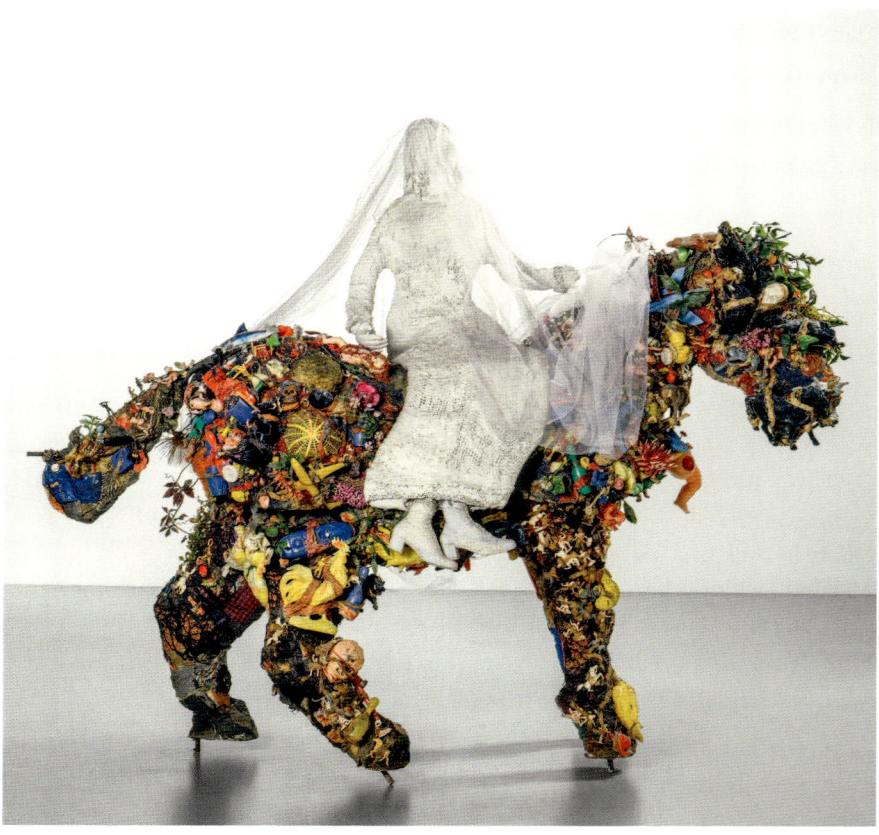

The Horse and the Bride
(Cheval et la Mariée), 1963
Fabric, toys, various objects, wire,
235 x 300 x 120 cm (92½ x 118⅛ x 47¼ in.)
Hanover, Sprengel Museum

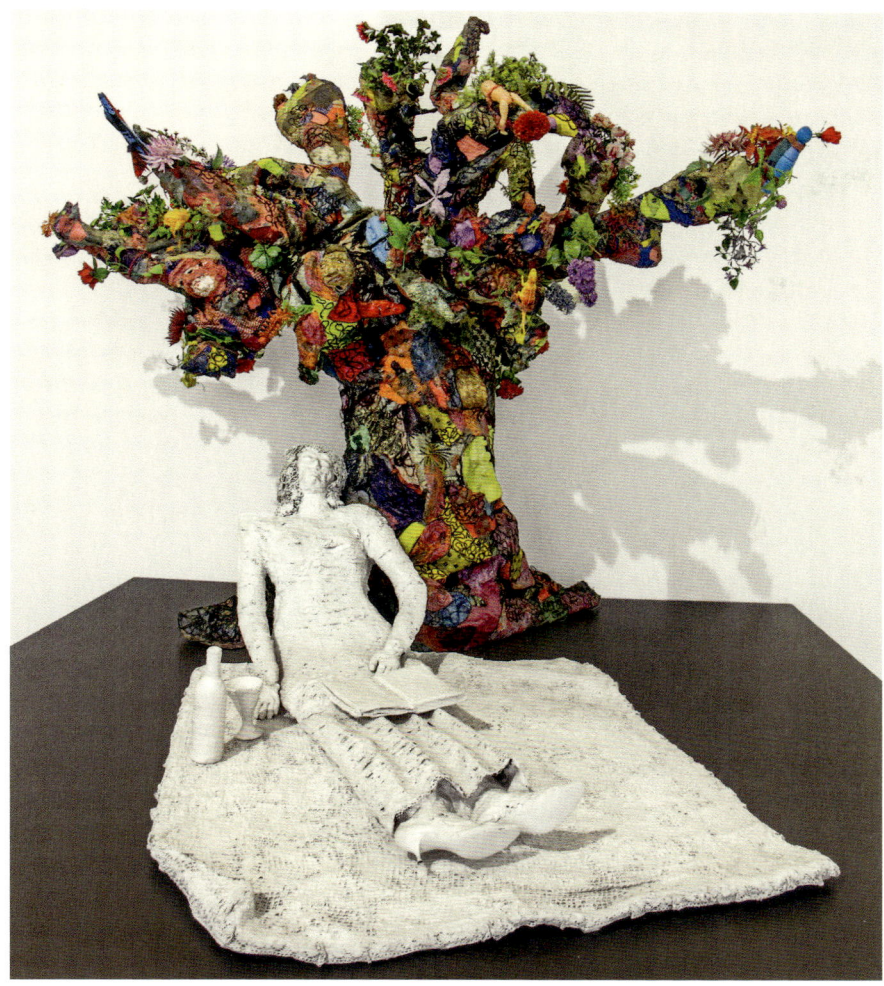

The Bride Beneath a Tree, 1963–64
Fabric, paint, toys, and various objects
on wire structure, 228 x 200 x 240 cm
(89¾ x 78¾ x 94½ in.)
Nice, MAMAC Collection

The freestanding bust *Marilyn* (1964) achieves an over-life-size, bully-like presence with a head sunken into the shoulders of a football player, rising up from the
dead, blue eyes glaring, with a skull for a brooch. She has metamorphosed from
two years in the afterlife and appears ready to do business. Marilyn Monroe had
died in August 1962 at 36 years old. Saint Phalle may have felt a gut wrench when,
two years later, she saw the magazine title "LIFE" floating above Monroe's face
on the cover from August 7, 1964. The *Life* cover portrait of the deceased actor
showed her like a bust, bare from the shoulders up. Like Monroe, Saint Phalle had
been a *Life* cover girl, had studied acting, and was a beautiful artist. Saint Phalle
had survived an early suicide attempt with pills, while Marilyn had not. The lines
accompanying Monroe's *Life* cover photograph say: "Marilyn Monroe eight years
before her suicide." The cover also promises an article about "What Really Killed
Marilyn," which relates the story of Monroe's childhood sexual abuse, unhappy
early life, and experience of dismal parenting, details that echoed Saint Phalle's
own life. Moving through the world, Saint Phalle was acutely observant of wom-
en's stories. She later expressed the "close call" feeling of seeing the female faces of
wanted terrorists pictured on airport posters in Stuttgart and speculated that she
might well have dipped into terrorism had she not become an artist.

Saint Phalle's large papier collé bust of Marilyn Monroe allowed the black-and-
white newsprint to show as skin tone. Isolated words and news images remain

visible, underscoring the way the press took ownership of Monroe, even to the point of following her into and past the grave. Saint Phalle's portrait is not a monument to female sex appeal, but to Monroe's magnified mythic power that has transformed her into a chthonic goddess. Saint Phalle lampooned the calculated way *Life* magazine instrumentalized Monroe's allure in order to sell its magazines. Anyone interested in meeting women of the mid-20th century on the emotionally torturous proving grounds of their everyday lives would do well to spend time looking at the advertisements and articles aimed at them in magazines like *Life* and *Ladies' Home Journal*.

Saint Phalle does away with the board background support again in *Leto or Crucifixion* (1965, p. 12), a work whose title has both Greek mythological and Christian connotations. Though Leto has no arms, this over-life-size female hangs on the wall as if crucified and extends from it about 20 inches (50 cm). Saint Phalle ridicules with excruciatingly sad detail how the crucified Leto suffered for her beauty. It was Leto's youthful looks that caught the eye of Zeus, who impregnated her with twins, a boy and a girl. Hera, Zeus's wife, then tormented Leto by ordering all lands to shun her, sending a python to pursue her, and prescribing painful extended labor during childbirth. Saint Phalle was "pursued by snakes" too, when her brother put a snake in her childhood bed, and it became

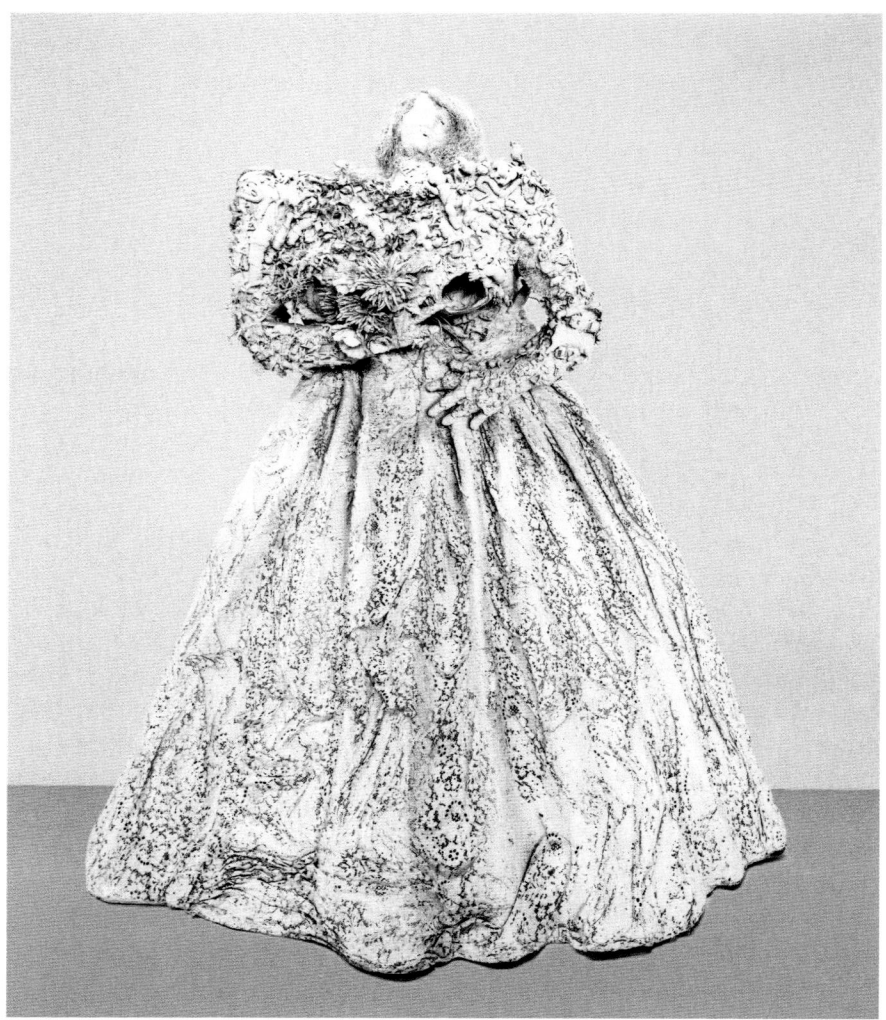

The Bride, 1963
Oil, various small objects on plywood,
226 x 200 x 100 cm (89 x 78¾ x 39⅜ in.)
Paris, Centre Pompidou

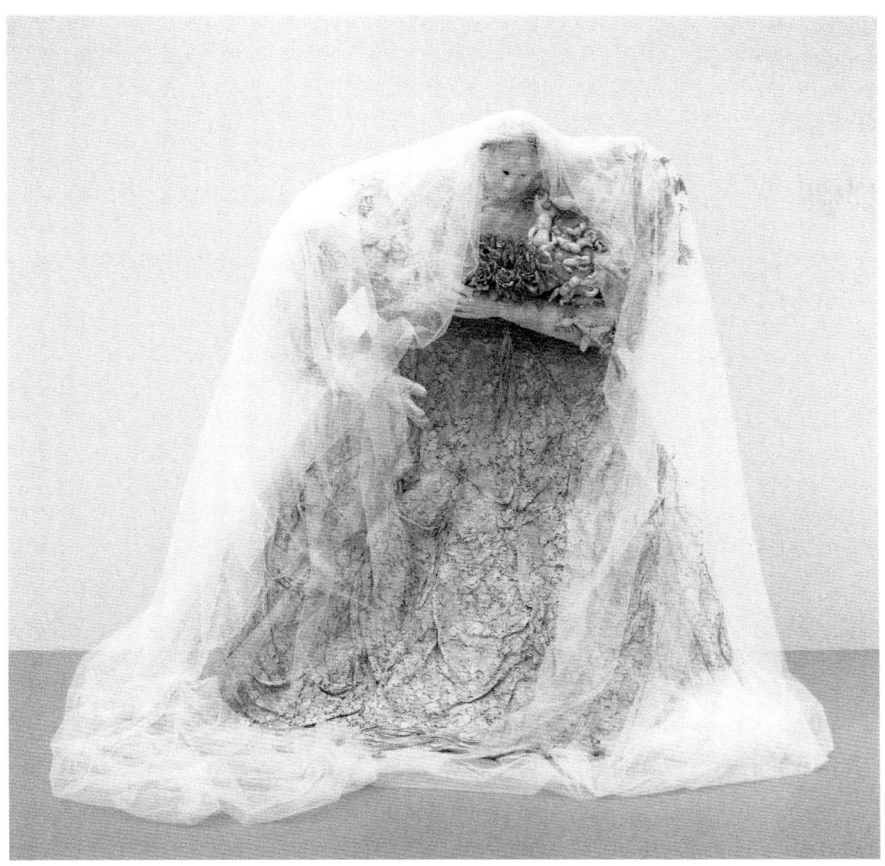

The Bride (or Miss Haversham's Dream, or When You Love Somebody), 1965
Fabric, toys, various objects, and wire mesh,
190 x 194 x 75 cm (74¹³/₁₆ x 76⅜ x 29½ in.)
Santee, Niki Charitable Art Foundation

linked in her mind to the "summer of snakes" when her father abused her.¹⁴ She also had a daughter and a son.

Leto's tiny head sports hair rolled up in curlers like the ones women wore to bed at night before blow-dryers became commonplace. A dainty trim of fresh daisies crisscrosses patchwork panties, but shaggy black pubic hair froths from the open crotch. A notably gigantic pink flowered garter belt and black floral lace stockings reach for each other over the expanse of Leto's thighs. Saint Phalle meditates here on the garter belt, that garment which until the mid-1960s, when pantyhose replaced it, functioned as the only way to hold up stockings. A garter belt was awarded in transition from girlhood (socks) to womanhood (stockings). Owning a garter belt—one article among an array of adult female underwear that should remain hidden—meant a girl had entered a more sexually objectified, anxiety-producing stage of being female. The exposed garter belt became a symbol for a sex worker. Saint Phalle circled around these nuances when she pointedly set up the garter belt's niceness against the shock of pubic hair and the sexy black stockings. Meanwhile, she used Leto's bodice to assemble infantilizing kitschy items. Artificial flowers, fruit, cute baby dolls, puppet heads (a white one and a Black one), toy animals and soldiers, a Campus Cutie doll, and the Tin Man from *The Wizard of Oz* jumble together there with all their associations.

 Thick in the middle and tapering out in the legs, Leto's body resembles a heavy, fraying package. Knees splayed out, she hangs more like a lowly thief crucified next to Christ instead of the savior himself, and her high heels become the nails that secure her feet to the imaginary cross. As she raises her flat, square,

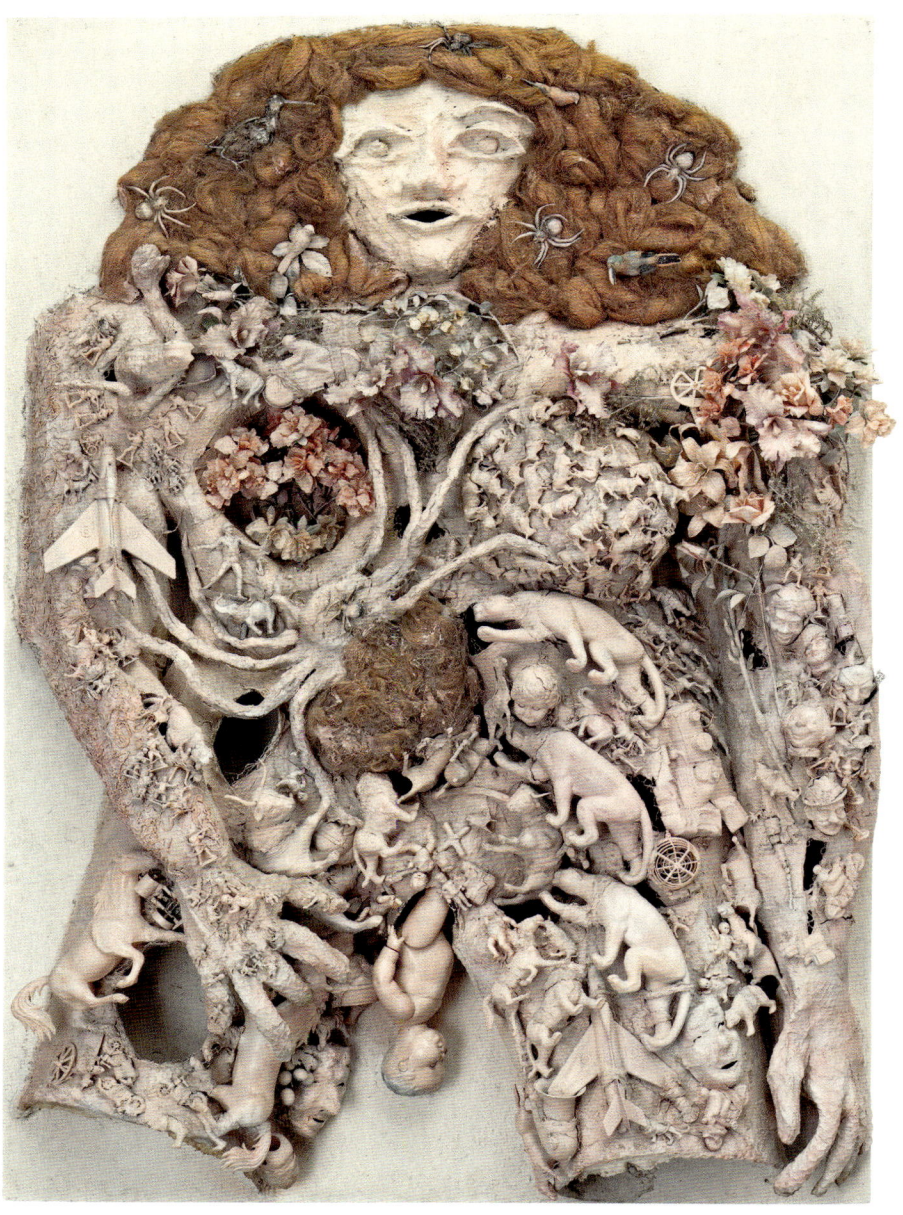

middle-aged face to a male Almighty, be it Zeus or God, she seems to be asking, "Why have you forsaken me?" This hanging Leto figure combines crossover attributes of housewife, whore, and Christ. Leto's lack of arms suggests an inability to achieve anything beyond what her trunk can offer—her body is a vessel for bearing children or being taken for sexual use.

Unlike any of the other New Realists, who were all men, Saint Phalle embodied a feminist consciousness and persisted in choosing depictions of women as her subject matter. In multiple sculptures she showed brides. To make these works, the artist purchased preexisting wedding gowns to dress bodies she fabricated herself. As a teenager visiting the Louvre, Saint Phalle had loved Rousseau's naive painting *War*, with its depiction of a bellicose woman clad in virginal white who charges forward on a horse, waving a weapon. Nothing could be further from the spirit of that artwork than Saint Phalle's *The Horse and the Bride* (p. 50) from 1963.

ABOVE
Pink Birth (Accouchement rose), 1964
Paint, toys, various objects, wire mesh on wood,
219 x 152 x 40 cm (86¼ x 59¹³/₁₆ x 15¾ in.)
Stockholm, Moderna Museet

OPPOSITE
Le monstre de Soisy, 1966
Paper maché, paint, fabric, wire mesh,
180 x 253 x 163 cm (70⅞ x 99⅝ x 64³/₁₆ in.)
Paris, Centre Pompidou

This life-size sculpture shows a small horse, perhaps a mare, mounted side-saddle by a veiled bride. The horse appears to be traveling slowly but inexorably. Its hide is an assemblage field of plastic toys and objects, while the passive bride—where are the reins?—remains defined only by her white dress, boots, and veil. Equally white, her face and hands make her appear ghostlike. One eye of the horse is a skull, and a naked doll's leg protrudes straight out of the horse's chest, two small details among the many assemblage pieces that raise sinister associations.

The Bride Beneath a Tree (1963–64, p. 51) allows the bride a book, a goblet, and a bottle of wine while she sits awkwardly under the tree, which, like the horse in *The Horse and the Bride* (1963, p. 50), bears the entire brunt of Saint Phalle's assemblage. Again, the puppet-like bride is entirely in ghost white, including her skin. She has shed her veil and summarily repurposed it as a picnic blanket at the tree's base. Saint Phalle had loved to draw trees as a girl at the Brearley School. She had decorated her children's room in Paris with her first ever sculpture, a tree, assisted by Tinguely's welding. The bride's tree is a version of the Tree of Life, an archetype found in many civilizations' mythologies and religions; here, it relates to knowledge.

Maybe the bride has skipped the wedding this time. A little drunk, she looks up from her book, imagining. Could she be reading Simone de Beauvoir's *The Second Sex* or Betty Friedan's *The Feminine Mystique*? Or a novel by Charles Dickens (1812–1870)? A classic Dickens work that became a movie Saint Phalle may have seen as a teenager stands behind *The Bride (or Miss Haversham's Dream, or When You Love Somebody)* (1965, p. 53). At the heart of the plot of Dickens's *Great Expectations* (1861), the character of Miss Havisham, jilted on her wedding day, is the subtitled subject of the large sculpture. In the book, Dickens's jilted bride doggedly cultivates her slight for two decades, still dressing in her wedding gown every day, exuding self-pity and a vengeful spirit.[15] Cobwebbed by her veil, mobbed by a mincemeat of little dolls and figures on her shoulder and holding the bouquet in the crook of her arm, with an airplane and an insect crawling up her sleeve, Saint Phalle's standing bride becomes a monument to her failed wedding ceremony. The event froze the bride's psychological and emotional chronology, but not her physical aging.

"Who is the monster, you or me?"

– NIKI DE SAINT PHALLE: WHO IS THE MONSTER, YOU OR ME? (DOCUMENTARY FILM DIRECTED BY PETER SCHAMONI, 1995)

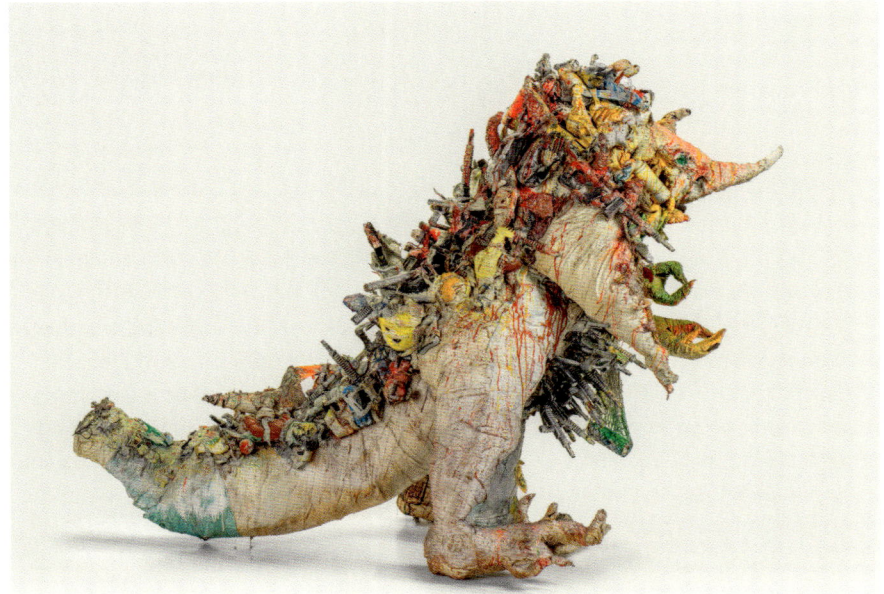

Women's Altar (Autel des Femmes), 1964
Oil, various small objects on plywood,
253 x 310 x 35 cm (99⅝ x 122 x 13¹³/₁₆ in.)
Hanover, Sprengel Museum

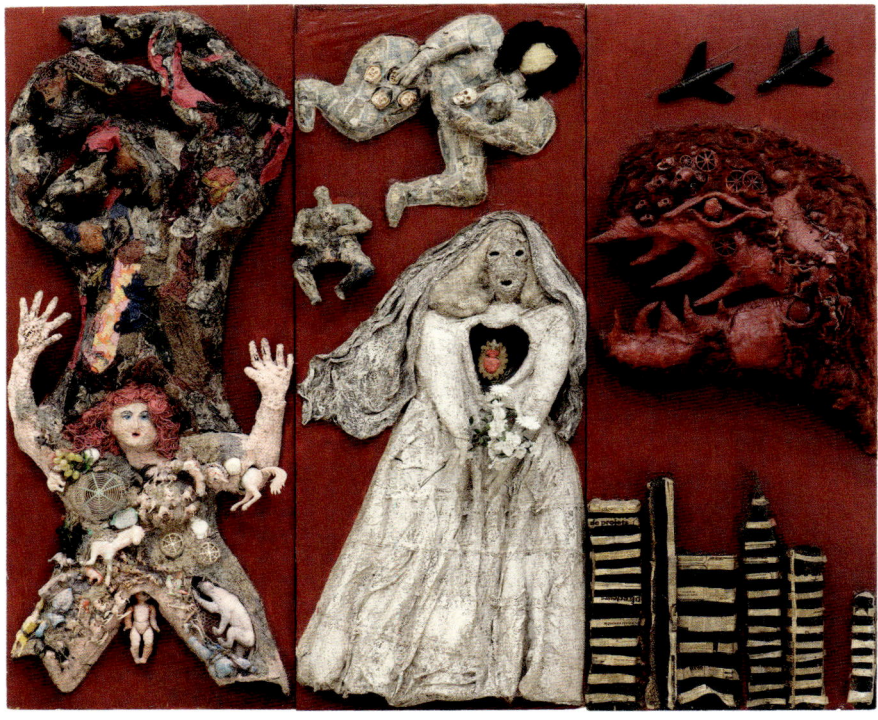

An entire chapter called "The Married Woman" in Beauvoir's *The Second Sex* discusses how a young woman becomes a bride and what happens to her if she does not: "for young girls, marriage is the only way to be integrated into the group, and if they are 'rejects,' they are social waste. This is why mothers have always at all costs tried to marry them off."[16] Saint Phalle herself had experienced and rebelled against her mother's idea of the socially acceptable mate. A conflicted attempt at marriage had ended in divorce, after which she freed herself. By choosing Miss Havisham as a subject, Saint Phalle condemned marriage as an institution of self-imprisonment. She fanned female rebellion. However, her focus on the bride as subject matter at this stage in her career may also be a statement of artistic allegiance. Her pessimistic view of marriage was shared by the man so influential in the art world of the 1960s and who married happily only late in life, Marcel Duchamp. In this respect Saint Phalle demonstrates an ambition to create work that was relevant to the insular art world, where she jockeyed for recognition.

Published in 1965, around the time that Saint Phalle was working on her bride assemblages, a book entitled *The Bride and the Bachelors: The Heretical Courtship in Modern Art* by Calvin Tomkins borrowed the courtship concept of Duchamp's *The Large Glass* to unite essays about Tinguely, Rauschenberg, and composer John Cage with an opening text about Duchamp, whose ideas reverberated in their work. The book mentions Saint Phalle only in passing in the chapter about Tinguely as "an attractive female *réaliste*, who invites spectators to shoot at her plaster-encrusted collages with a .22 rifle, thus breaking the bags of pigment concealed therein."[17] Tomkins does not mention her cathedral series, or her challenging assemblage sculptures dealing with women, which in fact did not sell well. He remembers only the spectacle of the *Tirs* and her own physical attractiveness. The prevailing tendency of critics to accord women's artwork less weight and importance may have prevented an essay about Saint Phalle being included in such a book, but she was about five years behind Tinguely and Rauschenberg in her career, and both men had been instrumental in her development. Around 1964, Saint Phalle made her heart-shaped assemblage called *My Heart Belongs to Marcel*, today in the Philadelphia Museum of Art where the largest repository of Duchamp works resides. Her appreciation no doubt had to do with Duchamp's utter lack of aesthetic concern in his art, his indifference to beauty, his refusal to make art for the eye instead of the brain.

Clearly, Saint Phalle did not fabricate beautiful brides or beautiful art. Like Duchamp, she chose fairly neutral or even abject, mass-produced, non-art materials to make her assemblages. Her subject matter was very important to her—the idea was everything, as Tinguely had reassured her. By reclaiming the bride in her own art, Saint Phalle opened a discussion about Duchamp's work grounded in her lived experience. She seems to say: beware of being almost married. Woman may become a crucified hanging sacrifice. A bride will have her whole life determined by one day in an encumbering white gown. Saint Phalle pictures no groom, no bachelors with the bride, just a horse, a book, and a tree. A passive bride will be pulled into a stifling life with an absent man who functions in a separate world, plagued by eros, or his desire for love. If she is not careful, she will become a ghost of her former self, delivered to the desires and forces of others. By the middle of the 1960s the artist had shifted her sense of the female prototype, as well as experimenting with different materials. Still a relief assemblage, *Women's Altar* (p. 56) from 1964 brings many of her subjects together on a red background. Suspended there between the tree and the bride, humming in the air almost like a fairy, levitates her first small, anonymous *Nana* figure, the next stage of Saint Phalle's artistic development.

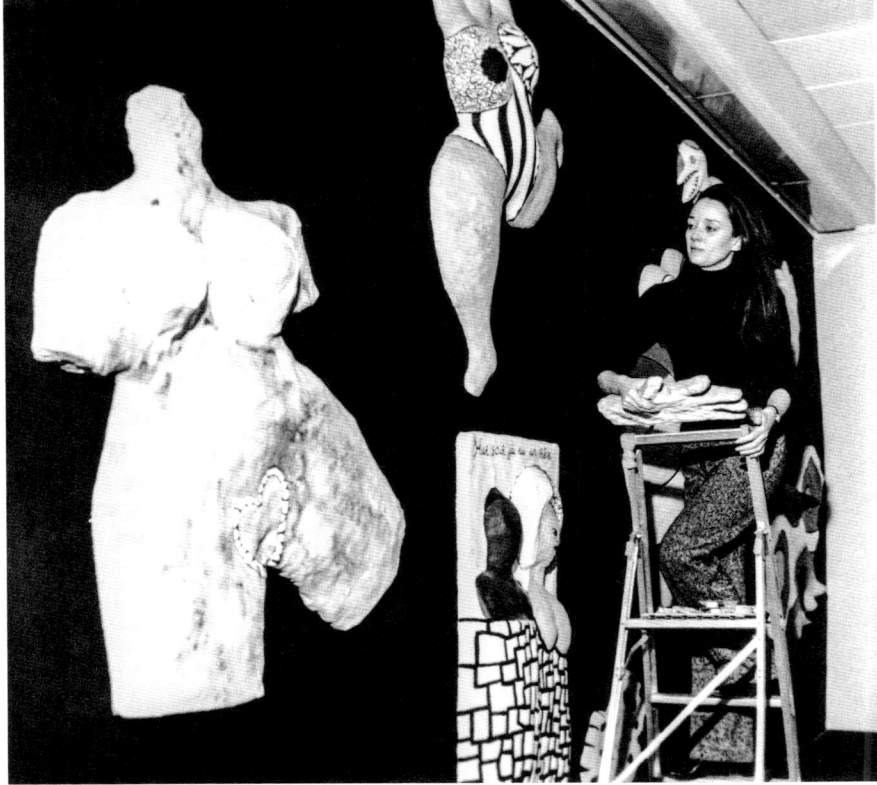

Niki de Saint Phalle during an installation at Alexander Iolas Gallery in Paris, 1968

By 1963, the mother of a burgeoning adolescent daughter, Saint Phalle began to make new, fully sculptural works together with Laura, and with technical help from Tinguely when necessary. The standing *Vénus* (1964) is made of wool yarn on wire mesh, not plaster, balanced on a rod fabricated by Tinguely. The suspended *Erica* (1965, p.58) floats, remote from Earth's gravitational pull. While *Venus* still uses embedded assemblage work, *Erica*'s surface is decorated only by soft textile materials, arranged in a predominantly pastel and neutral-colored patchwork pattern that recalls the shards that make up Saint Phalle's early *trencadis* self-portrait. A target marks one breast while the other cartoons a women's coiffed head, tipped to the side. The arrow pointing down towards Erica's genitals shows where the lines of wool yarn come together in a visible cleft between her legs. No plastic assemblage objects clutter the surface.

Saint Phalle named an ebullient pregnant woman, Clarice Rivers (1936–2024), as her inspiration for what would become known as her *Nanas*. Newly married, Americans Clarice Rivers and the artist Larry Rivers (1923–2002) had moved into the Impasse Ronsin in Paris in late fall 1961 and became friendly with Saint Phalle and Tinguely. A few years later, Larry Rivers collaborated with Saint Phalle

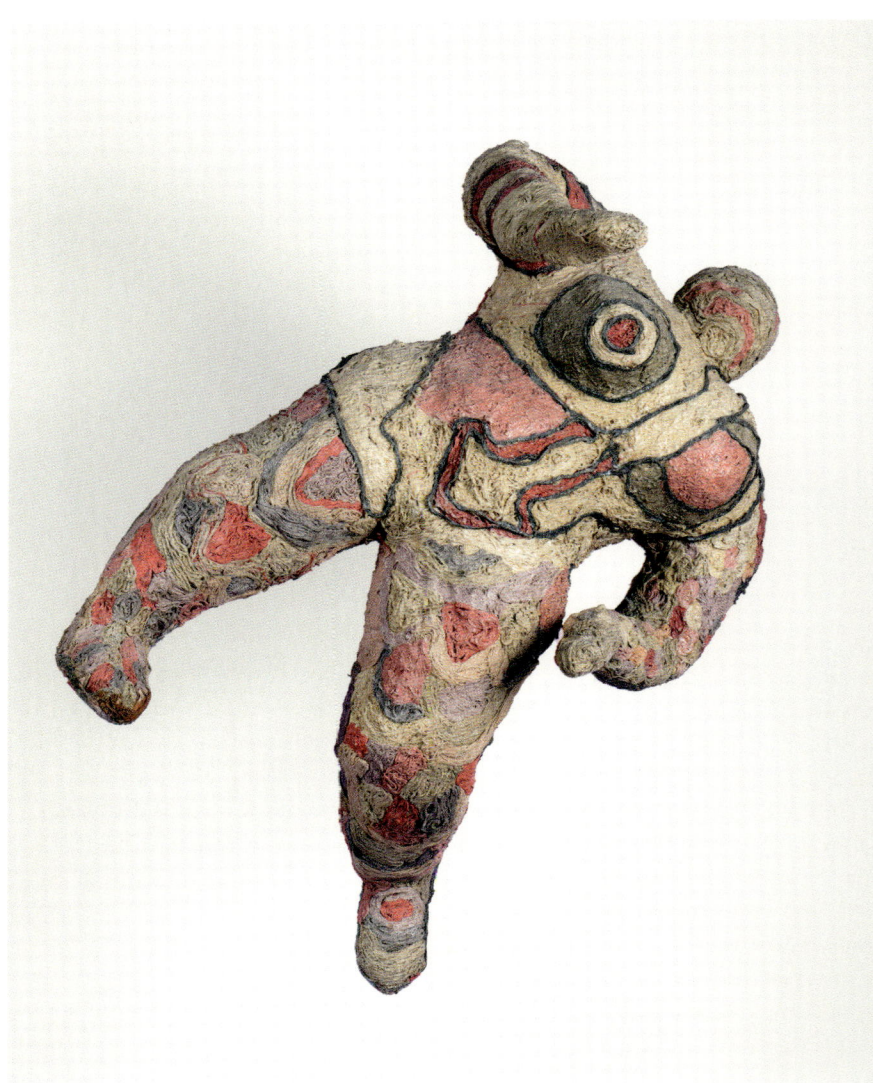

Erica, 1965
Wool, fabric, wire, 110 x 95 x 65 cm
(43⁵⁄₁₆ x 37⅜ x 25⁹⁄₁₆ in.)
Nice, MAMAC Collection

The early *Nanas* are named after real women friends and family members: *Bénédicte*, *Clarice*, and *Elizabeth* (1965).

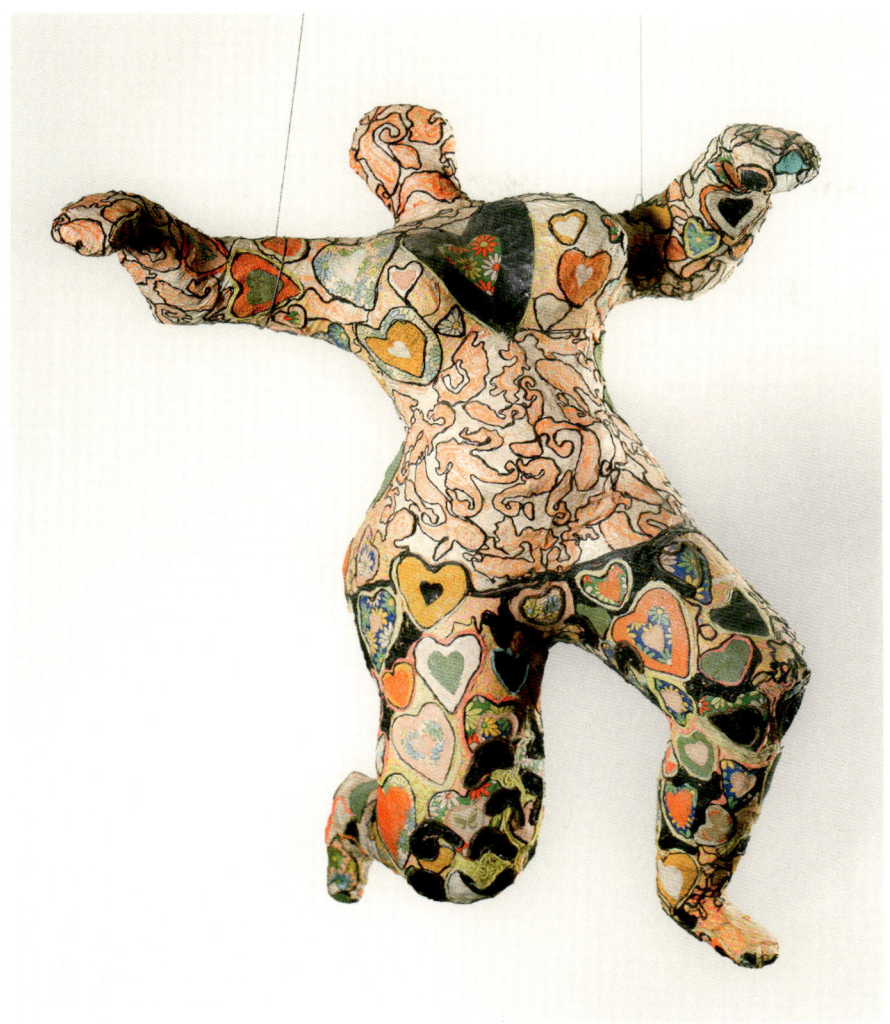

Samuela II, 1965
Paper maché, paint, fabric, wire mesh,
132.4 x 96.5 x 76.2 cm (52 x 38 x 30 in.)
Buffalo, Albright-Knox Gallery

on a drawing of the almost full-term Clarice Rivers, today in the Museum of Contemporary Art, Los Angeles (*Clarice Rivers*, 1964). While Larry realistically drew the face and body he knew so well, Saint Phalle patterned the body as she tenderly collaged Clarice's skin and crowned her with a headdress. The collaboration celebrated Clarice's rounded form as a site of fecundity. This image recalls Renaissance painter Sandro Botticelli's young Flora in his painting *Primavera* (*c*. 1477–82). Saint Phalle's sister, Elizabeth Marie Antoinette de Saint Phalle Rubin, was also pregnant at the time. Temporally distant from her own pregnancies and faced with the pubescence of her own daughter, Saint Phalle's ideas came together in the form of celebratory female figures, bursting with energy.

In the beginning, fabric patches and yarn patterned the skin of the *Nanas*, followed by painted plaster or resin. Their first showing in 1965 in Paris at the Alexander Iolas Gallery contained both media types. The large-scale *Nanas* were over six feet in height, plump or pregnant, with proportionally very small heads that made it seem like their bodies were gigantically looming. Saint Phalle chose an intentionally heroicizing body size to insist on female physicality, sexuality, and feeling, while the small, anonymous head de-emphasized rational thought and ignored the traditional sites of female beauty, such as the hair and eyes. The *Nanas* gyrate, caught in athletic, amusing, and immodest poses, like Matisse dancers that have broken out into three dimensions and are moving to thumping music. In another corner of that first Iolas Gallery *Nana* exhibition stood the monumental and somehow slightly sinister or frightening *Nana*, *La Waldaff* (1965), wearing a prim flower-print skirt and a blouse sorely challenged by her breasts, linebacker shoulders, and forearms. *La Waldaff* embodied both a more everyday yet more frightening type than the abstract *Nanas*, who were joyous and sexual.

Gallerist Alexander Iolas, who would give Saint Phalle a total of 17 shows during her lifetime, encouraged the artist to publish artists' books and to produce saleable graphic work that informed and accompanied her sculpture. For the 1965 exhibition Saint Phalle worked up her first artist's book/catalogue, where sketched *Nanas* disported themselves on pages enlivened and informed by her rounded handwriting. Pierre Descargues (1925–2012), a photographer, critic, and friend of Saint Phalle, fully appreciated the irreverence and humor of

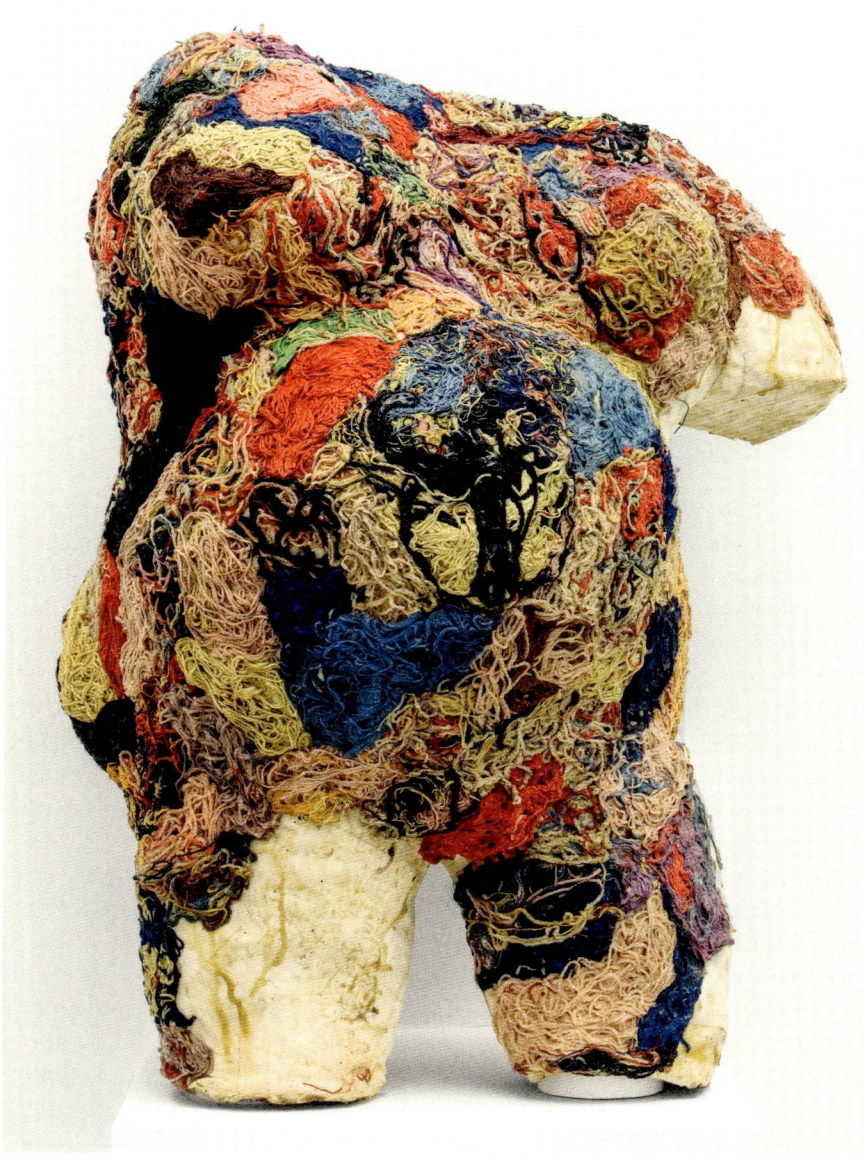

Nana boule sans tête, c. 1965
Fabric and wool on wire mesh,
75 x 50 x 35 cm (29½ x 19¹¹⁄₁₆ x 13¹³⁄₁₆ in.)
Nice, MAMAC Collection

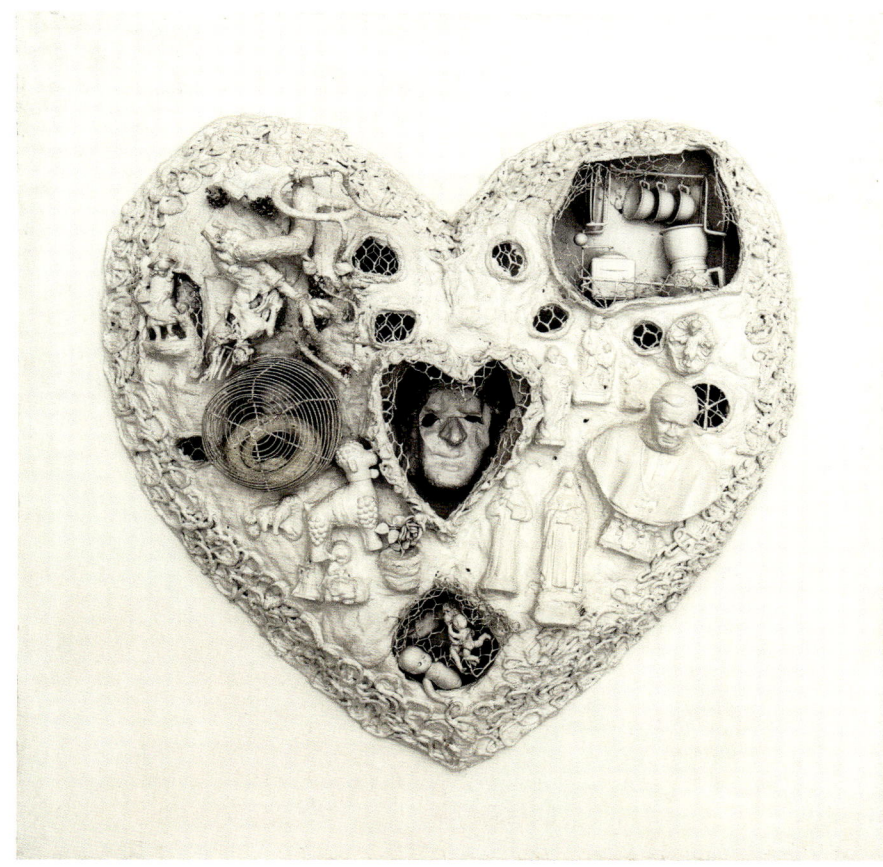

*Heart of Bigoted Old Woman
(White Heart),* 1964
Paint, wire mesh, and various objects on panel,
132 x 130 x 26 cm (52 x 51³⁄₁₆ x 10¼ in.)
Nice, MAMAC Collection

the *Nanas* when he wrote in that book about them in 1965. Certain male members of the European avant-garde favored Saint Phalle's attack on the patriarchy. One such figure was the choreographer, director, and dancer Roland Petit (1924–2011), who used the *Nanas* to stage a ballet, *Éloge de la folie* (1966). The portable papier-mâché sculptures were "danced" and manipulated by live performers. At one point in the ballet an enormous skirted sculpture, in the mode of *La Waldaff,* descended from the ceiling of the stage into the dancers' upheld hands, slowly crushing them into a heap. An awkward giantess, *La Waldaff* and other similarly dressed, big female figures Saint Phalle made, who are carrying purses or just standing, bear an uncanny resemblance to the non-human servant/destroyer Golem from the 1920 expressionist movie *The Golem* by Paul Wegener. The film's Golem character is shown being created from clay and then given life via magic, to help protect the Jewish people. In one scene the Golem carries his basket to market looking much like Saint Phalle's sculptures of women carrying a pocketbook. The Golem becomes enraged and turns his strength against humans, as *La Waldaff* did against Petit's dancers.

As a monster produced by man, the Golem might well be a camp, humorous reference to early cinema, but also to how women could turn on the society oppressing them. Saint Phalle's exaggeration of female body size and her chosen intense stylization and unnaturalness of "woman" correspond to Susan Sontag's discussion in her 1964 essay "Notes on 'Camp.'" This essay put its finger on the pulse of a sensibility that reigned in sophisticated circles at the time, which recognized the perverse appeal of a bygone, corny, and exaggerated style of a thing or phenomenon—a "camp" object. The 1933 movie *King Kong* is

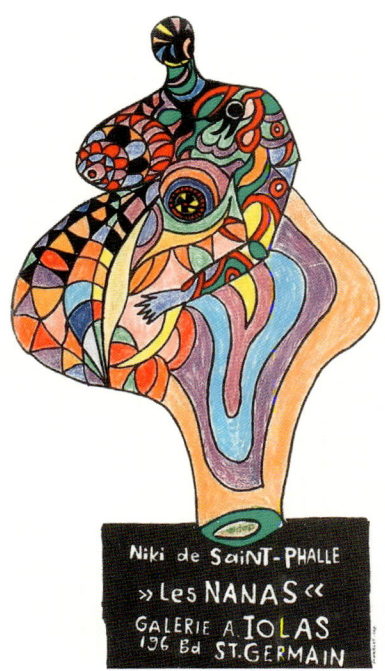

Poster for Les Nanas *exhibition*
Paris, Alexander Iolas Gallery, September–
October 1965

specifically mentioned in Sontag's essay as an example of something that was considered camp by 1964, as was Gaudí's architecture. Saint Phalle demonstrated a sophisticated camp sensibility when she used old movies to make the connection between wronged creatures on a rampage and wronged women who could potentially let loose and take a swing. Roland Petit thought the *Nanas* expressed symbolically and with great humor the power of women in contemporary society. Involved as a partner in Petit's ballet project, Tinguely contributed a kinetic backdrop that provided contrast to the moving bodies of Petit's dancers and the *Nanas*.

In 1966, the Swedish director of Moderna Museet, Pontus Hultén, invited Saint Phalle and Tinguely to come to Stockholm. He envisioned an exciting, audience-interactive exhibition similar to one held in Amsterdam at the Stedelijk Museum in 1962 called *Dylaby*, which Tinguely had co-curated. Hultén hoped for a new collaboration between Saint Phalle, Tinguely, and the Finnish artist Per Olof Ultvedt (1927–2006). According to Saint Phalle, the form this collaboration took came together during a group discussion in Stockholm, and was ultimately suggested by Hultén, though completely informed by Saint Phalle's work up to that time: it was to be a house-sized, pregnant *Nana*, lying on her back with legs parted so that the public could enter through her vagina. The sculpture was given the Swedish title *Hon–en Katedral* (She–a Cathedral, p. 65), at the suggestion of Ultvedt.

This idea held inherent compositional similarities with Saint Phalle's cathedral works and her female assemblages. Naturally, the idea of entering and exiting a woman's body through her vagina is built into life itself. However, there were also some close art historical precedents for what happened in Stockholm. Salvador Dalí had created a pavilion called *Dream of Venus* for the World's Fair in New York in 1939, whose entrance between visible stockinged female shins meant a woman's knees were apart and her skirt was up. Visitors to the pavilion bought their tickets at a booth between the shins, which was shaped like an inflated puffer fish. Dalí's pavilion was luridly sexual and objectified the female body in multiple ways. A 1939 watercolor of the event by Reginald Marsh shows the public filing past a reclining female body made of rubber that had been painted suggestively with a piano keyboard. Live topless women and some clad in bathing suits activated the space. Saint Phalle had visited the fair as a nine-year-old

RIGHT
Lysistrata, Maquette for Stage (for the production of Aristophanes's Lysistrata *by Rainter von Diez, Staatstheater Kassel)*, 1966
Painted plaster, 112 x 74 x 45 cm
(44¹/₁₆ x 29⅛ x 17¾ in.)
Hanover, Sprengel Museum

OPPOSITE
Gwendolyn, 1966-90
Coated polyester on metal base,
252 x 200 x 125 cm (99¼ x 78¾ x 49¼ in.)
Hanover, Sprengel Museum

After the unveiling of a city commission for three large *Nanas* in Hanover, Germany, the reaction was strong. The controversy and the *Nanas*' fate was settled by a public tug-of-war. The younger side won, and the *Nanas* stayed.

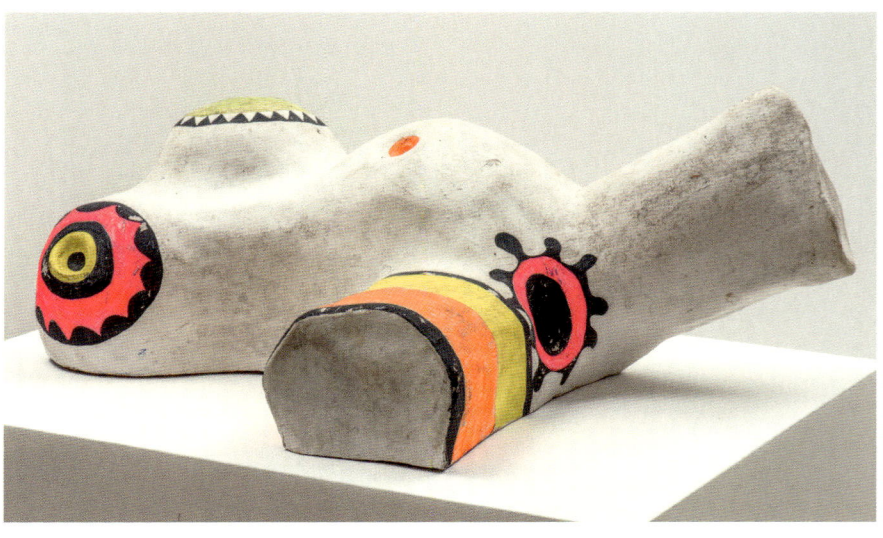

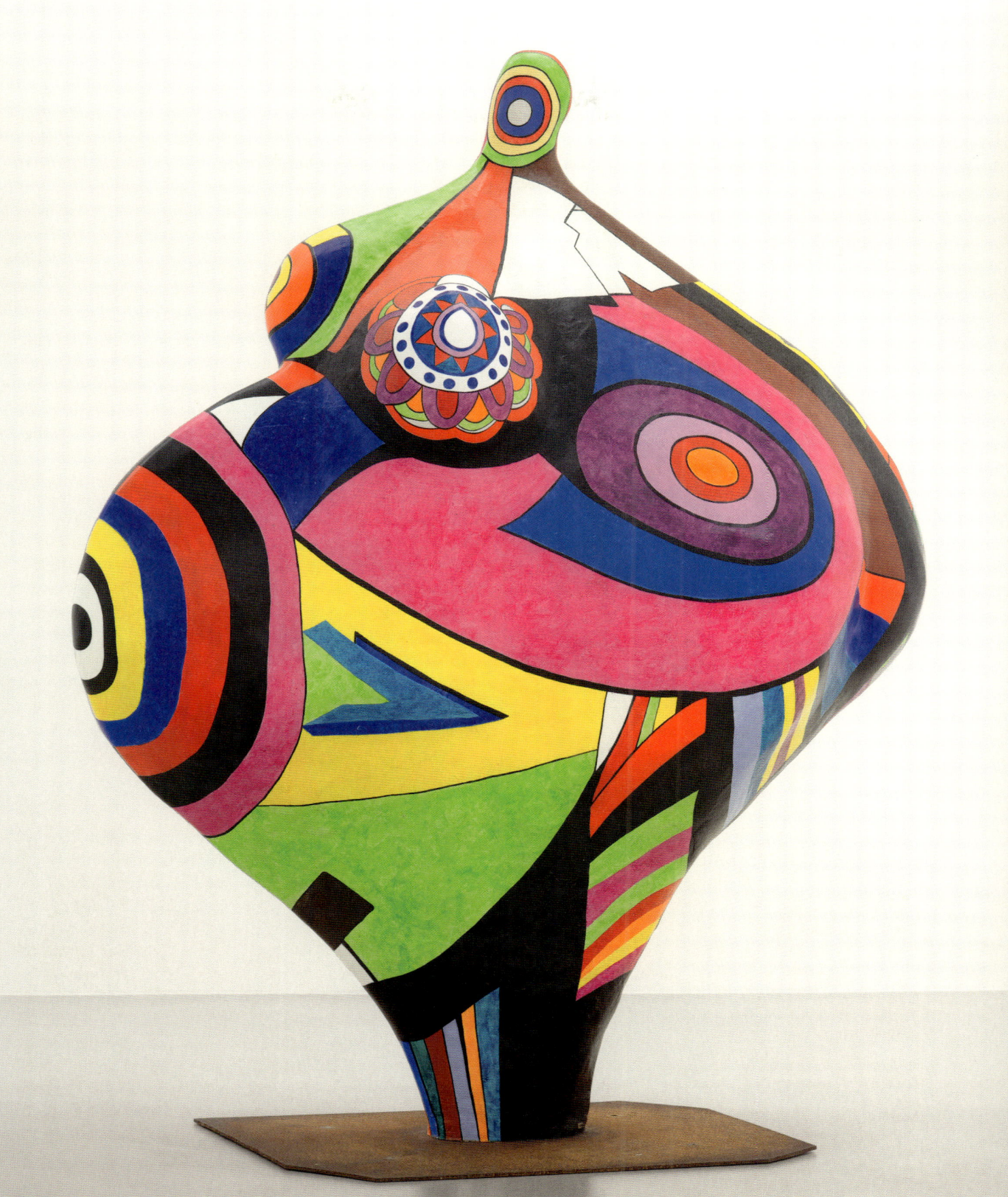

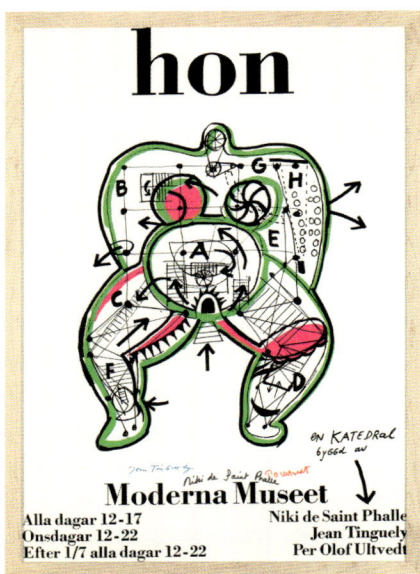

Poster for Hon–en Kathedral *exhibition*
Stockholm, Moderna Museet, 1966

OPPOSITE
Hon–en Kathedral, 1966
Stockholm, Moderna Museet
Photograph by Hans Hammarskiöld

The pose of *Hon* mirrored that of a woman on a gynecological table, knees lifted, heels planted, as if she were being examined or giving birth. The public approached down the "corridor" of her parted legs and entered the rounded door of her vaginal opening. Not a slit or a mandorla shape, the odd portal recalled the softened pointed arch doors and windows that Gaudí had designed for the Palau Güell in Barcelona (1886–88).

child; her biographer Catherine Francblin makes a case for Dalí's pavilion influencing her later *Nana* architecture, although Saint Phalle did not mention this in her autobiographies or in connection with *Hon*.

Another work that may have precipitated *Hon* is Duchamp's complex tableaux construction *Étant donnés*. Duchamp had worked on it for a very long time in secret and although it was completed in 1966, it was still unknown to the public at the time of the Stockholm exhibition. Hultén, Ultvedt, and the Moderna Museet curator and art critic Ulf Linde (1929–2013) had all been recently involved in making copies of Duchamp's works for exhibition purposes. (It was more practical to remake them than to borrow them to show in Europe.) Linde had worked in close consultation with Duchamp for this, and Duchamp authorized and signed the copies of his *Large Glass* and readymades. Duchamp probably showed his New York studio to Linde and Hultén during this collaboration. Of course, Tinguely and Saint Phalle knew Duchamp, too, and had been introduced to Dalí by him in Spain.

Completely different in mood and scale from *Hon*, *Étant donnés* confronts the viewer with the spread legs of an inanimate nude female in a marshy landscape who holds aloft an illuminating lamp. Duchamp planned this work to be installed behind a weathered, lumber wall with two peepholes at eye level for the viewer to peer through. Because of the separating wall and the awkwardness of using the peepholes, the viewer in no way enters the scene, but is forced to become the voyeur of what looks like a crime—the figure could be a rape victim abandoned in a remote setting. Despite it being the focus of the work, the female's genital area looks disfigured or anatomically edited in relation to the otherwise comparative realism of the scene. *Étant donnés* was installed at the Philadelphia Museum of Art only a year after Duchamp's death in 1968, and only after that did it become publicly known. But some insiders in the art world could have heard and seen what Duchamp was doing. It would have been clear that *Étant donnés* focused on the parted thighs of a naked figure. One might argue that whatever else this work could mean, it showed that the female body was still employed as a field of combat where male artists fought their aesthetic battles at woman's cost.

In contrast to *Étant donnés*, *Hon* was planned as a temporary exhibit and had to be made quickly. Hultén made sure the work on *Hon* remained a secret from the press until the opening. If there was to be a scandal, it needed to happen once the construction could no longer be stopped. The daring, taboo-breaking hilarity of *Hon* made it an adventure to work on, but the artists also knew that they were pioneering an art exhibition of unprecedented scale.

A monumental 9 x 30 x 20 feet (280 x 900 x 600 cm) in dimension, *Hon* became a building within a building, completely filling in both height and breadth the largest room of the museum. It took a team of people working with hive-like concentration to build the structure within 40 days ahead of the opening. Saint Phalle, Tinguely, Ultvedt, and Hultén (who was very hands-on for a museum director) all worked on fabricating the sculpture which, because of its form, would go down in history as the ultimate expression of Saint Phalle's art. Rico Weber (1942–2004), a young Swiss barman at the Moderna Museet's restaurant, was tapped to help, and he became a trusted assistant to Saint Phalle and Tinguely for 15 years to come, as well as being an artist in his own right.

First, a welded rebar skeleton established the general anatomical form of the reclining *Nana*, which was then covered with chicken wire mesh. Layers of fabric glued to the wire mesh provided a thick enough skin for Saint Phalle to paint. A base coat of white covered the body, and then wide bands of color,

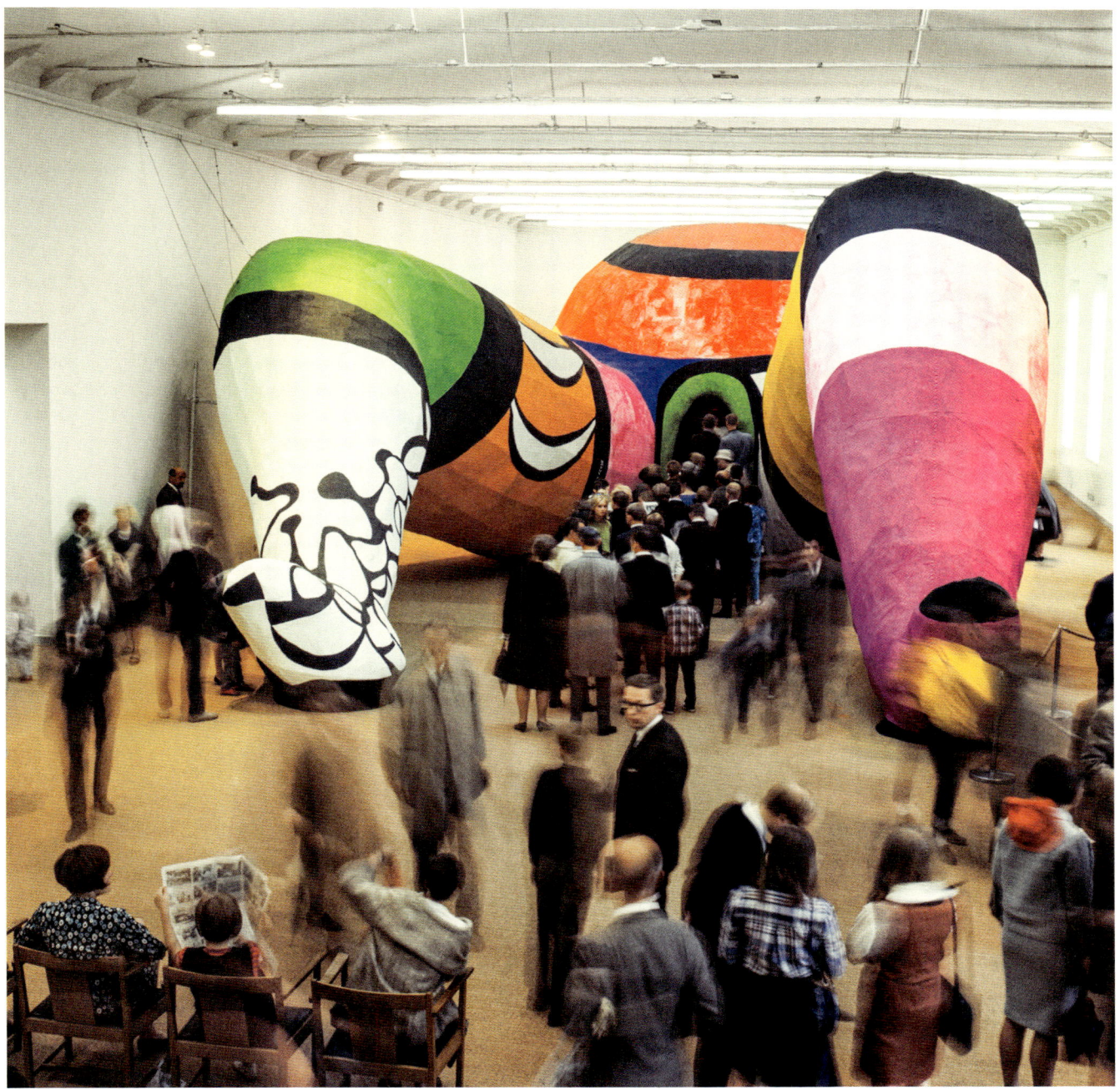

black line, and some crescent and concentric designs "clothed" *Hon*. While Saint Phalle painted the exterior of her "goddess," as she called her, Tinguely and Ultvedt conceived the interior, orchestrating the events, mechanics, and artworks inside of *Hon*.

Painted black inside, and offering just enough light, visitors found doors and ladders that led to distinct areas with things to see and experience. In her 2018 essay in *Stedelijk Studies*, Annika Öhrner uses archival documents from the Moderna Museet to discuss the curation of this work and lists the entertainment features inside *Hon*.[18] Interpretations and memories vary in the literature, as do available photographs, but it is possible to assemble some idea of the experiential features offered by the exhibition. Near the entrance, in place

Could We Have Loved?, 1968
Color silkscreen on wove paper,
59 x 74 cm (23¼ x 29⅛ in.)
Washington, D.C., National Gallery of Art,
Corcoran Collection (Gift of Olga Hirshhorn)

of a beating heart, stood a raw wood kinetic sculpture made by Ultvedt of a man in a chair, getting a massage and watching a cardboard television set that showed waves and a sinking boat. In *Hon*'s right leg was a ramp/slide adjacent to stairs where, seated on a toy tiger, child viewers could zip past paintings that were done in the styles of known contemporary artists and were labeled as "fake." (These were painted anonymously by Linde, who had been involved in the reproductions of works by Duchamp.) In the left leg, a ladder offered access to a higher level, where the visitor happened upon a sandwich automat and a milk bar in the right breast. A chute leading from the milk bar allowed for the disposal of bottles, and they descended to a noisy bottle-crushing machine below, which had been built by Tinguely. A planetarium filled the left breast. A coin-operated telephone booth made communication possible from inside *Hon* to the outside world. A cinema for 12 people was built into the left arm, where, accompanied by music by Johann Sebastian Bach, a screen showed the 1922 silent movie *Luffar-Petter*. The film featured Swedish bathing beauties frolicking in the summer countryside. Noted for employing the glamourous Swedish actor Greta Garbo in an early role, the film reminded visitors of being outside with women while being inside a woman. It also reflected the summer

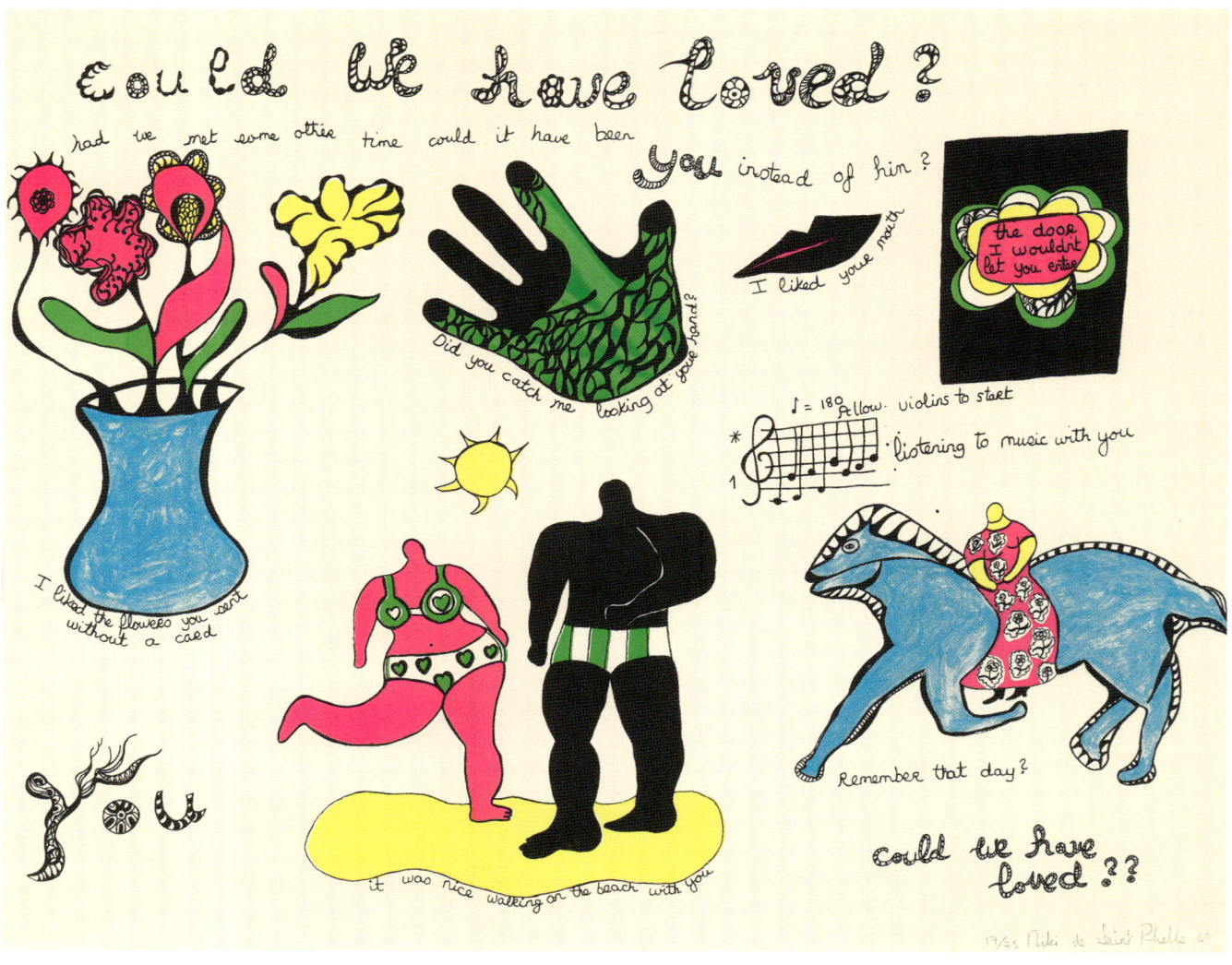

running time of the show, from June 4 through September 4, 1966, after which it was dismantled.

A red velvet loveseat in *Hon*'s knee provided a rather plush, Victorian-style place for couples to sit together. Wired with a transmitter, any private conversation there could be heard in the bar "upstairs." Near that loveseat was a pond with goldfish, corresponding to the probable location of *Hon*'s womb. (Saint Phalle and Tinguely occasionally liked to include living animals in their works.) A sketch of *Hon* used for the front page of the catalogue shows the pond labeled as an "aquarium," but it was irregular and rounded in shape, not a glass box, and the swimming fish likely embodied reproductive swimmers—sperm—at least in the imagination of some visitors.

A rearview mirror near the loveseat made it possible to view postcards of artworks from the shop of the Moderna Museet that were mounted behind it, twice removed from reality as reflections of miniaturized reproductions. On top of *Hon*'s pregnant belly, a panoramic terrace allowed viewers to look down and see fresh viewers arriving, adjusting their facial expressions to their first ground-level impressions of Hon's parted thighs. This vicarious experience of seeing people seeing was planned, and part of the fun. But an inscription on

Sweet Sexy Clarice, 1968
Color silkscreen on wove paper,
59 x 74 cm (23¼ x 29⅛ in.)
Washington, D.C., National Gallery of Art,
Corcoran Collection (Gift of Olga Hirshhorn)

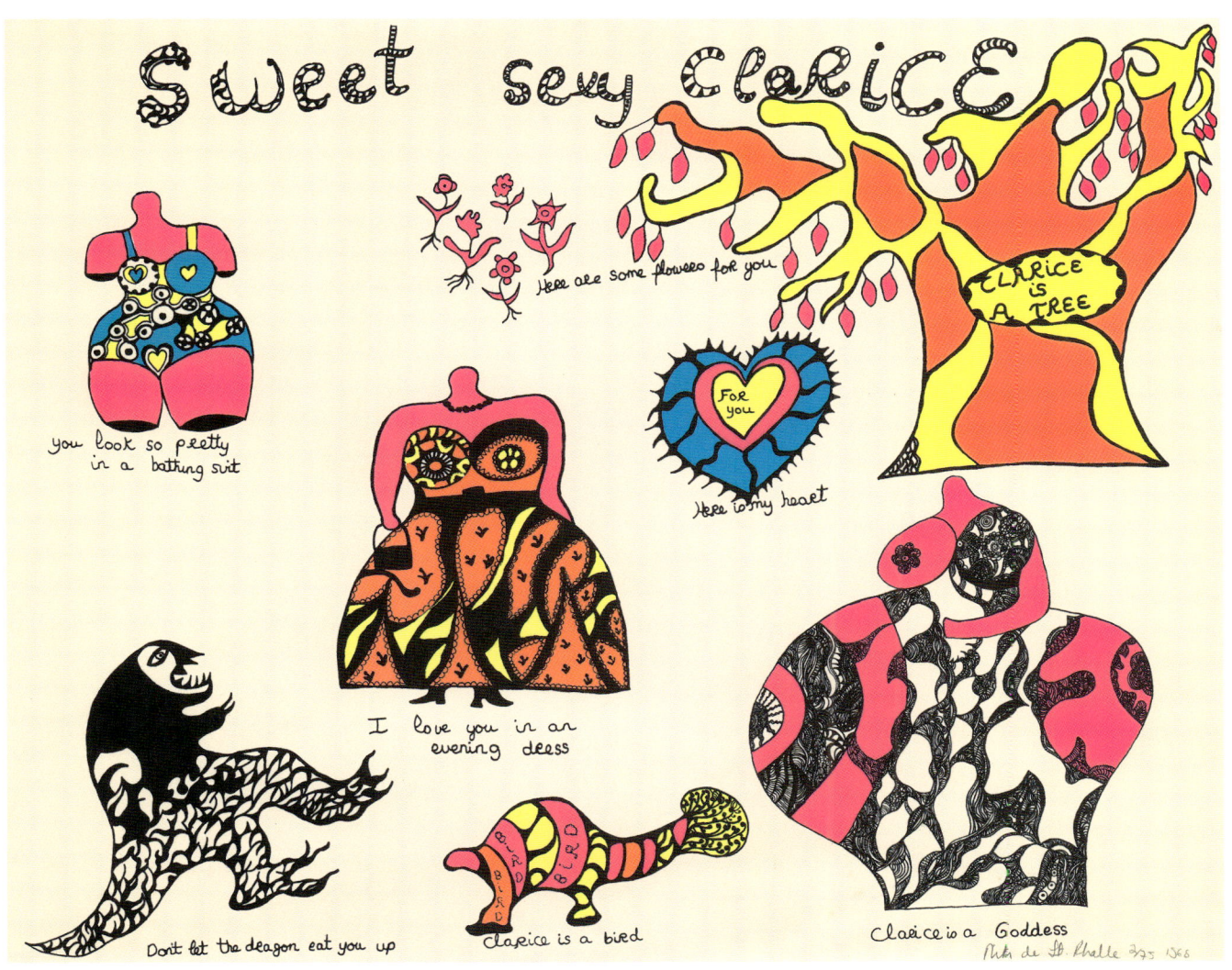

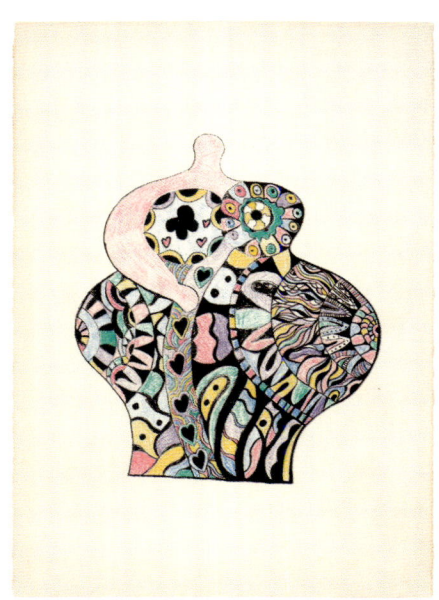

Nana Enceinte (Pregnant Nana), 1968
Oil crayon on laid paper,
90 x 63.5 cm (35⁷/₁₆ x 25 in.)
Hanover, Sprengel Museum

Hon's inner right thigh admonished visitors who were about to enter not to have bad, perhaps obscene thoughts: *Honi soit qui mal y pense*, it said, which is the Anglo-Norman maxim, "Disgraced be he who thinks ill of it."

The spelling similarity between "Hon" and the French "Honi" (the word for "disgraced" or "shamed") may have had associative meaning for Saint Phalle, as this French phrase inscribed on the thigh went back to the chivalric tales told to the artist during her childhood about her Saint Phalle ancestors who had fought in the crusades, vanquished infidels, and battled alongside Joan of Arc. *Honi soit qui mal y pense* is the motto of the Order of the Garter, the world's oldest chivalric order, which can be traced to 1348, when French was still spoken at the English court. On *Hon* it occupied the place of a thigh garter, instead of the traditional knee garter.

Judging from photographs, the Stockholm public encountered *Hon* in good spirits and with an open mind, dressed as if for church and accompanied by their children. While waiting in line for their turn to go in (green and red traffic lights regulated the entry point), some people quickly educated themselves by reading a museum publication, a "catalogue" printed in the form of a newspaper. The exhibition was a great success. Saint Phalle and the Moderna Museet liked to take credit for a rise in the Stockholm birth rate the following year. Saint Phalle, in response to a reporter's question, agreed that some might see *Hon* as a big whore, taking in thousands before releasing them, transformed. Yet if *Hon* was a whore, her visitation implicated an entire society. *Hon* certainly threw open the doors to many discussions about accessing and understanding a woman's body. It ignited questions about female roles within human society and the ways women should be respectfully depicted. *Hon* also went down in exhibition history as a show that changed ideas about what a museum could do. Almost exploding the spatial limits of the Moderna Museet, shows like *Hon* pushed artists to look for bigger and more democratic venues, such as the factories that would soon be deserted by industry and repurposed into art venues.

Only a short time later, Tinguely and Saint Phalle planned another large collaboration. Conceived for the roof of the French Pavilion, *The Fantastic Paradise* was a love game between six of Tinguely's black kinetic machines and nine of Saint Phalle's *Nanas*, in which the dark male machines "attacked" the colorful, curvy *Nanas*. Saint Phalle explained the playful dynamic as the opposition of two gendered forces as "lovers' battles," "a war without victors or vanquished."[19] To move the *Nanas* outdoors for the Expo 67 project, Saint Phalle shifted from using wool, paper, and plaster as materials to polystyrene, polyester, and fiberglass. Nonporous and waterproof, these materials could be painted easily with opaque, bright colors. The works exchanged a matte finish for a glossy look. *The Fantastic Paradise* later traveled to Albany and New York City, before being donated to the Moderna Museet in Stockholm, where it stands outdoors today. When the sculptures came to New York's Conservatory Garden in Central Park for a year in 1968, Saint Phalle's sister Elizabeth produced inflatable plastic *Nanas*, designed by Saint Phalle in three different sizes and colors and intended as affordable works of art that anyone could own. *Vogue* magazine pictured them in April 1968. You can still buy one. And while their sale once helped finance the building of Saint Phalle's monumental projects, today they contribute to the maintenance of her sites. A sculpture curator from Israel who saw the installation in New York in 1969 would later commission a public sculpture by Saint Phalle: her first public commission, *The Golem*, which took the form of a children's slide. A version of the playful creative dialogue between Saint Phalle's colorful sculpture and

Tinguely's black machines was achieved again later in the *Stravinsky Fountain* (1983) installed next to the Centre Pompidou in Paris, where 16 sculptures, moving and spraying water, stood for the works of the composer Igor Stravinsky.

After two decades of producing the *Nanas*, Saint Phalle grew to understand them as the harbingers of a new matriarchal society that could solve world problems caused by men, their machines, and their wars. The *Nanas* represented for her a brand of independent, kind, good mother, and that was why some people disliked or even hated them. In her eyes, her sculptures forced the public to confront their own feelings for their mothers. While today the *Nanas* as a whole are heralded as Saint Phalle's most beloved sculptures, because of their brashness, their bright—to some eyes garish—colors, and the way their overt curves affronted propriety while concomitantly showing disdain for anatomical accuracy, they were by no means uncontroversial in their time.

Last Night I Had A Dream, 1968
Color silkscreen on wove paper,
50 x 70 cm (19¾ × 27¹¹⁄₁₆ in.)
Washington, D.C., National Gallery of Art,
Corcoran Collection (Gift of Olga Hirshhorn)

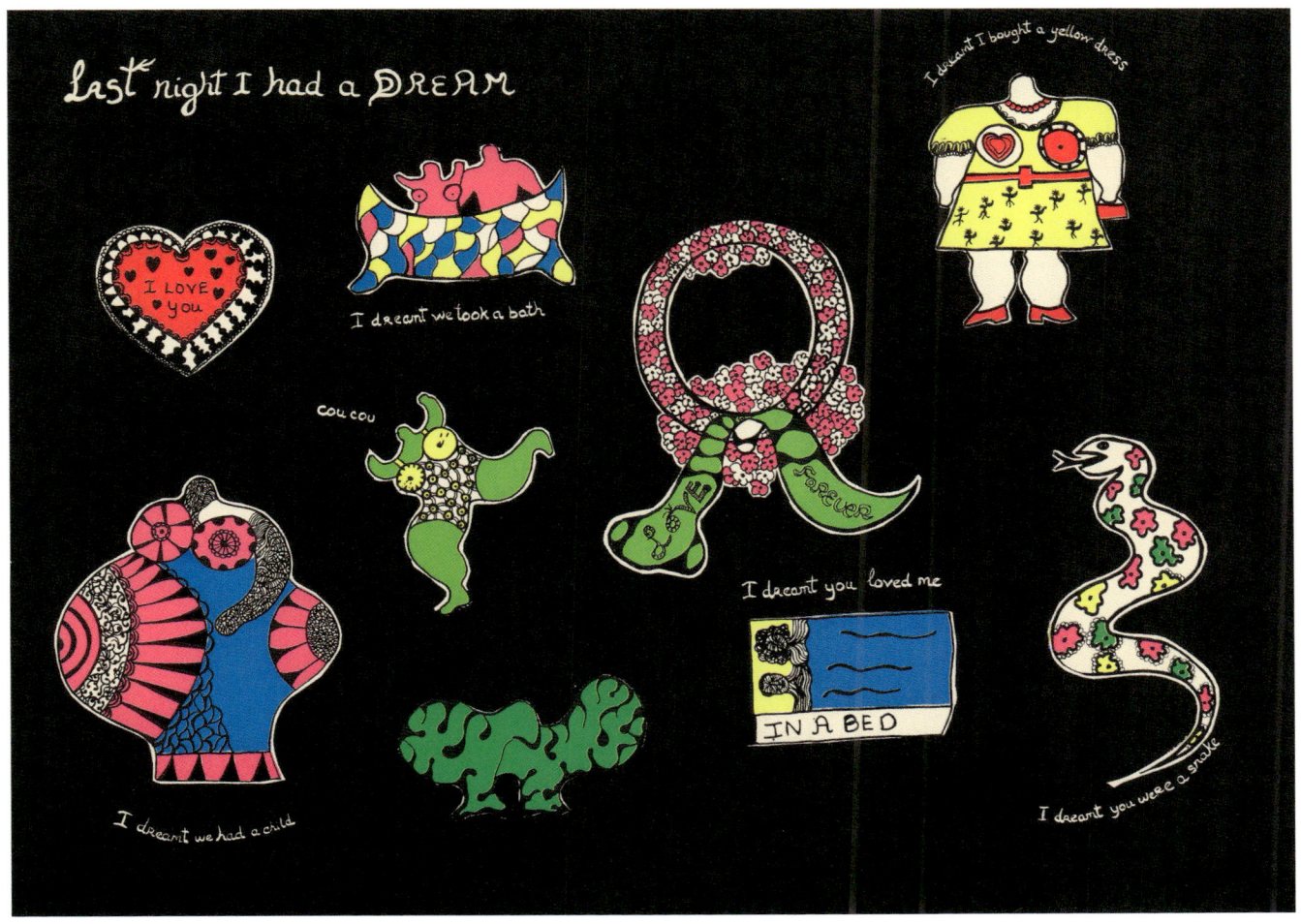

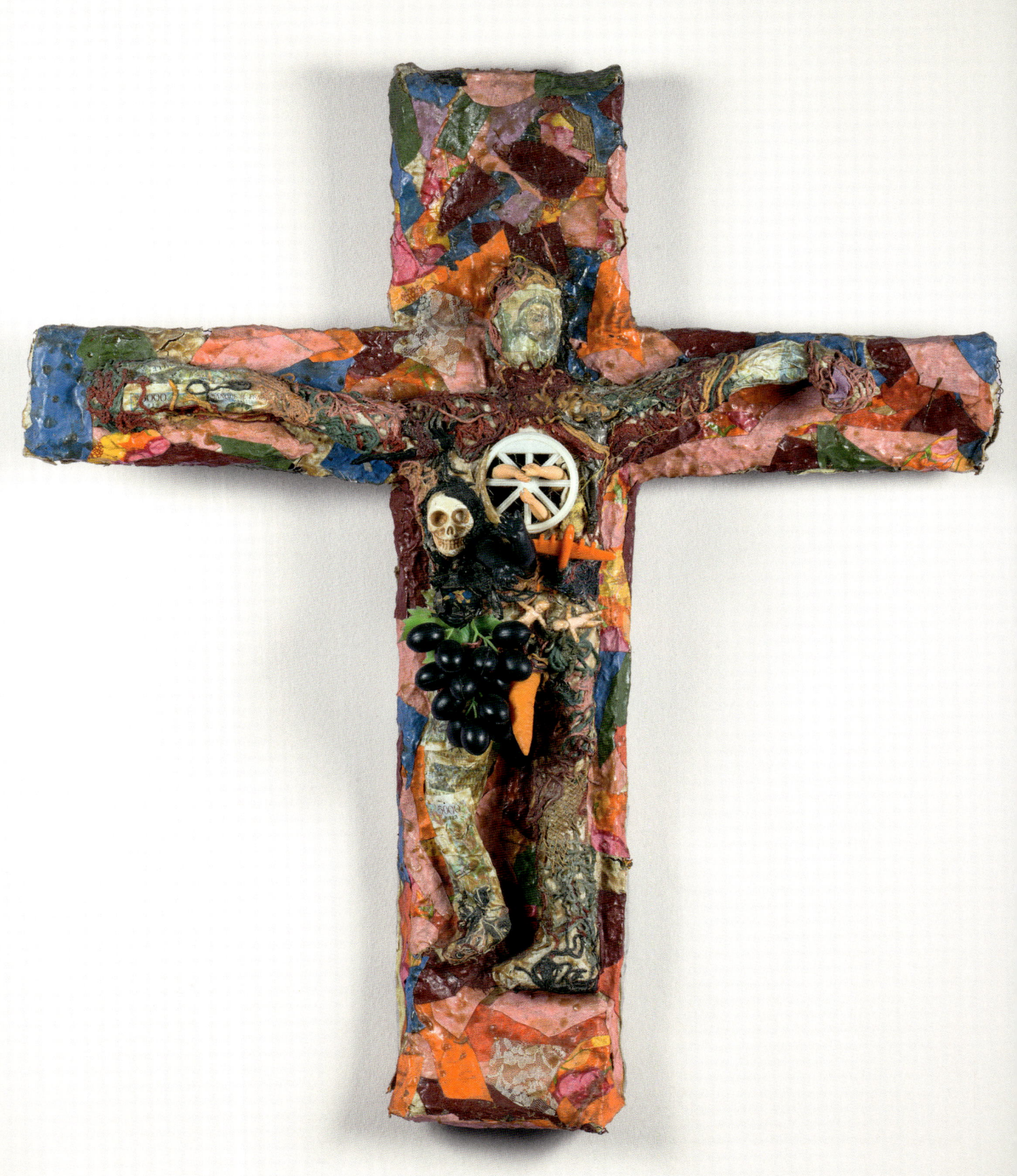

The Artist's Cosmos

By the 1970s, Niki de Saint Phalle considered experimenting with making films. Animation interested her, and offered a natural fit with her drawing. However, she also wanted to conceive stories with actors, use location, costumes, and props (including her own artworks), and direct and act herself. She finished two movies, which are not often screened. The general public may well have a hard time finding them to watch, though Peter Schamoni used original footage from both of them in his documentary about her life, *Niki de Saint Phalle: Who is the Monster, You or Me?* Both of the films that Saint Phalle made show extremely surreal events that correspond to the fantastical motifs of her drawings and the habitable structures she designed. In a sense, the films continue where her architecture left off, adding the dimension of time to the unfolding of her art and taking a dark, comedic turn. Camped up scenes of sex and violence expressed by intentionally deadpan or histrionic acting have the ability to disturb the viewer, without committing to realism.

Her first film, *Daddy* (1973, pp. 71, 72–73, 75), co-conceived by British filmmaker Peter Whitehead (1937–2019), dared to explore her past as a psychosexual reckoning with her childhood abuse and the development of a girl's sexuality. It dealt out an uninhibited take on incest, sadomasochism, bisexuality, and masturbation, and employed an amateur "family" of Saint Phalle's personal friends and former lovers as actors. Rainer von Hessen played Daddy. Clarice Rivers played Saint Phalle's mother, and the child Gwynne Rivers played Saint Phalle as a child. For the final cut, another actor, Mia Martin, was hired to play Saint Phalle as an adolescent. Much of the film was made at the Chateau du Beauregard in the Loire Valley, a Renaissance castle that the artist rented for the project. Whitehead called it a "pseudo-fictional biopic."[20] Saint Phalle herself commented that the film was not in any way a faithful portrayal of her parents, but rather a story of how people in a family devour each other.

In one scene her dead father's body lies in an open coffin, metamorphosed into a gigantic, gray phallus, a punned embodiment of the family name Saint Phalle. The content of the film still challenges taboos—an excellent account of the film's action and its relation to the confessional poetry of Anne Sexton (*To Bedlam and Part Way Back*, 1960) and Sylvia Plath ("Daddy," 1965) is given by Joanna Bourke in a 2011 article in *The Journal of Cinema and Media*.[21] Even though the filmmakers shared the sensibilities of poets, Whitehead and Saint

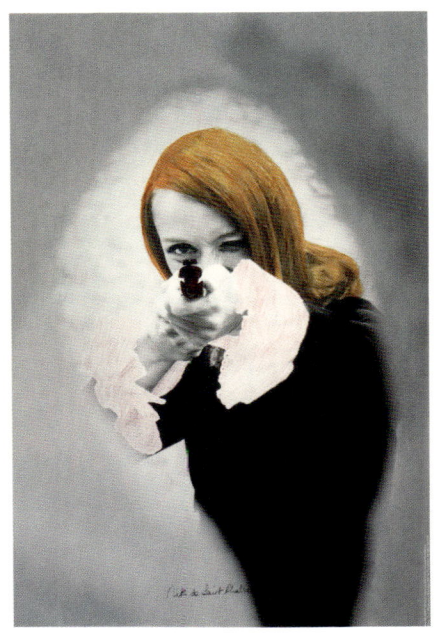

OPPOSITE
Daddy: crucifix, 1972
Film prop. Various small objects on wire mesh, 90 x 80 cm (35⁷/₁₆ x 31½ in.)
Nice, MAMAC Collection

ABOVE
Saint Phalle pointing gun, black-and-white photograph hand-colored with wax crayon. Promotional image for the film *Daddy*, 1973. Photograph by Peter Whitehead

Phalle tread rough ground with this painful film about incest, the repudiation of patriarchy, and family dysfunction.

The artist directed her second film herself: *Un rêve plus long que la nuit (A Dream Longer than the Night)* (1976, p. 74), a fairy tale with medieval, monster movie, and cartoon inflections. It features a princess, played by Saint Phalle's 25-year-old daughter Laura Duke Condominas, who had recently starred as Guinevere in Robert Bresson's film *Lancelot du Lac* (1974). In *A Dream Longer than the Night* (sometimes also called *Camelia and the Dragon* or *Camelia's Dream*), the princess is transformed into an adult, encounters a fantastical dragon, passes through seven doors, and discovers what the unsettling world has to offer. An early painting like *Pink Nude with Dragon* (p. 21) already prefigures the dream-like atmosphere and the teaming up of woman and dragon. Dragons, those staples of medieval lore, offered the personification of evil against which a hero could measure themselves. Various types of dinosaur-like monsters put in multiple appearances in Saint Phalle's *Tirs* and drawings. Dragons had inhabited her emotional world since childhood, when she and her brother John had been told stories about their medieval ancestors. Derived in part from medieval myth, like the story of Saint George, who was patron saint of the Order of the Garter

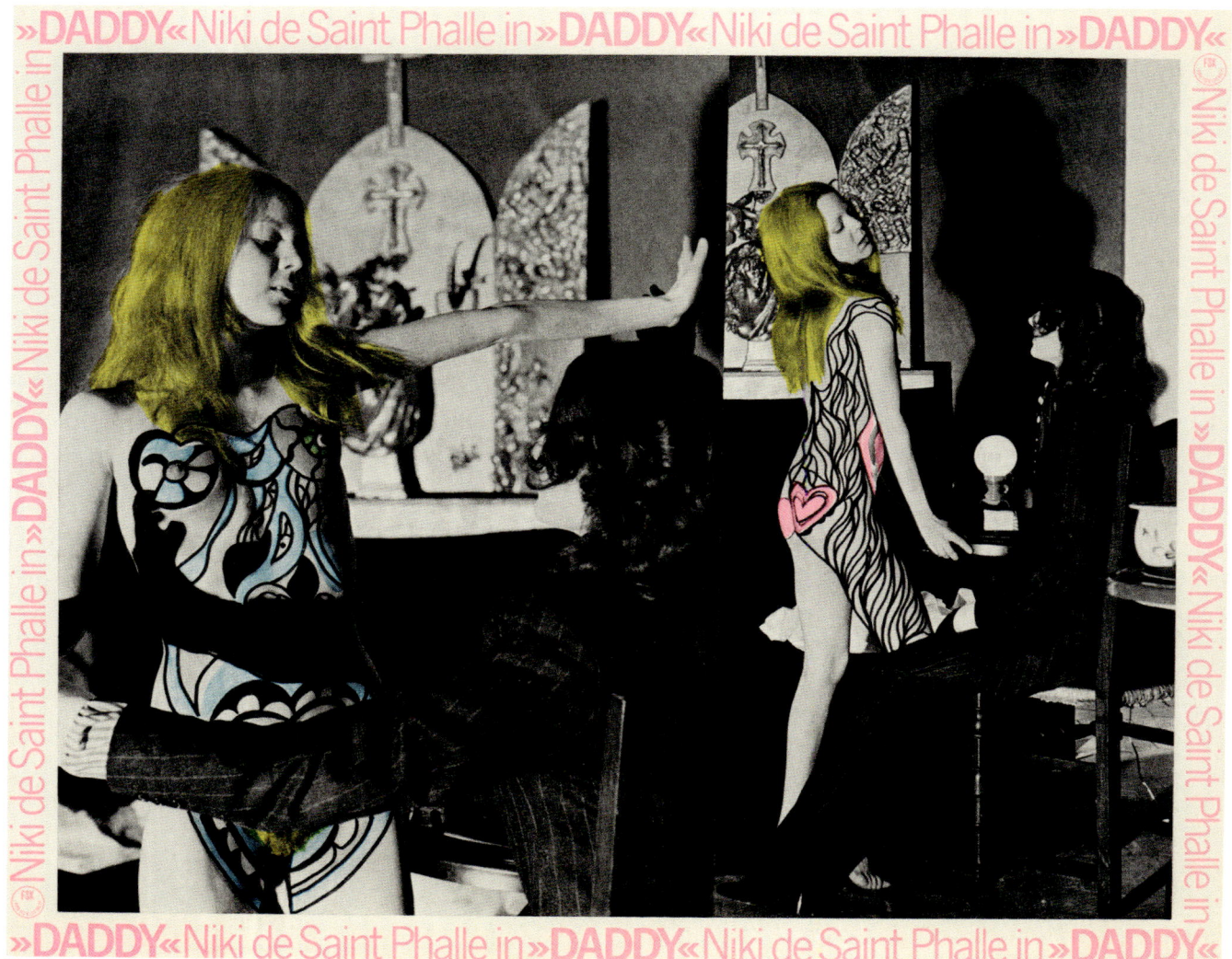

(the order's slogan *Honi soit qui mal y pense*—"Disgraced be he who thinks ill of it"—had ornamented the thigh of *Hon*), and in part from her beloved monster movies, Saint Phalle's dragons do not succeed in being truly ferocious. In *Un rêve plus long que la nuit* the character of the dragon is instantly recognizable as a man lumbering about in a homemade dragon suit. (Rico Weber wore the suit.) Yet the dragon stands for something to be vanquished. The act of vanquishing dragons is existential, a serious test upon which all else depends.

Saint Phalle used the film to portray men as makers of war and prisoners of eros. Tinguely, strapped with a helmet and a giant penis, played a general armed with a penis-shaped cannon taller than himself. He gives enthusiastic, uninhibited performances of male zaniness in battlefield and brothel scenes. As a filmmaker, Saint Phalle mines Tinguely's forceful appetites in loving acknowledgment of his nature. Around the time Saint Phalle was experimenting with film, as well as working on other projects, her breathing problems flared up again, and put her in the hospital in 1974. Afterwards she went to St. Moritz, Switzerland, for some skiing and the fresh, cold air. While recuperating in the jet set spa town and staying at the house of gallerist Bruno Bischofberger, who was a friend of Tinguely, she met an old friend of her own from her modeling days in

OPPOSITE AND BELOW
Daddy, 1973
Promotional material for the film: black-and-white photograph with color retouching, 23.9 x 29.8 cm (9⅜ x 11¾ in.)
Paris, Bibliothèque Kandinsky, Musée national d'art moderne, Centre de création industrielle

The artist herself plays a kind of "red witch" in the film; unable to separate herself from trauma, her character passes the trauma on.

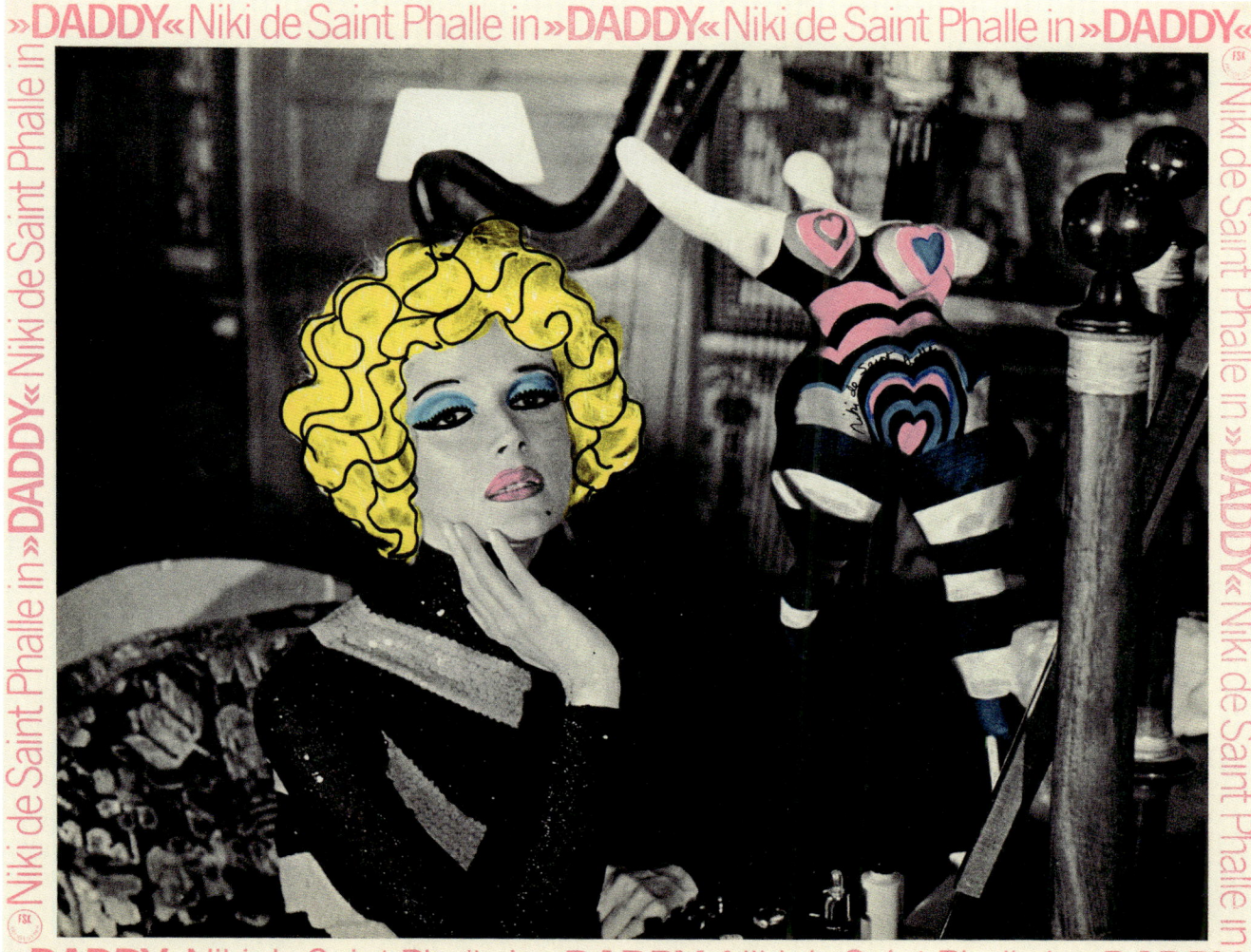

Un rêve plus long que la nuit (A Dream Longer than the Night), 1974
Silkscreen on paper,
65.5 x 42.5 cm (25¹³⁄₁₆ x 16¾ in.)
Nice, MAMAC Collection

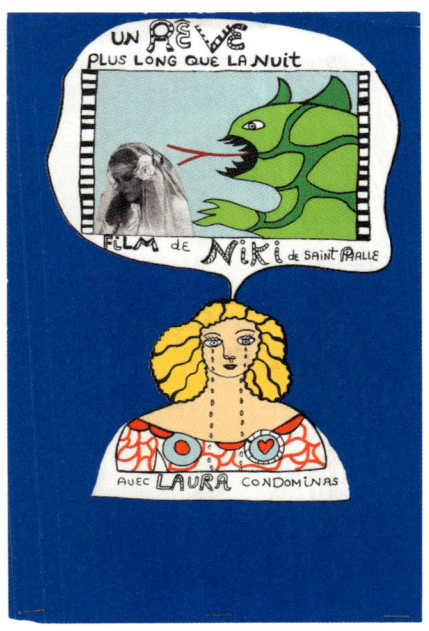

New York, Marella Caracciolo Agnelli (1927–2019), who had worked as an assistant to the photographer Erwin Blumenfeld. Like Saint Phalle, Agnelli had an American mother and a European father, had modeled, and was well connected through her own family and through marriage. Surrounded by the beautiful Alpine countryside of St. Moritz, Saint Phalle did not talk about her ambitions for making movies, but instead told her friend about her longstanding desire to build a sculpture garden inspired by Gaudí's Park Güell in Barcelona. The theme of the garden was to be a pack of cards: the tarot deck.

According to her biographer Catherine Francblin, Saint Phalle had first been introduced to tarot cards by sculptor Eva Aeppli, her old friend and Tinguely's first wife. Then in 1976 the avant-garde filmmaker Alejandro Jodorowsky (b. 1929), a serious student of tarot and a collector of tarot decks, interpreted the cards for Saint Phalle in such a way that she became interested in working with them. Jodorowsky had heard about tarot from Surrealist André Breton, and he helped restore the original 17th-century Marseille deck for modern printing. Jodorowsky believed that tarot can teach a person how to create their own soul, to go from a wandering fool to being linked to everything in the world, an idea that appealed to Saint Phalle.

A resurgent interest in tarot cards had spread during the 1960s and 1970s. The cards became popular because they could be used as an interpretive tool to understand oneself. The evolving feminist, anti-war, and civil rights movements of that era had people questioning themselves. Society as a whole demanded personal readjustment, the finding of the "me" that Saint Phalle had wanted to depict in her movie about Camelia's dream. In particular, the Rider–Waite–Smith tarot (1909) and 17th-century Marseille tarot inspired Saint Phalle. She went on to become familiar with early tarot cards such as the Visconti Tarot by Bonifacio Bembo (*c.* 1450), the Tarocchi of Mantegna (*c.* 1465), and tarot images inlaid in the marble floor in Siena Cathedral (14th to 16th centuries). During the 1960s and 1970s, graphic artists designed many new sets of tarot cards that interpreted traditional tarot imagery going back centuries to the first existing Italian and French decks.

Marella Agnelli listened with interest to Saint Phalle's wish, and even had a suggestion about where such a tarot garden might be located: in the south of Tuscany, on 14 acres of property that her two brothers owned and which had been an ancient Etruscan site. The land was sloping. An abandoned quarry left an amphitheater form with multiple levels in the landscape, on top of which olive trees and rosemary bushes had grown.

Saint Phalle was very happy with this idea and made some first models to propose the plan to the brothers, Carlo and Nicola Caracciolo, who agreed to a garden smaller than what it grew to be. Generally considered the pinnacle of her career, Tarot Garden brought together Saint Phalle's aesthetic sensibilities like no other single project. Work on the garden began in earnest in 1978. Saint Phalle moved to Garavicchio, Italy, a medieval hamlet, and began the sculptures that corresponded to the 22 named cards of the tarot deck known as the Major Arcana, considered the karmic cards of destiny. (There are a total of 78 cards in a tarot deck. Saint Phalle did not directly address the 16 court cards, or the remaining 40 cards of the Minor Arcana, four groups of 10 suit cards representing the four elements.)

Major Arcana cards represent life lessons, karmic influences, and the archetypal themes that make up an individual's life journey. The cards are numbered from 0 to 21, and each card shows a figure. The digit 0 stands for the main

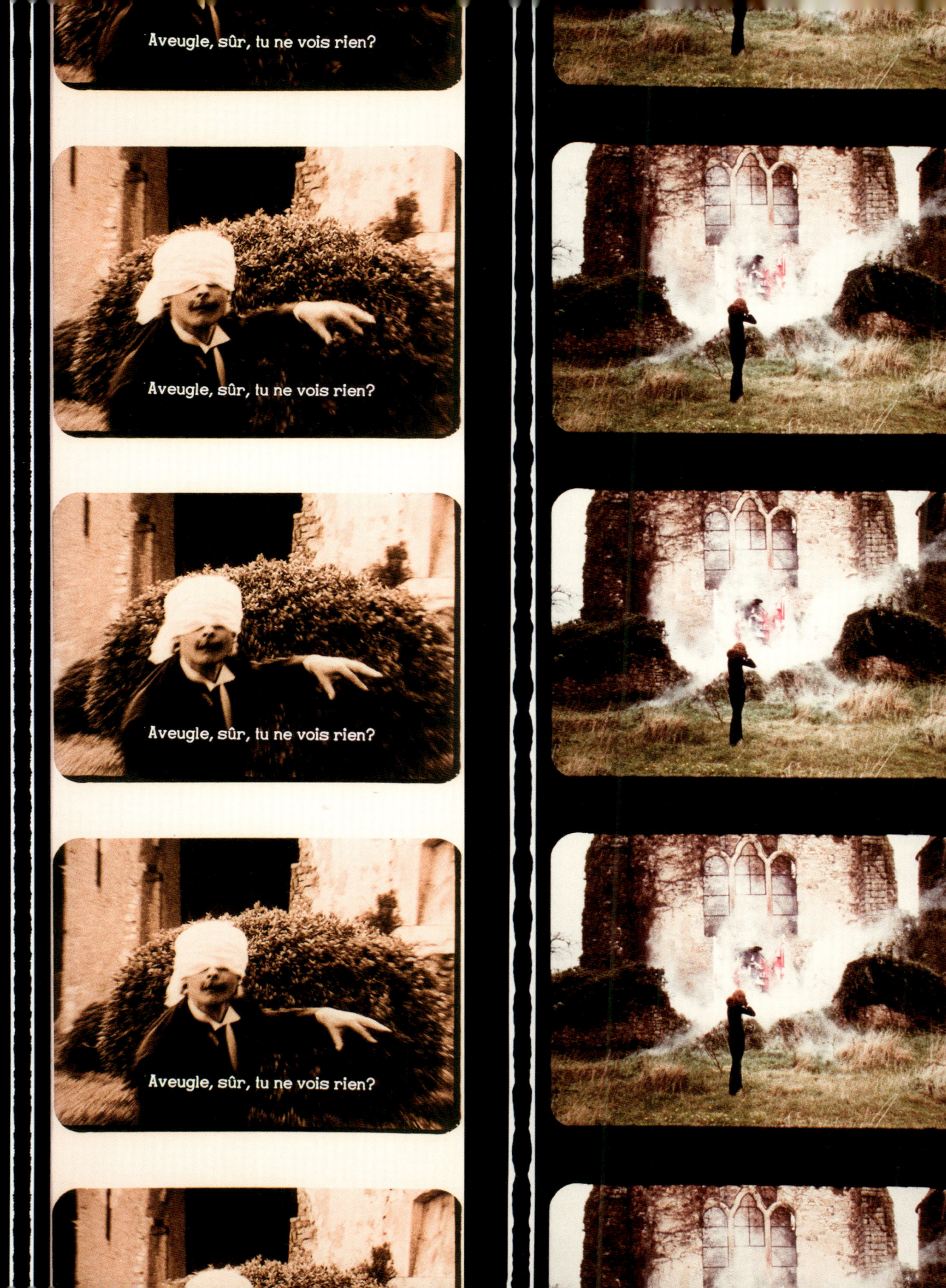

character of the pack, the Fool, who travels through the entire deck and meets all of the other characters. Each character has something to teach the Fool, until he reaches the final card, the World card. The characters are The Fool, The Magician, The High Priestess, The Empress, The Emperor, The Hierophant, The Lovers, The Chariot, Strength, The Hermit, The Wheel of Fortune, Justice, The Hanged Man, Death, Temperance, The Devil, The Tower, The Star, The Moon, The Sun, and Judgment, followed by The World.

For Tarot Garden, Saint Phalle would make 22 weatherproof sculptures, some of them four to five feet (120 to 150 cm) high. Some were painted polyester and reinforced concrete, others covered with mosaics of ceramics, glass, and pieces of mirror. Faced with an enormous project and unknown costs, Saint Phalle was buoyed in her garden ambition by the architectural magic of her heroes, Gaudí, Cheval, and Rodia, who had also worked for years on their projects. But quite near to her Tuscan garden site lay another artful garden populated by fantastical features: the mannerist Garden of Bomarzo. Sometimes called The Sacred Grove or Park of Monsters, its grotesque, quasi-architectural sculptures and small buildings had been nestled into the natural landscape and bedrock of northern Italy during the 16th century. Saint Phalle had visited Bomarzo in 1962 and brought Jean Tinguely with her.

Commissioned by a grieving and untethered Pier Francesco Orsini after the death of his beloved wife Giulia, Bomarzo's design features, like its leaning house and its hell mouth, may have mirrored the widower's sense of loss. As a retort to rational, classicizing Renaissance garden planning, Bomarzo spoke to those who did not feel all was right with the current order of the world. Saint Phalle took inspiration from Bomarzo. From 1979 until its opening in 1998 and beyond, Saint Phalle designed, continually fundraised for, and built, piece by piece, her ideal garden in the Tuscan landscape. She used her own money, raised in part by products she designed, such as a signature perfume, her *Nana* inflatables, jewelry, furniture, and prints, not to mention her sculptures. Her first husband,

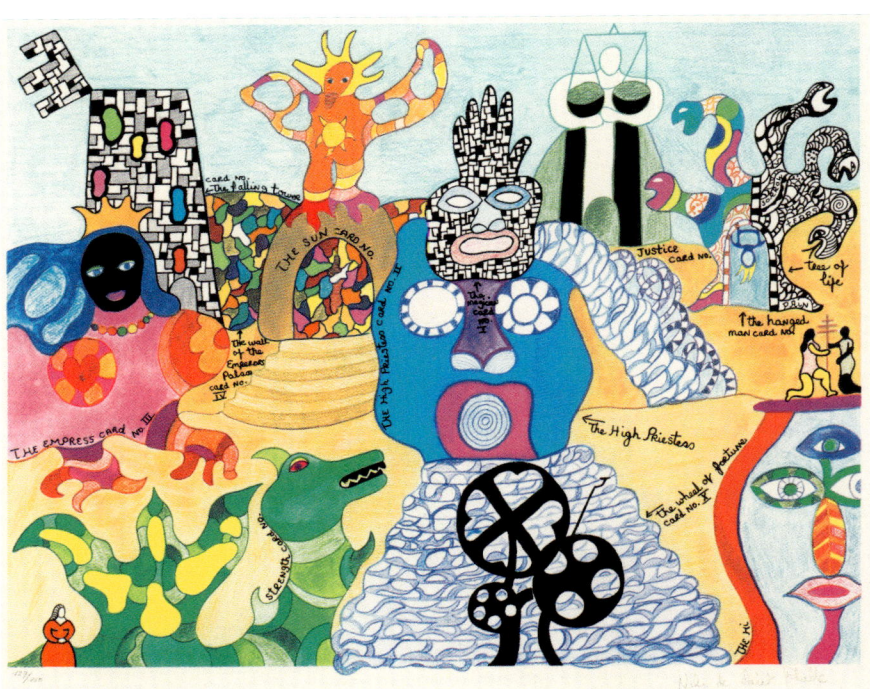

Tarot Garden, 1991
Color lithograph on Arches Velin,
49.5 x 64.3 cm (19½ x 25⁵⁄₁₆ in.)
Hanover, Sprengel Museum

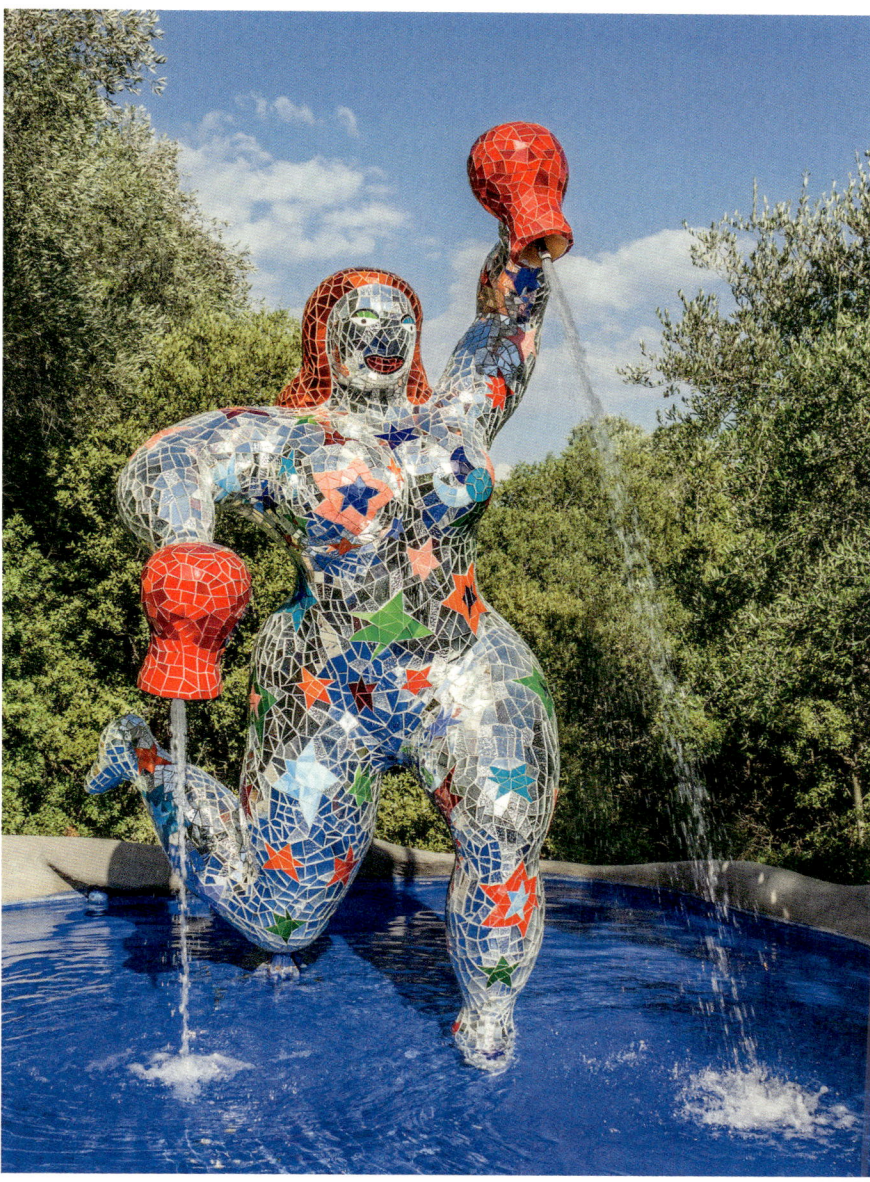

LEFT
The Star as installed in the Tarot Garden in Garavicchio, Italy

PAGES 78–79
Overview of the Tarot Garden in Garavicchio, Italy. Photograph by Laurent Condominas

For many years, the acreage in Garavicchio was alive with artists and craftspeople working towards a common goal. like a medieval work site.

Harry Mathews, contributed financially, as did Tinguely and an unknown British aristocrat, and the Caracciolo brothers, who had donated the land. Saint Phalle was essentially her own boss. She employed and managed local artisans and trained others, including—and this must have satisfied her enormously given her admiration of letter carrier Cheval—the local postman, Ugo Celletti, who worked there until his death in 2016, surviving Saint Phalle by 14 years. Those who contributed to Saint Phalle's garden believed in her vision and trusted her as one of their own. The scale of the garden required Tinguely's collaboration, and he was not only significantly involved with construction, welding fully half of the garden sculpture armatures with Rico Weber, but upon Saint Phalle's request added features of his own. Tarot Garden became another place where the two artists remain in dialogue with each other through their art, even today.

From the road, the first sculpture that comes into view for the visitor about to enter Tarot Garden is the rising of a monstrous head. It stares out, a large,

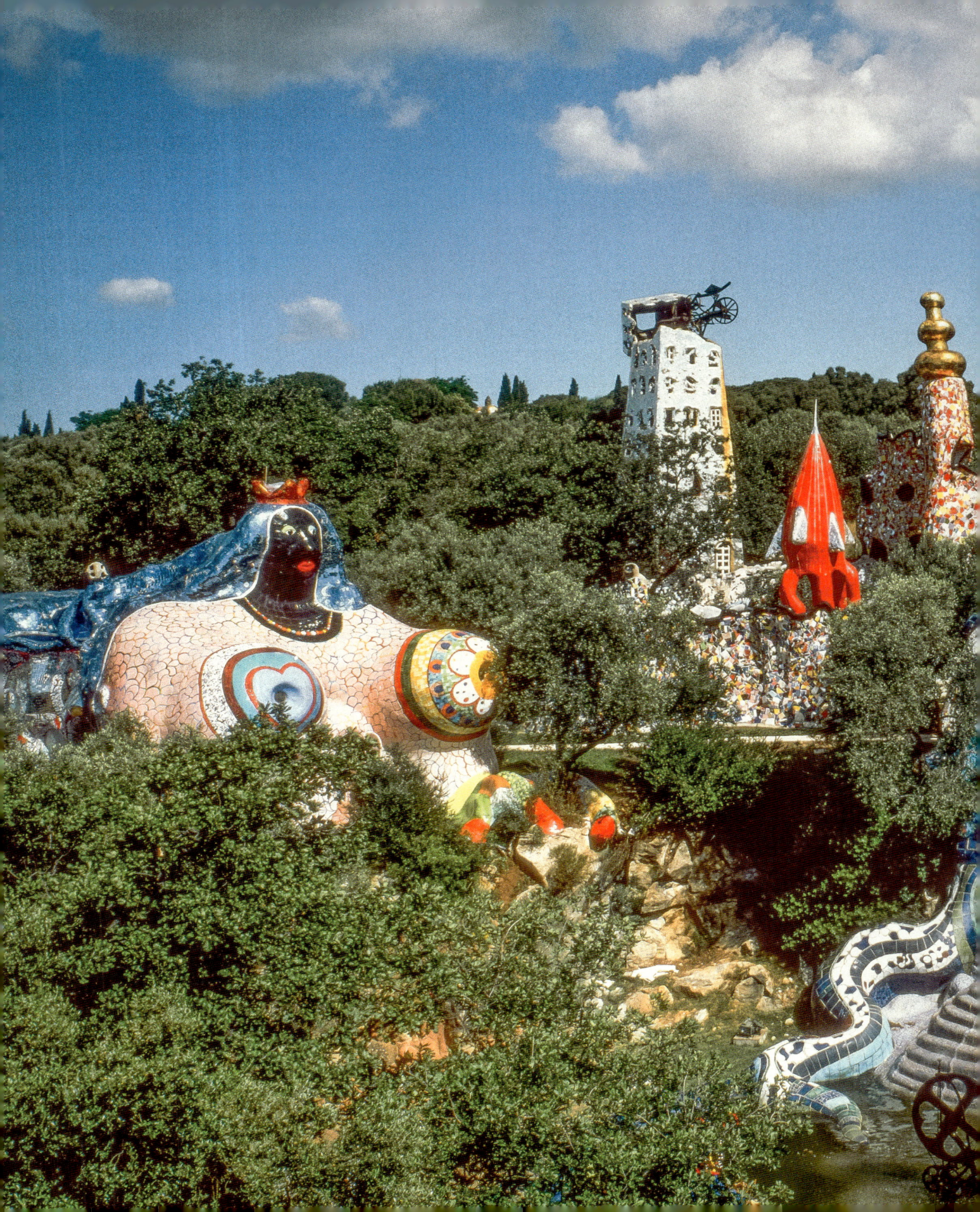

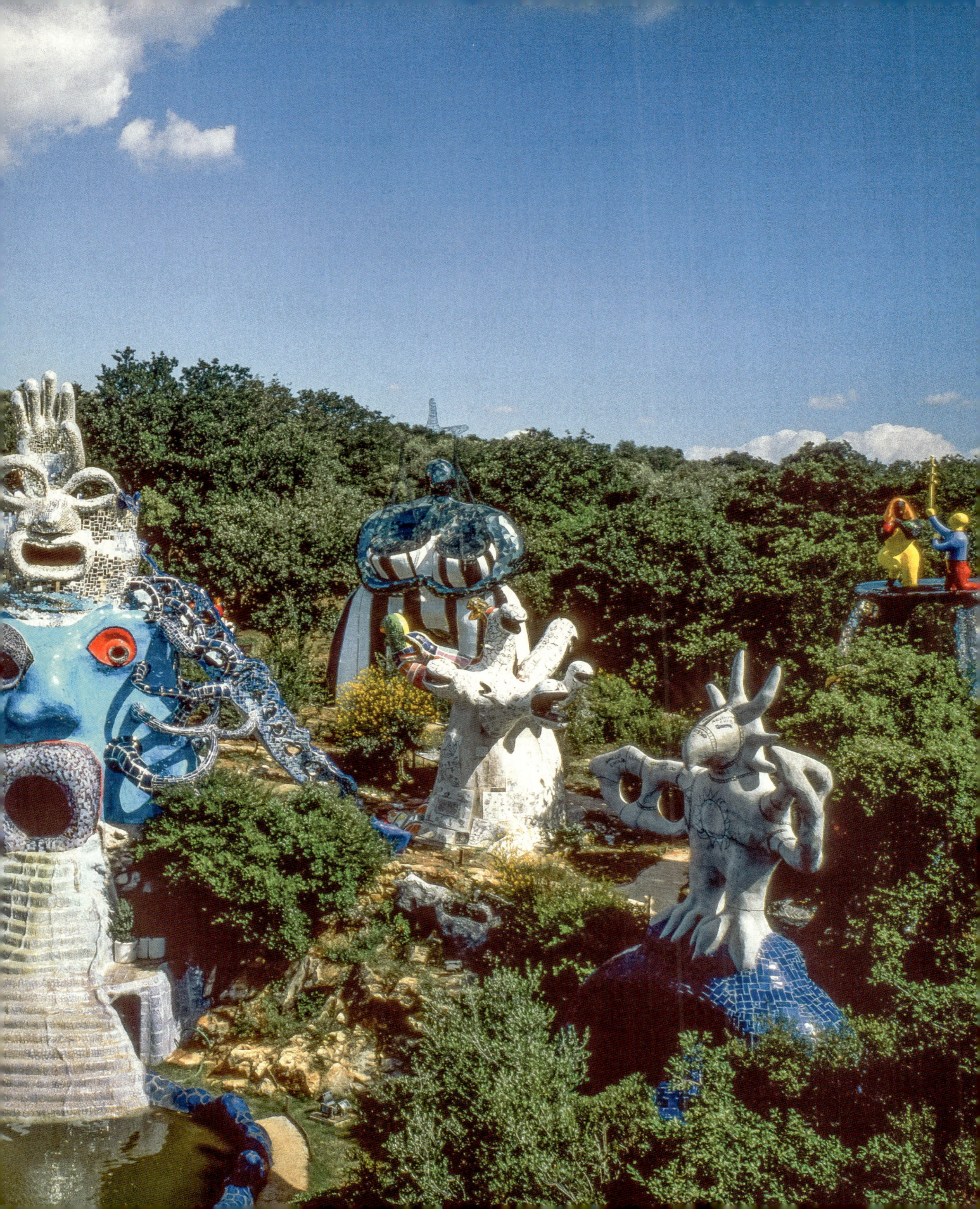

Tarot (The Devil), 1987
14 x 8 cm (5½ x 3³/₁₆ in.)
Published by Editions Acatos

Tarot (The Empress), 1987
14 x 8 cm (5½ x 3³/₁₆ in.)
Published by Editions Acatos

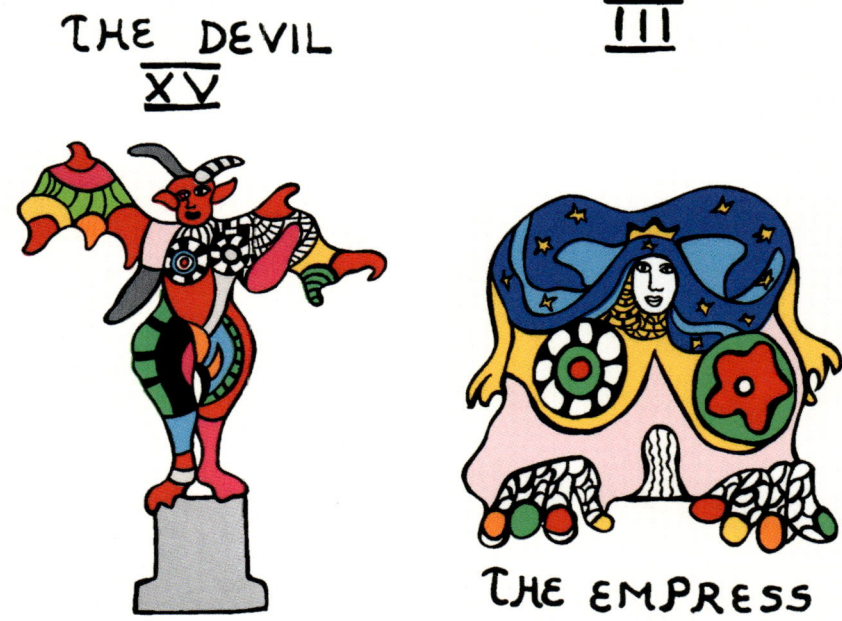

BELOW
View of Antoni Gaudí's Park Güell in Barcelona, Spain

The Emperor has a red, phallic rocket ship and chess piece aspects that give it a skyline like the Palau Güell. The Emperor also quotes Park Güell's esplanade, with its curving bench around a Greek theater.

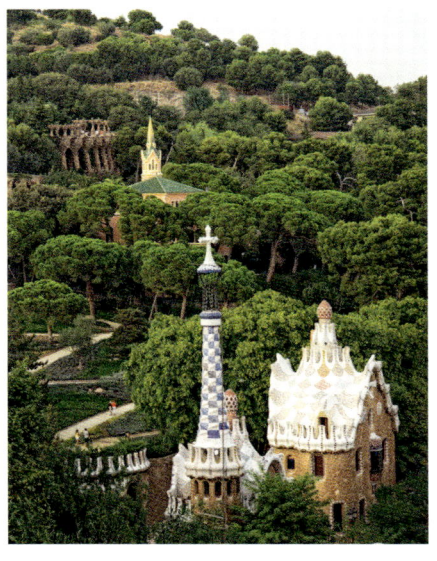

bright blue face with empty eye sockets and a round, open mouth. Although there is nothing notably feminine about it, this sculpture is called *The High Priestess* (she embodies card number two), and is evocative of dreams, intuition, and the subconscious. *The High Priestess* quotes the *Orcus Mouth* (p. 81) at Bomarzo in its proportions and facial features, but adds color. Vines grow out of the side of her face. Water pours from her mouth and cascades down shallow, softly widening, azure-patterned steps into a pool, where a kinetic fountain machine by Tinguely stands in the water and represents card number 10, the *Wheel of Fortune*. Appropriately for a water feature, the retaining wall of the pool undulates, covered with unique ripple-like pieces of blue tile, thus complementing and providing a resting place for the lively body of an enormous, multicolored snake that raises its head next to the top of the cascade steps, and whose tail is submerged. The snake pays tribute to Park Güell's step-guarding great lizard. Producing such irregularly shaped structures with complicated, nuanced surface detail was only made possible through the use of reinforced concrete. Ceramic, glass, and mirror pieces were embedded into the concrete using the *trencadis* technique. This consistent surface treatment throughout the park created patterning that unified the whole in its non-uniformity. Some discrete individual sculptures were made with painted polyester.

Slightly behind and stacked on top of *The High Priestess* floats yet another unearthly face, also with wide open features that are silvery and highly reflective. A shiny right hand emerges in greeting or benediction from the top of the equally shiny head, like a feather plume from a turban. This second face and hand represent *The Magician* (card number one), an archetype responsible for determination, skill, focus, and the manifesting of things. The hand refers to the "sleight of hand" of a magician; in the Rider–Waite–Smith tarot deck, the Magician raises a hand holding a wand to the sky. By combining the High Priestess and the Magician archetypes, and thus also male and female, Saint

Phalle commands both the instinctual imagination and the concentration of the visitor: the Tarot Garden will raise the big questions of life. *Strength* stands near to *The High Priestess* and *The Magician*, elevated by a stone outcropping. Her help will be needed. These figures, together with *The Empress* (card three), were the first to be created for the garden between 1980 and 1983, and define a semi-circular gathering space.

Sited on the ledge of the quarry amphitheater, *The Empress* guards her realm as a sentinel figure. The idea of the reclining sphinx as bedroom, conceived ten years previously for *The Bird's Dream*, is realized in *The Empress*, which became a habitable structure. Saint Phalle was able to move into it by 1983 and from then on operated from it as her headquarters, living in relative isolation with a German shepherd and, judging from some photos, a yellow labrador retriever. *The Empress* was not heated, and over the course of her work on the garden Saint Phalle developed debilitating rheumatoid arthritis, which made her work and her life painful. She depended on her assistant Ricardo Menon (1952–1989) for help with physical and personal tasks, as she was occasionally even unable to walk or care for herself.

The interior of *The Empress* gradually became more opulently decorated with Saint Phalle's personal iconography and angular mirror pieces. Her bedroom and bathroom, which had a showerhead shaped like a snake, occupied a breast, and the kitchen filled the other breast. Inside the many-faceted, reflective belly of *The Empress* stood the long, mirrored table she called the Monastery Table. That is where she made models, dined, and conferred. The table became the center of the studio/living room where she met employees and offered them food and

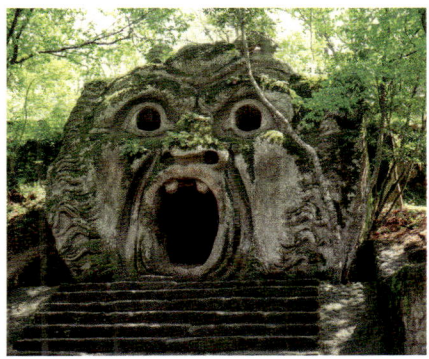

ABOVE
Simone Moschino, *Orcus Mouth,* 1550
Bomarzo, Italy

BELOW
Detail of **The Devil** in Tarot Garden. Photograph by Laurent Condominas

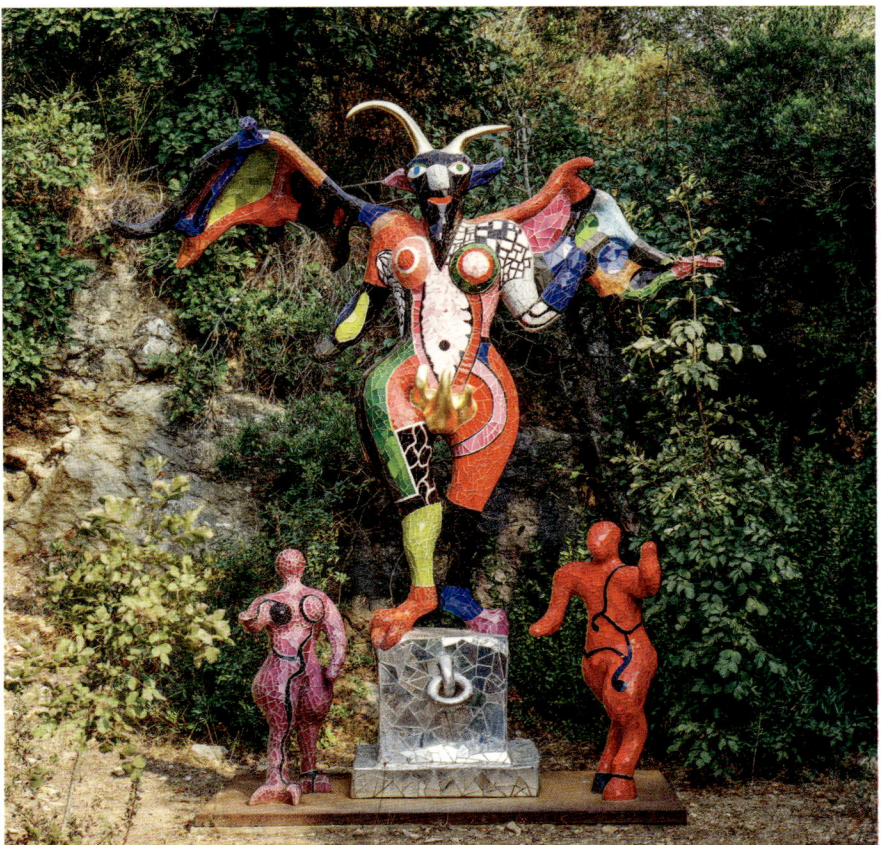

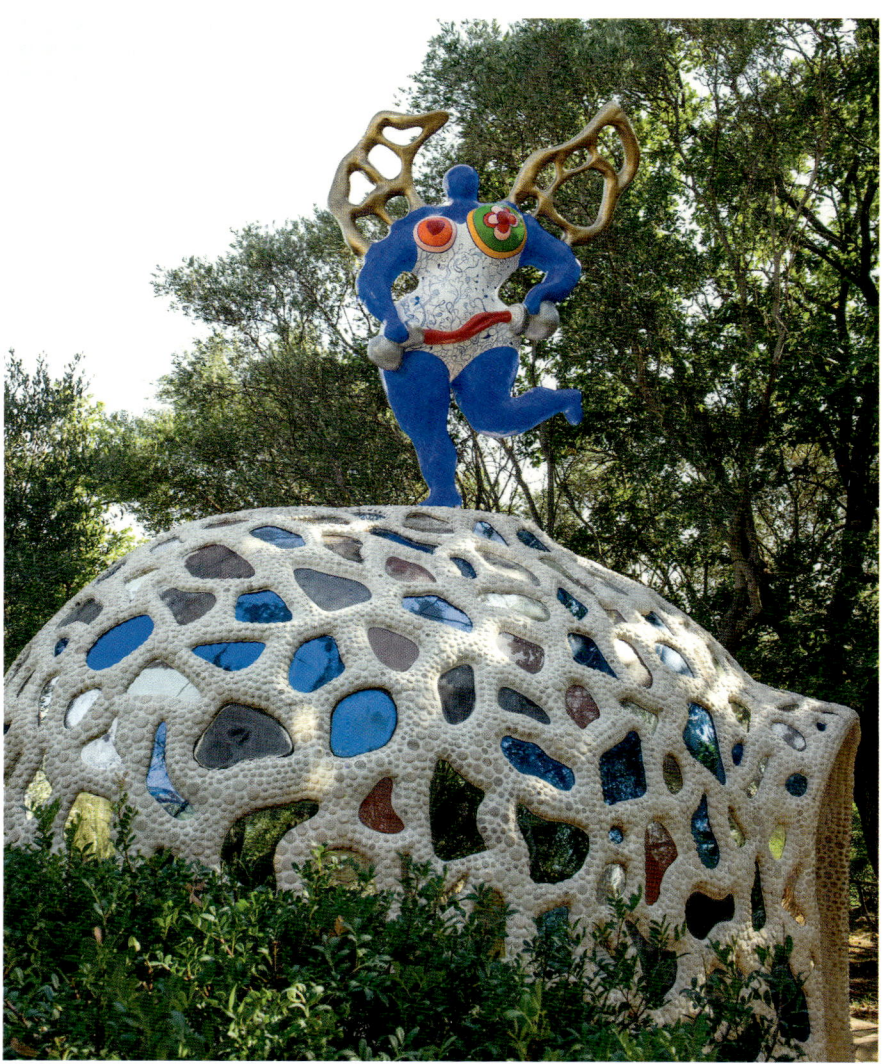

coffee breaks. The prismatic walls of the highly reflective room arc from its floor with the irregularity of a cave's interior, though the space also evokes an expressionist, Bruno Taut-inspired crystalline chapel with porthole windows. Saint Phalle believed it was possible to get her tough, macho Italian workmen to "impose her vision" on the garden if she treated them like a mother would, and she did this by gathering them around her table. However, the workers enjoyed the experience of being inside the work. "On all she exerted a fatal attraction," Saint Phalle said of *The Empress* in *The Tarot Garden* (1997), her handwritten artist's book about the project.[22]

Featured on the cover of the *Tarot Garden* book, *The Empress* has black skin and multicolored lion paws. She wears a small, bright red crown over a heavenly blue cloth sprinkled with many stars that flows over her back to her haunches. The sphinx's breasts are tiled with concentric rings of color; the nipples, which are also windows, are framed by a heart and a flower. Abundantly proportioned, the breasts appear to be popping out of a pink brocade dress, and are as multicolored as her paws. Although inspired by ancient mother goddesses in spirit, the sphinx is wearing a dress with a 1960s princess neckline, tastefully accessorized by a string of graduated beads. Solidly grounded and alert, *The Empress* exudes regal self-confidence. She holds court, more dignified than her sisters, the *Nanas*. Her imperative is color.

To enter the garden walk the visitor passes under a blue tile arch supporting a red and orange bird with a sunburst on its chest. As the creature that flies closest to the sun, Saint Phalle has made her bird the symbol for card number 19, The Sun, which traditionally also depicted a scene of joyful play in the foreground. After entering the garden, the visitor encounters the *Tree of Life*, and two paths behind it that force a choice. Which way? The walk is not predetermined. Tarot archetypes appear, the order of encounter determined by the visitor's choice of direction. In a sense, the encounter with a sculpted figure is like pulling a card. The interpretation of the encounters is left to the visitor, who may or may not know the meanings of the Major Arcana cards and may be happy enough just to see the works as sculptures. Following traditional depictions, Saint Phalle outlines *The Fool* in blue, crisscrosses his tunic with colorful lines, and gives him a walking stick and a red bundle tied to a stick over his shoulder. Also depicted as *Skinnys* are *The Hanged Man* (card 12), not executed but suspended by his ankle, and thus able to view the world differently from others and exist apart from it; and *The Moon* (card 18), which appears to be a self-portrait of Saint Phalle. *The Moon* looks up, questioningly and with hope, into the sky. Saint Phalle uses line to portray herself in profile, a drawing set into a landscape. Her page boy haircut takes the shape of a crescent moon, supported by a red crayfish, which in turn is supported by a wolf and a dog. These narrative elements are taken very literally from the Rider–Waite–Smith tarot pack Moon card, and even the sculpture's placement, further out from the center of the garden, seems to reflect the card's landscape imagery. The light wings of the flying, full-bodied *Temperance* are also "drawn" with the *Skinny* technique. *Temperance*, an angel, appeared later in a slightly different, suspended version called *Guardian Angel* in the main train station in Zurich (1997). Both figures pour a red liquid from jug to jug—in Zurich, sequenced lighting gives a dynamic illusion of flow. Saint Phalle designed the Zurich sculpture after she left Europe for California because her doctors told her the climate there would ease her breathing, and she donated *Guardian Angel* to the Swiss city. The tarot

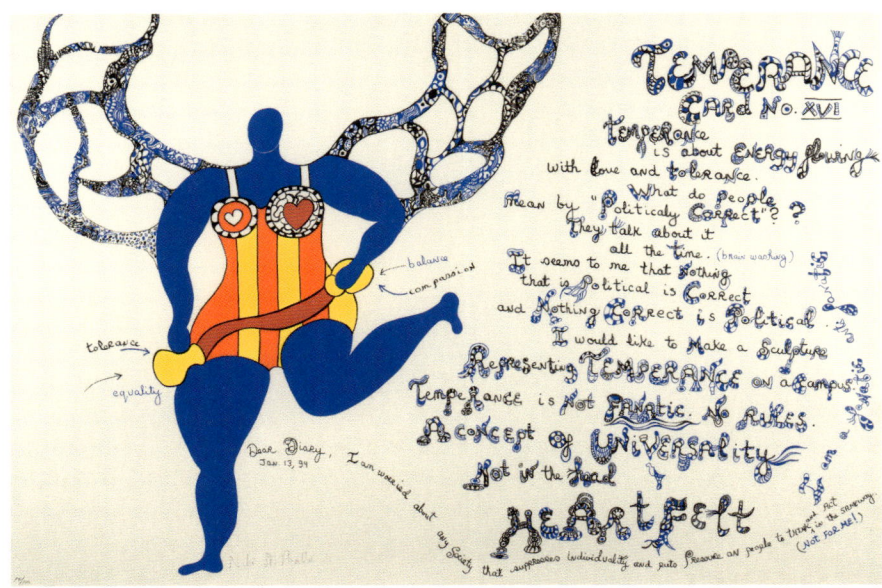

OPPOSITE
Temperance as installed in the Tarot Garden in Garavicchio, Italy

LEFT
California Diary: Temperance, 1994
Serigraph print,
80.4 x 119.8 cm (31⅝ x 47³⁄₁₆ in.)
Nice, MAMAC Collection

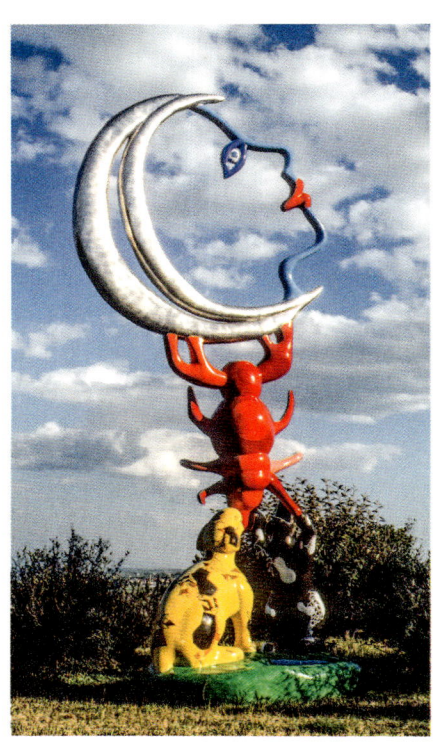

Temperance card, with its meanings of peace, moderation, and balance, may have been most appropriate to Switzerland's tradition of neutrality.

In Tarot Garden, *The Falling Tower* (card 16) and *The Emperor* (card 4) stand adjacent to each other. Both of them are masculine cards. Saint Phalle does not depict them as character figures, but more abstractly as architecture. *The Falling Tower*, also sometimes called the *Tower of Babel*, has a formal predecessor in Bomarzo's *Leaning House*. The top of Saint Phalle's tower has been shaved off by a "bolt of lightning" that sticks out of the building, and this is embodied by a black metal kinetic sculpture that Tinguely made. This structure was also habitable, and some of Saint Phalle's workers lived there during the construction phase of the garden.

Tarot Garden was intended to bring joy and inspire growth. Immeasurably appreciative of their help and friendship, Saint Phalle made sure that the workers would not be forgotten, so their names on tiles and their faces as ceramic masks were built into Tarot Garden. In November of 1993, two years after Tinguely passed away and five years before Tarot Garden officially opened, Saint Phalle moved to San Diego, California, on the recommendation of a doctor. She had to complete the final details of Tarot Garden mostly from a distance, visiting the site about twice a year. Saint Phalle would live for almost another decade and continue to design other public sculpture venues and many individual works of art. However, Tarot Garden stands as her crowning achievement, a cosmos of sculptures dedicated to an esoteric meditation on life's choices.

ABOVE
The Moon as seen in the Tarot Garden.
Photograph by Laurent Condominas

RIGHT
Sphinx, 1978
Painted polyester,
30 x 28 x 28 cm (11¹³⁄₁₆ x 11 x 11 in.)
Hanover, Sprengel Museum

OPPOSITE
The Empress as seen in the Tarot Garden.
Photograph by Laurent Condominas

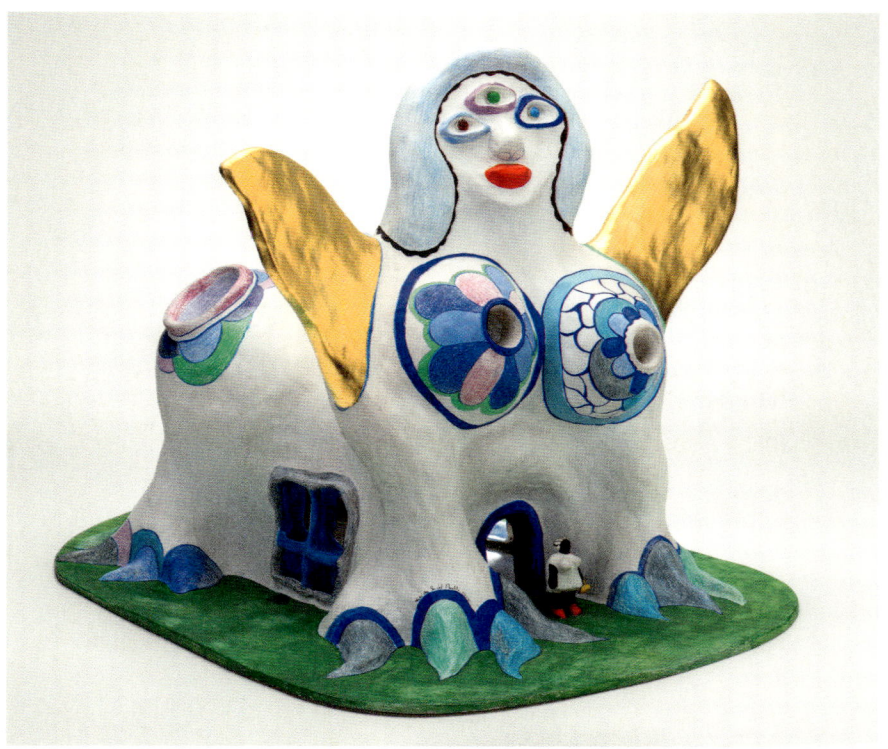

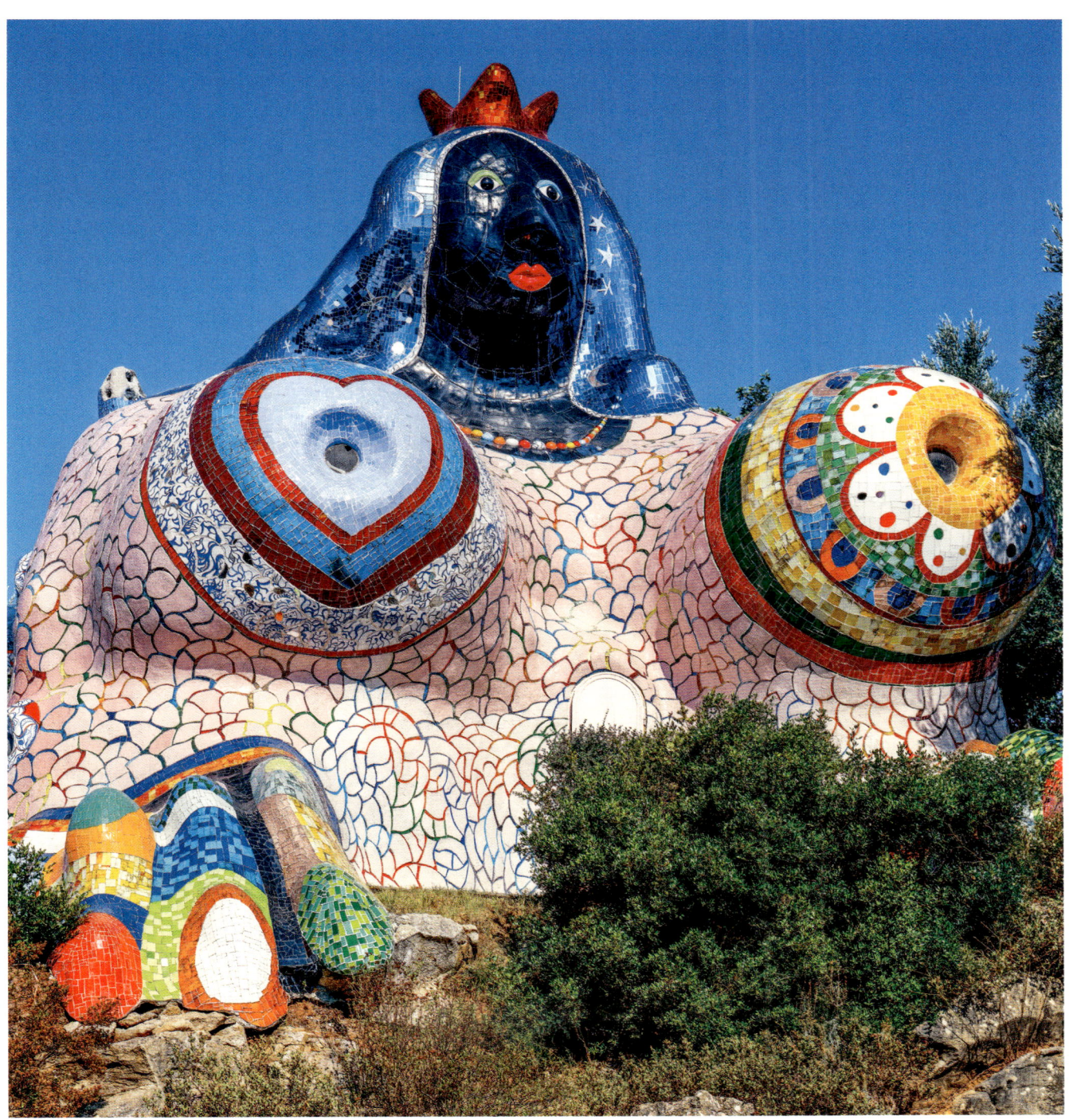

Niki de Saint Phalle

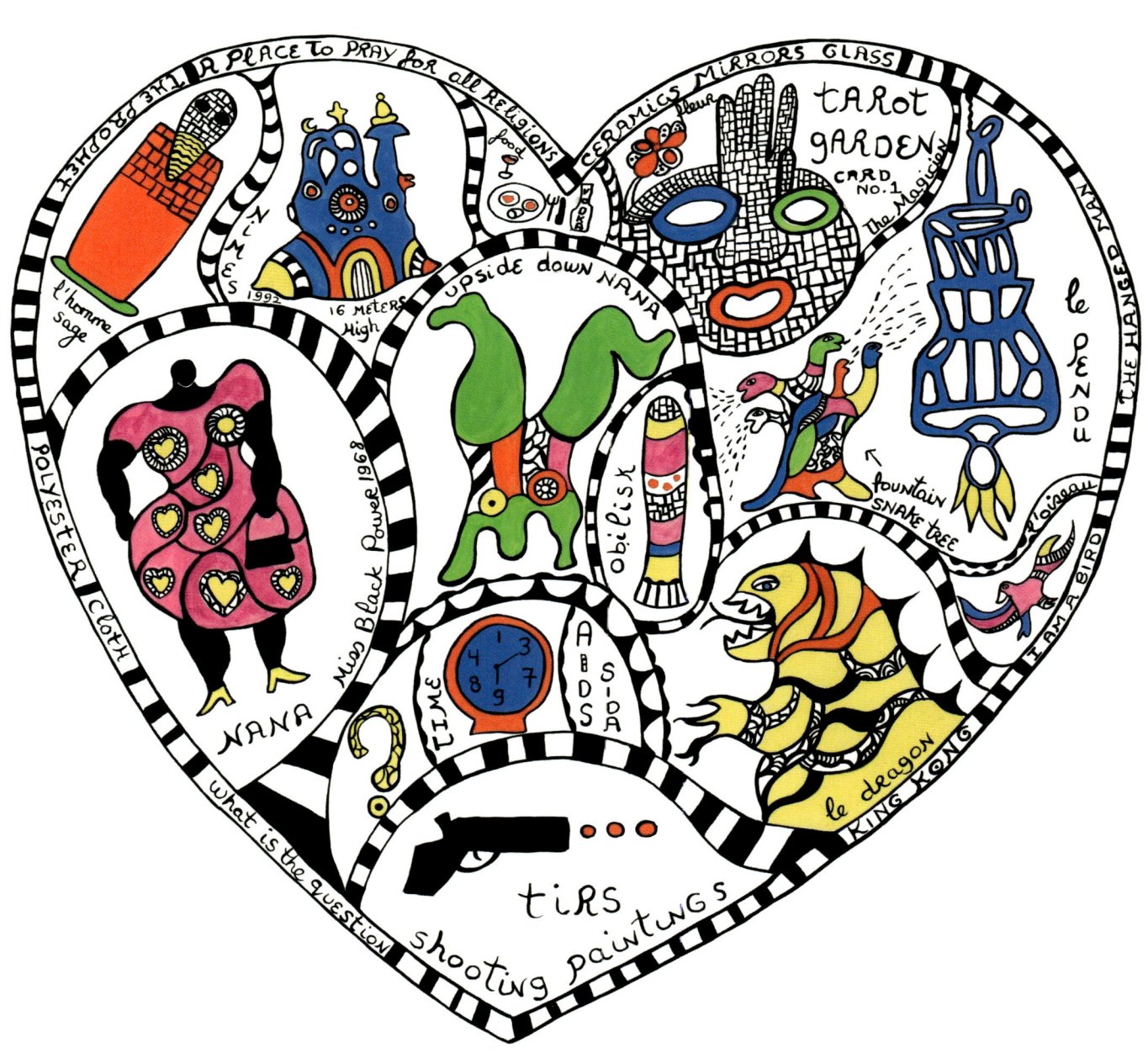

A Wild, Wild Weed

As a child, Saint Phalle had loved penmanship in school, and she never lost her enjoyment of the physical act of handwriting. Her writing unspooled from her pen as she talked to herself or an imaginary other. She left it as it arrived, correcting it with carets and cross-outs, and boosting it with drawings. Saint Phalle told the story of her own life in illustrated artists' books, which were mass produced. *Traces* (1999, p.13) and *Harry and Me: The Family Years* (2006, p. 87) use handwritten and typed text and many photographs and drawings to tell her story in an engaging way. *Mon Secret* (1994, p.89), about her childhood sexual abuse, takes the form of a handwritten letter to her daughter, Laura, with only two illustrations, on the cover and title page.

These books surprise and enthrall the reader through the insight they give into the artist's mind, but also because they are colorful and unpretentious, generous and empathetic. In 1968, when Saint Phalle was hospitalized for one of her many illnesses, a doctor asked her to produce a silkscreen to raise funds for cancer research. That silkscreen print became her first "letter." She found the work so entertaining that she continued with it and made a whole series of epistolary silkscreen prints. She enjoyed disguising her texts as handwritten letters to friends, allies, and family members, dead or alive—letters that were never sent to them but summoned them in her mind as she addressed them. Saint Phalle worked well when she was talking with someone she loved. The "letter writing" parallels her delight in collaboration and explains why she assembled loyal families of collaborators to help her realize her projects. Saint Phalle returns again and again to her central themes of love, family dysfunction, the emancipation of the self, the power of women, the need to overcome war and destruction as cultural givens, and increasingly as she ages, love again, protecting, and giving joy. Her books reveal her inhibitions, her feelings about her body, her emotional vulnerabilities. They communicate a sense of touch, with color marking the touch spots: people touching people, monsters and snakes seeking to touch people, flowers begging to be touched. Her graphic production often looks like another incarnation of her books, or vice versa.

The Devouring Mothers, printed in Milan but made for the London gallery Gimple Fils in 1972, had 26 color plates between two cardboard covers. It was bound only by two punched holes secured with twine. It pretended on the first page to be an innocent children's book, but the vignettes are hardly for children.

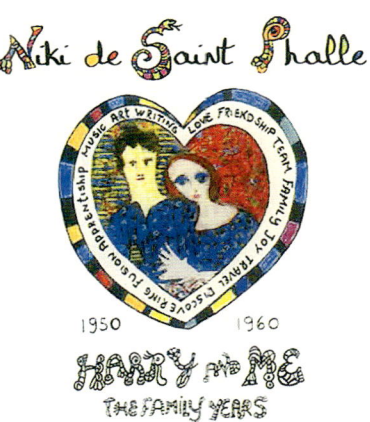

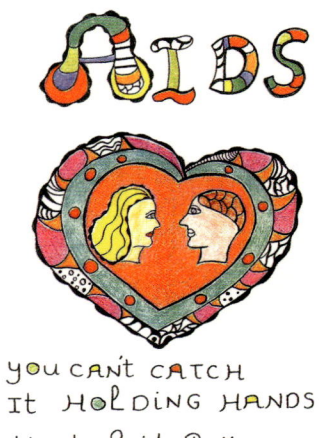

It successfully drives home Saint Phalle's idea that families devour themselves from within.

Sometimes Saint Phalle helped enhance catalogues written by museum directors and curators. One example of this is a small publication produced for an early retrospective exhibition of her works organized by the Lehmbruck Museum in Duisburg, Germany (1980). Although the museum concentrates on 20th-century sculpture, particularly that of Wilhelm Lehmbruck, the curators chose to exhibit a complete overview of Saint Phalle's work in all media. However, Saint Phalle emphasized the primacy of three dimensionality in her work by having the catalogue's white cardstock cover die cut in the shape of a blue, dancing *Nana* wearing a colorful bathing suit so that the *Nana* could pop up. Through a second cut on the inside flap of the cover, a small tab can be pushed up to hold her in a position perpendicular to the cover, like a paper doll with a folded stand. At the opening of the Lehmbruck Museum retrospective, which went on to travel through four other German museums, Saint Phalle autographed catalogue covers along the curve of *Nana's* left leg for those lucky enough to attend. A small detail like this shows the love she put into her work, and how she reached out to a public unable to afford more substantial works. *Nana* "stood up" as a symbol of personal freedom in every conceptual version of herself.

Saint Phalle made one very important book in 1987 as a public service. She wrote the book together with the Swiss immunologist Silvio Barandun, in the guise of a letter to her son Philip, which made it seem motherly and concerned, not coldly scientific. *AIDS: You Can't Catch It Holding Hands* (p. 88) was about the international AIDS crisis and offered practical, preventative, frank, and even humorous advice. The book set out the facts. As a sexy, non-scolding voice of reason, Saint Phalle produced a colorful picture book with handwritten explanations that also gave courage to journalists trying to educate the public about the disease on television and radio. Because she addressed the book to her son, she acknowledged publicly that he might be at risk.

ABOVE
AIDS: You Can't Catch It Holding Hands, 1987
Artist's book, 20 x 25 cm (7⅞ x 9¹³⁄₁₆ in.)
Published by Lapis Press, Culver City, California

BELOW
My Love, 1971
Artist's book, each page 19 x 19 cm
(7½ x 7½ in.)
Published by Gallimard, Paris

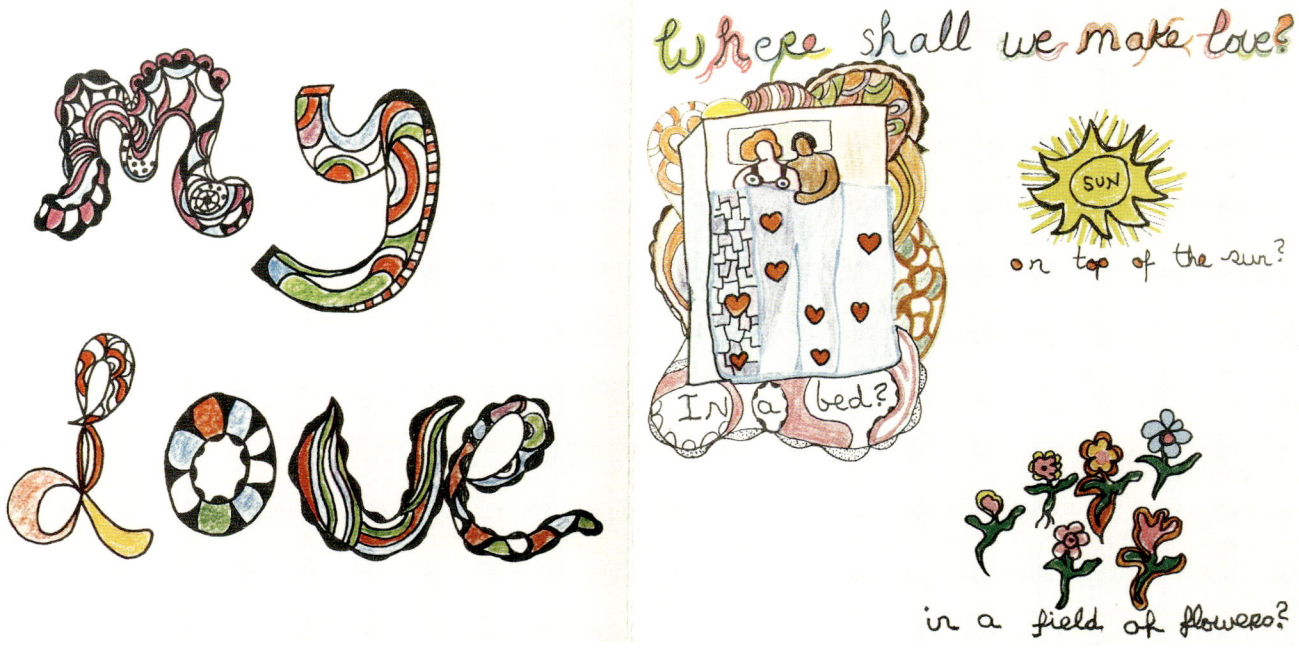

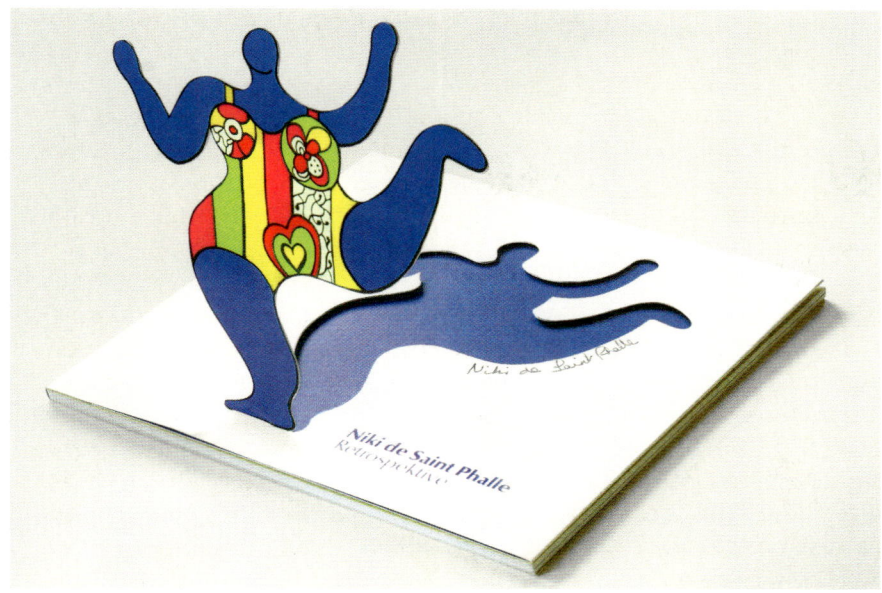

LEFT
Niki de Saint Phalle, 1976
Artist's book, 15 x 18 cm (5¹⁵⁄₁₆ x 7¹⁄₁₆ in.)
Published by Lehmbruck Museum, Duisburg

BELOW
Mon Secret, 1994
Cover for artist's book,
65.5 x 42.5 cm (25¹³⁄₁₆ x 16¾ in.)
Published by des femmes, Paris

Saint Phalle's large, rounded handwriting and
her drawings—somewhat akin to doodling—go
hand in hand. As she pens text, she may stop
and let people and animals, real and fantastic,
form on the page, as well as flowers, trees, and
buildings. The forms of the letters and the creatures mirror each other. She "illuminates" her
texts in the spirit of medieval manuscripts, or a
storyboard for the film of her life.

AIDS haunted the art world, especially from the late 1980s onwards, before
medication made it a treatable disease. Saint Phalle's gallerist Alexander Iolas died
of AIDS in 1987. Karl-Egon Vester, one of the curators of the 1980 Saint Phalle
retrospective at the Lehmbruck Museum, died of the disease in 1988 in Hamburg,
where he had become director of the Hamburger Kunstverein, never having
made his infection public. Saint Phalle's assistant Ricardo Menon, who at first hid
his infection from her and then moved away, died in 1989 in Paris. Artist Keith
Haring, who had once stayed in Saint Phalle's *Dragon of Knokke* and obtained her
permission to paint a mural inside it, died of the chronic condition in 1990. These
are only some of the people who died of AIDS whose lives had touched Saint
Phalle's. By the late 1980s, numerous individuals in the art world were infected
and fear reigned in many quarters. The public often shunned those perceived as
gay or ill, even when they were dying. *AIDS: You Can't Catch It Holding Hands*
was an early, brave book that destigmatized the disease, informed people, and
gave the public behavioral suggestions. You will need these, as Saint Phalle said
in the book, "if you're no angel." Published in English, it was translated into four
other languages and distributed widely to schools in France.

The cover of *AIDS: You Can't Catch It Holding Hands* features a heart that
encloses the profiles of a heterosexual white couple, face to face. Saint Phalle
intentionally makes the cover look like a homemade Valentine's Day card. The
colors pop off the clean white background and the handwritten title makes
it seem friendly, easy to read. The book starts off with "Dear Philip," and she
begins by telling her son what she has learned from the doctor. The reader then
turns the page to find a threatening green dragon—the kind of monster Saint
Phalle has often pictured as something that can be overcome by strength of
will. The book ends with love and kisses and a sprinkling of hearts. Saint Phalle
would go on to ask her son to make an animated film of the book; a series of
animated public service announcements were also made for France. She continued to assist in the STOP AIDS campaign by decorating a giant condom for an
AIDS information bus and making a series of erect, condom-covered, phallus-
shaped sculptures. A drawing by Saint Phalle of a colorful, erect condom featured on a Swiss postal stamp in 1994. She designed grave markers for two men

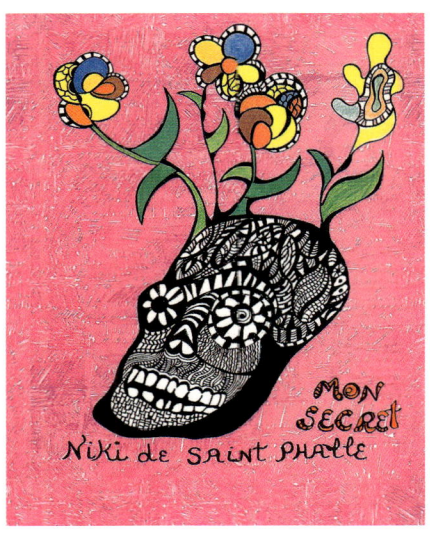

who died of AIDS: Menon and Jean-Jacques Goetzman, the latter of whom had been cared for by her son. Both men are buried at the Cimetière Montparnasse in Paris.

Saint Phalle had already made a book about love in 1971. The Moderna Museet in Stockholm published the book in the form of a leporello (a folded accordion-pleat style volume). Called *My Love* (p. 88), the cover is almost identical to the later AIDS book cover, although the couple within the heart are pictured with different skin colors—love can be interracial. The book's touching images reproduce Saint Phalle's original black marker and colored pencil drawings. The reader follows Saint Phalle's all-consuming passion page by page, seeing all the tender things she has enjoyed with her lover, until a recurring bad dream (a dragon) interrupts her thoughts. When the dragon returns, heartache ensues. The book shifts into a "remember" mode, as if something is over. Towards the end of her life, Saint Phalle called her work her "secret jealous lover."[23] She compared work to Count Dracula, always waiting in a long black cape. With *The Night Bat* (1983–86), she assembled a creature of the night, half marked by death and devourings, and half capable of transcending those things with color as it takes wing.

Her designs for public sculpture, playgrounds, and parks were overshadowed by the constant production of smaller-scale work for galleries. After settling in in California, Saint Phalle began her *Californian Diary* (1993–94), a folio of eight silkscreen prints in which she responded to her new life and the landscape around her in La Jolla. On one print she inscribes diaristic entries into the depicted hillsides, as well as telling what she knows of the mythical story of Queen Califia, who formed and ruled California. As a visual diary, the folio is talkative, presenting an open conversation with herself. Saint Phalle chose Queen Califia as the subject of her last major sculptural garden project. *Queen Califia's Magical Circle* (p. 91) honored the Black warrior queen who ruled over a mythical realm—the "island" of California—and led a Black warrior tribe who lived like Amazons without men. The original source for Califia's story was the kind of tome Saint Phalle appreciated: *The Adventures of Esplandián* by Garci Rodríguez de Montalvo, a Spanish epic novel of chivalry from the 16th century.

"I have been a wild, wild weed. Done everything."

– TRACES: AN AUTOBIOGRAPHY (1999)

Wounded Animals, 1988
Artist's book, 22 x 24 cm (8¹¹⁄₁₆ x 9⁷⁄₁₆ in.)
Published by Gimpel Fils, London

I have always been crazy about b i r d s ever since I can remember. I wanted to have one of my own.
This I managed to have when I was six years old. I refused to learn to read until my father offered me a bird as soon as I could read. I learned to read almost immediately.
Unfortunately all my birds have an unhappy ending and that is why I don't own any today.
One spring night when I was twelve years old I left my bird in its cage in the garden: an animal came and ate him. There were only some bones and feathers left in the morning.
I felt like a murderess.
Later I was to fall in love with falcons and a falconer.
Birds have been a constant theme in my work. Immortal birds. Sad birds. Triumphant birds. The Hungry bird.
When my father died in 1967 of a heart attack I made a portrait of him in his coffin. Next to him a red bird was crucified on a golden cross.
In the Skinnys Sculptures there are birds, in the Strawinsky Fountain there are two birds. In the Tarot Garden a huge joyous bird is uses as the symbol of Card N° XIX, the S U N
This spring of 1988 I have made a relief in ceramic and glass of
The p h e n i x resurrecting from the sea.
I have also a bird in flight one of whose wings has been shot. Birds are messengers from our world to the next.
My Guardian Angel is a bird.

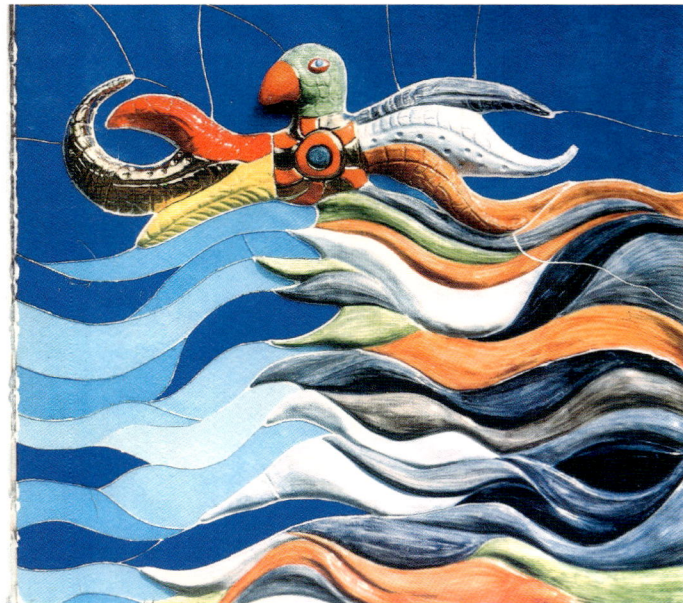

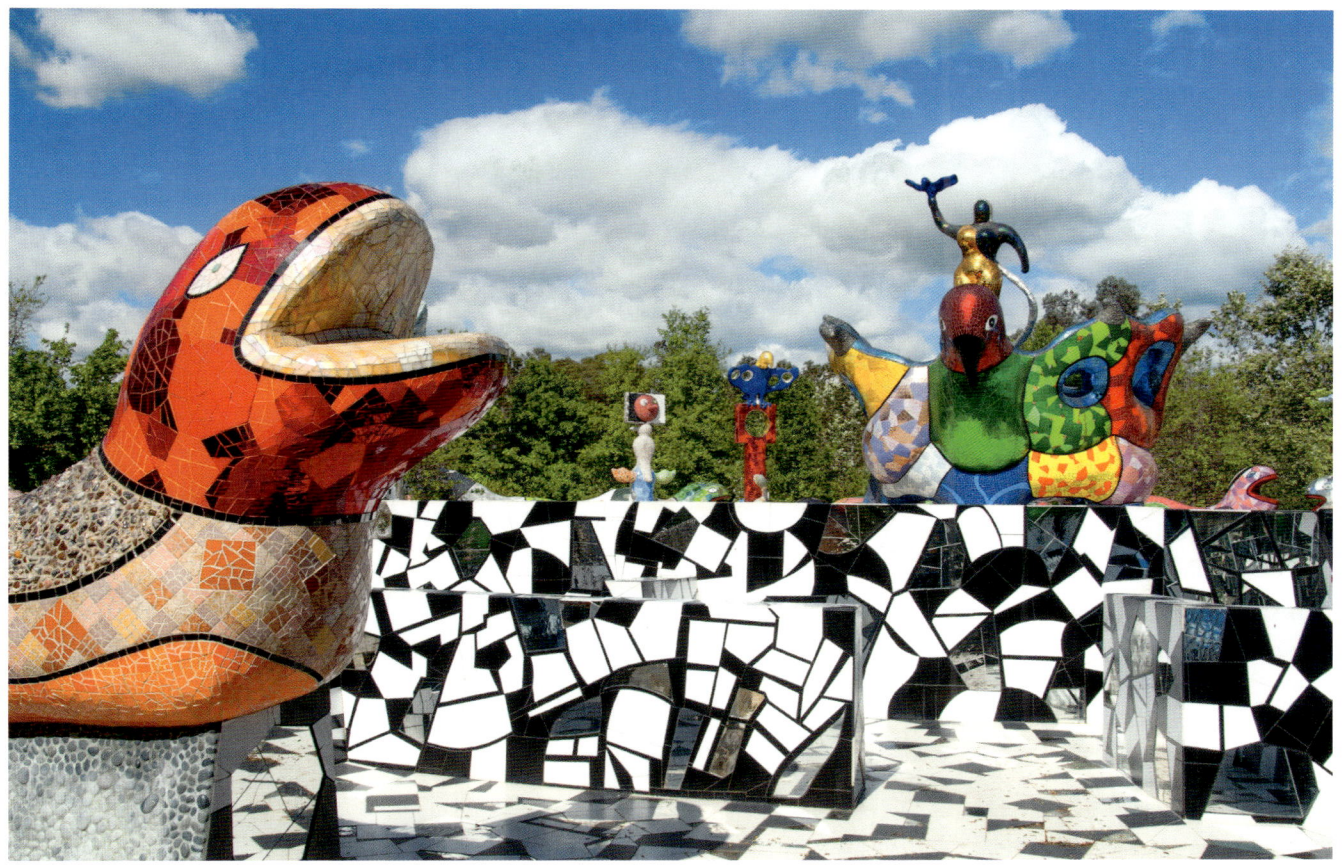

Queen Califia's Magical Circle, 2003
Escondido, California

The great Queen Califia stands 11 feet (about 335 cm) high on a 13-foot-tall (about 396 cm), five-legged eagle in the center of the garden, holding aloft a small blue bird. Openings between the eagle's legs allow the visitor to stand under a shaded space, something like an outdoor pavilion chapel with a ceiling symbolic of heaven. A golden egg fountain fills the center of the space. Totem figures inspired by Pacific coast, pre-Columbian, and Mexican art surround Queen Califia and her eagle.

The park was Saint Phalle's gift of thanks to California for granting her more time. It opened to the public in October 2003, a little more than a year after Saint Phalle's death and just a few days short of what would have been her 72nd birthday. Niki de Saint Phalle, who had been born with her umbilical cord wrapped around her neck, died of a chronic respiratory ailment on May 21, 2002, surrounded by her children and her first husband, Harry Mathews. Saint Phalle wanted no gravesite, and her daughter, Laura, scattered her ashes in the Pacific Ocean.

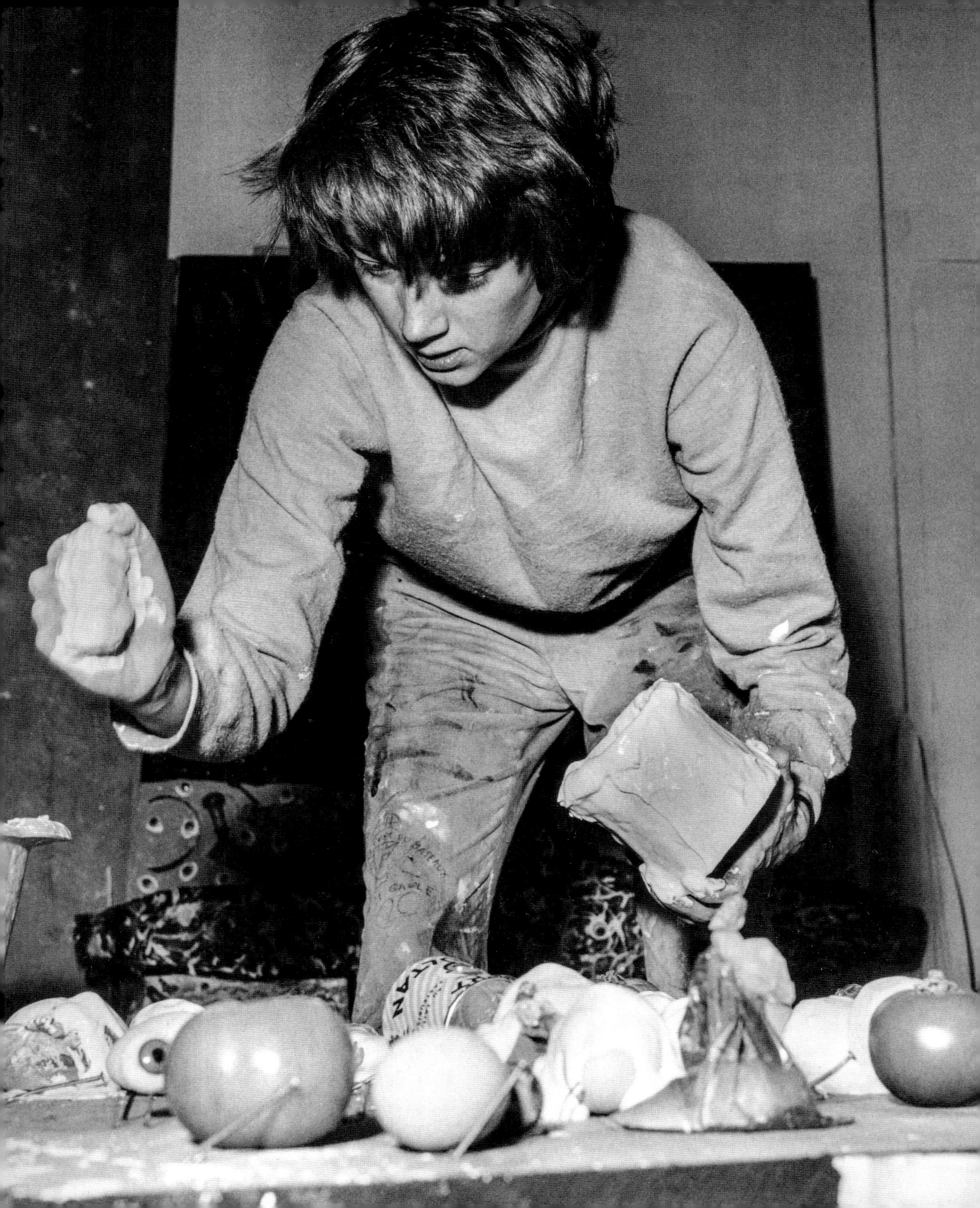

Niki de Saint Phalle
1930–2002
Life and Work

1930 Catherine Marie-Agnès Fal de Saint Phalle is born in Neuilly-sur-Seine, France, as the second of what will become a family of five children. Her parents are Jeanne Jacqueline (born Harper) and Count André-Marie Fal de Saint Phalle. Saint Phalle's mother changes Marie-Agnès's name to "Niki" in 1934.

1936–41 The family lives in New York on the Upper East Side. She writes the play *Meat Without Coupons.*

1942 Saint Phalle matriculates at the Brearley School. She develops an anti-authoritarian personality. After entering a third and then a fourth school, she finishes her secondary education in 1947.

1948–51 Saint Phalle works as a fashion model for *Life, Vogue, Elle,* and *Harper's Bazaar.* When she turns 18, she elopes with Harry Mathews, and they move to Cambridge, Massachusetts, where she studies theater and acting. Their first child is born in 1951, a girl named Laura.

1952–55 After the Mathewses move to Paris in 1952, they travel to cathedrals and museums and lead a bohemian life. In 1953 Niki Mathews has a nervous breakdown diagnosed as schizophrenia, which is treated in Nice, France, using electroshock and insulin treatments. Making art becomes part of her therapy, and she resolves to become an artist. A son, Philip, is born in 1955 on the Spanish island of Mallorca. After returning to Paris, she and her husband get to know the artist couple Jean Tinguely and Eva Aeppli in the Impasse Ronsin, which houses many artist studios.

OPPOSITE
Saint Phalle in the studio at Impasse Ronsin, 1961. Photograph by Shunk-Kender

RIGHT
Saint Phalle with (from left to right): Bloum, Laura, and Jacqueline de Saint Phalle, La Commanderie, 1973. Photograph by Laurent Condominas

1956–58 Niki Mathews has her first one-person show at Galerie Gotthard, St. Gallen, Switzerland and shows works mostly painted on Mallorca. In 1958, for her health, Niki Mathews and her family move to Lans-en-Vercors in the French Alps.

1960 Niki Mathews separates from her husband and their children; they move out. The artist assumes her maiden name. She starts working on assemblages featuring sharp implements and weapons as well as toys. She begins her target assemblages. By the end of the year, Saint Phalle has moved in with Tinguely in the Impasse Ronsin, where they share a studio. She meets curator Pontus Hultén.

1961 Saint Phalle's target assemblages give way to the *Tirs,* or *Shooting Paintings.* Pierre Restany invites Saint Phalle to join the New Realists; she becomes the only female member of the group. Saint Phalle participates in the group show *Moving Movement* curated by Tinguely, Spoerri, and Hultén at the Stedelijk Museum, Amsterdam.

She has a solo show at the short-lived Galerie J in Paris, co-founded by married couple Restany and Jeanine de Goldschmidt. Marcel Duchamp

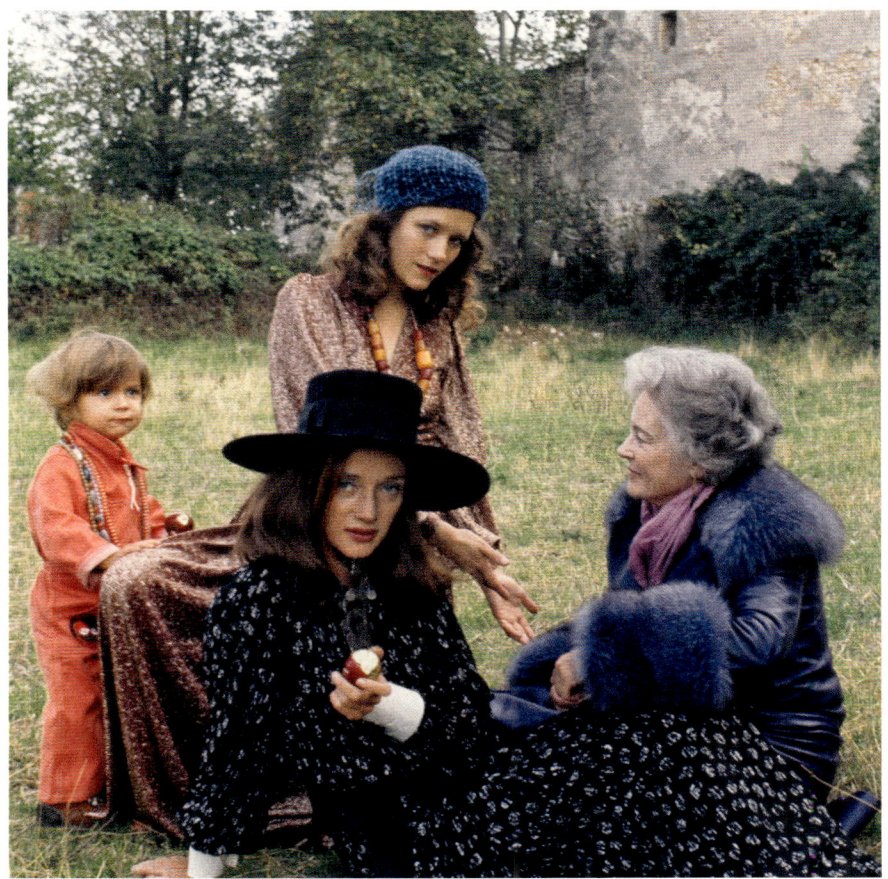

introduces Saint Phalle and Tinguely to Salvador Dalí in Spain, where they participate in a Dalí celebration by exploding a papier-mâché bull in a public bullfighting arena. Saint Phalle participates in *The Art of Assemblage* at the Museum of Modern Art in New York.

1962 Saint Phalle and Tinguely travel to California. The Everett Ellin Gallery in Los Angeles sponsors her first shooting action in the United States. Installation artist Edward Kienholz helps Saint Phalle by organizing a second shooting event at the Malibu home of gallerist Virginia Dwan. Saint Phalle assists Tinguely with a happening in the Nevada desert that is broadcast by television channel NBC. She appears in the play *The Construction of Boston* by Kenneth Koch. At a one-person show in Paris, Saint Phalle's work attracts the notice of gallerist Alexander Iolas, who offers her an exhibition in New York that takes place in October. Saint Phalle collaborates with Robert Rauschenberg, Tinguely, Per Olof Ultvedt, and others on the exhibition *Dylaby* in Amsterdam.

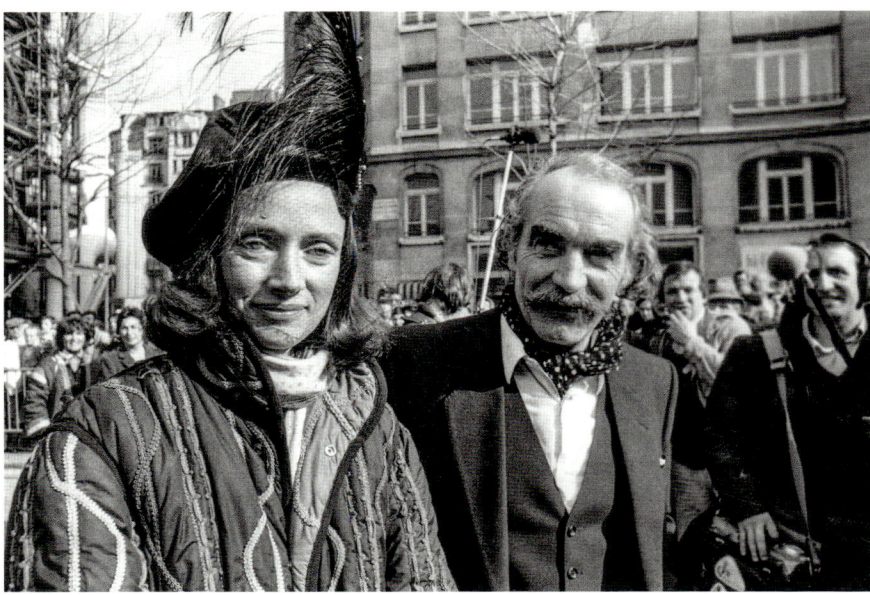

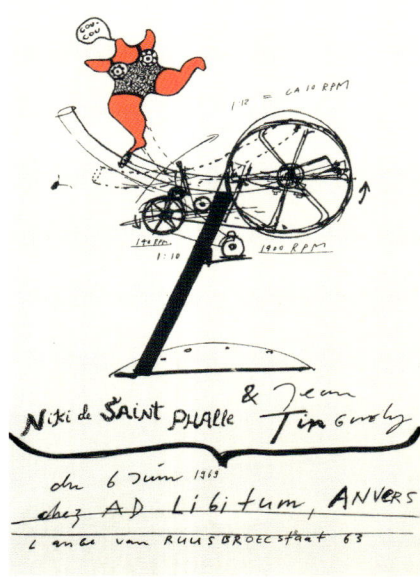

1963–64 Saint Phalle is invited to exhibit at the Dwan Gallery in Los Angeles and works on her assemblage/painting *King Kong* there. She and Tinguely move their studios to Soisy-sur-École, outside of Paris. Saint Phalle begins to make assemblages featuring single female torsos, then shifts to three-dimensional tableaux, including assemblages of brides. Saint Phalle and Harry Mathews officially divorce.

1965 In April, inspired by her friend Clarice Rivers's pregnancy and working with her daughter, Laura, Saint Phalle begins the *Nana* series using papier-mâché and textile materials. The Alexander Iolas Gallery in Paris gives the first showing of the *Nanas*.

1966 Saint Phalle collaborates with Tinguely and Ultvedt on *Hon–En katedral (She–a Cathedral)* at the Moderna Museet in Stockholm, a sculpture/building in the shape of a reclining female that can be entered through her vagina. In Stockholm Saint Phalle and Tinguely get to know artist Rico Weber, who will become a long-term production assistant. Saint Phalle collaborates on ballet and theater productions with her sculptures and costume designs.

1967 Commissioned by the French government, Saint Phalle and Tinguely collaborate on a sculptural installation, *The Fantastic Paradise*, for Expo 67 in Montreal, Canada. Saint Phalle begins working with polyester as a medium for this project. The Stedelijk Museum organizes her first one-person show in a museum, *Nana Power*, which includes the architectural *Nana Dream House* and *Nana Fountain*.

1968 Saint Phalle writes the theater piece *ICH: All About Me* with Rainer von Hessen (a.k.a. Rainer von Diez).

1969–70 Saint Phalle works on the outdoor summer residence *The Bird's Dream* for von Hessen. She travels to Morocco, India, and Egypt.

1971 Saint Phalle and Tinguely marry and travel to Morocco together, although they live apart and have other romantic alliances. Saint Phalle becomes a Swiss citizen through her marriage and a first-time grandmother when her daughter, Laura, has a child with Laurent Condominas. She designs her first pieces of jewelry and exhibits works called *The Devouring Mothers*.

1972 She completes a commission for a children's playground in Jerusalem: *The Golem*, a monster with three tongues as slides, one for each of the city's major religions.

1973 Saint Phalle constructs the children's playhouse *The Dragon of Knokke* for a Belgian collector. Saint Phalle and Peter Whitehead work on a second version of *Daddy*, which is shown at the 11th New York Film Festival.

1974 Saint Phalle makes a model for a church, *The Ideal Temple or Church for All Religions*, designed to combat religious intolerance. Saint Phalle is hospitalized in Bern for a serious lung illness.

1975–77 The artist recuperates in Switzerland, where she runs into her friend Marella Caracciolo Agnelli in St. Moritz. Agnelli offers land in Tuscany that belongs to her brothers as a possible site for Saint Phalle's *Tarot Garden*, which will become the artist's main project for the next 20 years. Saint Phalle writes, directs, and acts in her film *A Dream Longer than the Night*, working together with her daughter, Tinguely, and other artist friends. She designs furniture and props for the film. Tarot Garden takes shape in her mind. She meets Ricardo Menon, who becomes her personal assistant.

1978–96 Saint Phalle designs and begins to produce Tarot Garden, which will include 22 monumental sculptures.

1982 Saint Phalle designs a perfume bottle and scent for Jacqueline Cochran Cosmetics in New York, the sale of which will help to finance Tarot Garden.

1983 Saint Phalle moves into *The Empress* in Tarot Garden. She and Tinguely design the *Stravinsky Fountain* for a site next to the Centre Pompidou in Paris.

1986–87 Saint Phalle writes and illustrates *AIDS: You Can't Catch It Holding Hands*, published in lished in 1987. She works with her son Philip on an animated film based on the book.

1991 Saint Phalle designs *The Ideal Temple,* a large-size maquette for an architectural project that was never finished. In August, Tinguely dies in Switzerland, and Saint Phalle will make *Meta-Tinguelys,* kinetic sculpture/pictures that honor him.

1994 Saint Phalle moves to La Jolla, California, for her health. Peter Schamoni films a documentary about her, *Niki de Saint Phalle: Who is the Monster, You or Me?* (released 1995). She publishes her book *Mon Secret.*

1998 Tarot Garden opens officially to the public in May. Saint Phalle and Mario Botta design a children's park in Jerusalem based on Noah's Ark, for which she makes the animals. Saint Phalle writes her autobiography, *Traces.*

1999 *Traces* is published and Saint Phalle starts to write the second volume of her autobiography, *Harry and Me: The Family Years,* which will only appear in English in 2006, after her death.

2000 Saint Phalle introduces a model for *Queen Califia's Magical Circle* for a public park in Escondido, California. She donates a representative selection of over 360 of her works to the Sprengel Museum in Hanover and becomes the first woman to be awarded honorary citizenship of the city.

2001 Saint Phalle donates almost 200 of her works to the Musée d'Art Moderne et d'Art Contemporain (MAMAC) in Nice.

2002 Saint Phalle's health worsens and she enters palliative care. She dies on May 21 from her chronic respiratory disorder, at the age of 71. Her ashes are scattered in the Pacific Ocean by her daughter, Laura.

2003 Inauguration of a 330-year-old grotto Saint Phalle redesigned in Hanover. *Queen Califia's Magical Circle* opens to the public.

OPPOSITE ABOVE
Saint Phalle with Jean Tinguely at the inauguration of the *Stravinsky Fountain*, Paris, March 16, 1983

OPPOSITE LEFT
Poster for exhibition of work by Niki de Saint Phalle and Jean Tinguely, 1969 43 x 30 cm (16 15/16 x 11 13/16 in.) Nice, MAMAC Collection

BELOW
Saint Phalle in her studio at work on the fountain of Château-Chinon, 1992. Photograph by Laurent Condominas

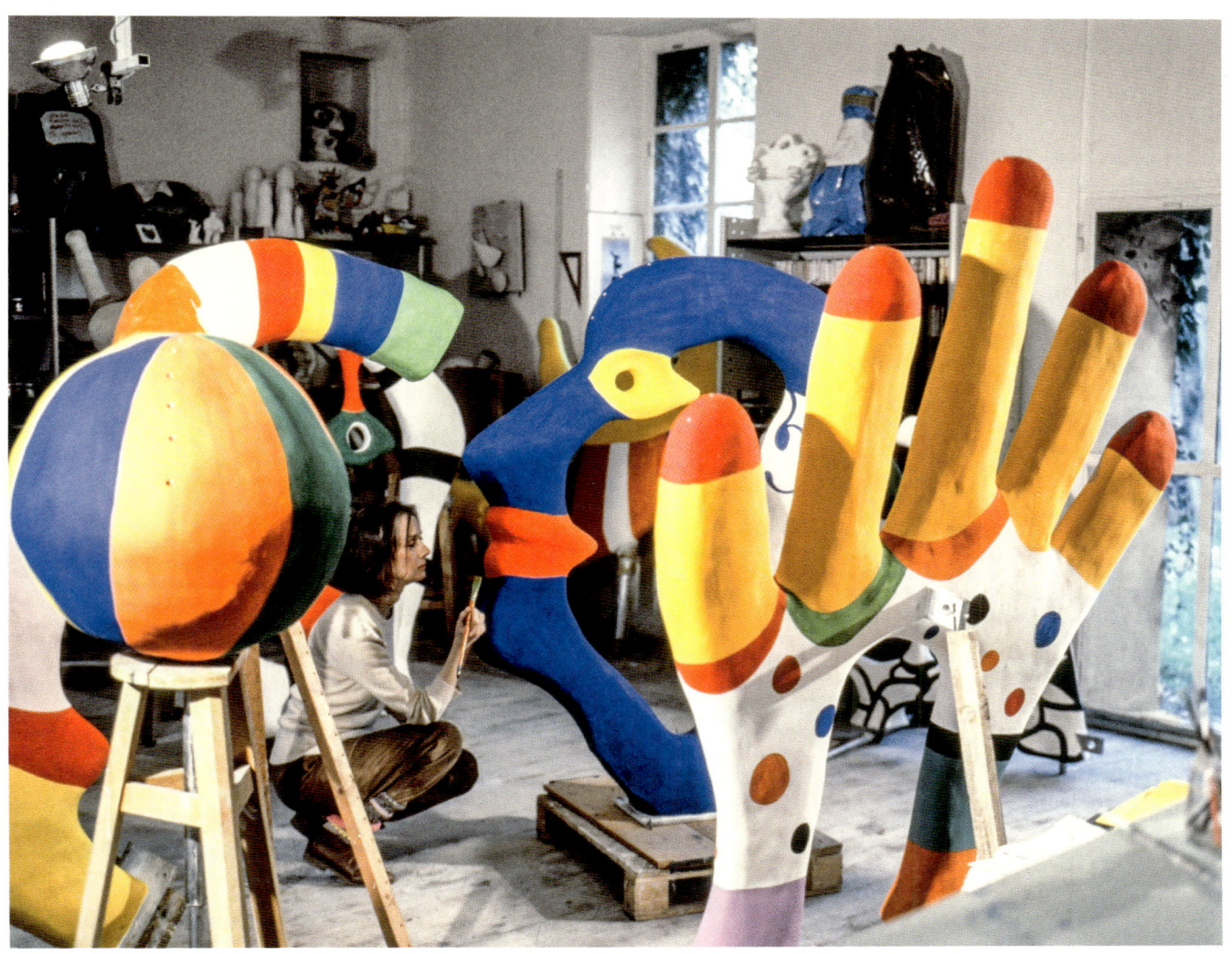